# THE DOCTRINE OF GOD

ALBERT C. KNUDSON
Dean of Boston University School of Theology, and
Professor of Systematic Theology

THE ABINGDON PRESS
NEW YORK CINCINNATI CHICAGO

Printed in the United States of America

DEDICATED

TO

MRS. GEORGE LOUIS RICHARDS

AND TO

THE MEMORY OF HER FATHER

MR. ROSWELL RAYMOND ROBINSON

BOTH GENEROUS BENEFACTORS

OF

BOSTON UNIVERSITY SCHOOL OF THEOLOGY

# CONTENTS

## CHAPTER III

### SCIENCE AND THEOLOGY



## CHAPTER IV

### PHILOSOPHY AND THEOLOGY

## CHAPTER V

### SOURCES AND METHOD



# PART II. THE DOCTRINE OF GOD

## CHAPTER VI

### THE EXISTENCE OF GOD

## CHAPTER IX

### The Goodness of God

## CHAPTER X

### THE TRINITY

## PREFACE

THIS is the first of two independent volumes that together will cover the field of Christian theology. The second volume will be entitled *The Doctrine of Redemption,* and will deal with the world, man, sin, and salvation through Christ. The present volume, as the title states, has to do with the doctrine of God, but it also deals in an introductory way and at considerable length with the nature of theology in general and its place in modern thought.

The current prejudice against theology, insofar as it has a rational basis, is due to the modern revolt against authoritarianism and metaphysics. These twin evils are supposed to attach to theology, and as far as the second is concerned I see no way of escaping the charge. Authoritarianism belongs to the past. Progressive Protestant theology has set it aside. But metaphysics has to do with ultimate reality; it has to do with what "God" stands for in religion. Theology, therefore, could not renounce it without ceasing to be theology. One might, it is true, expound the biblical doctrine of God without relating it to one's total world-view and without seeking to ground it philosophically. But this would be a superficial mode of procedure. Such a theology would be metaphysical in content without being metaphysical in method. Metaphysics, as William James said, is only "an unusually obstinate effort to think clearly and consistently," and this kind of obstinacy can hardly be avoided in a theology worthy of the name. Most of the crudities and vagaries of current popular and so-called "scientific" theology are due to a lack of metaphysical insight. To eschew metaphysics in the field of theology is to fall back into a shallow ecclesiastical or sense dogmatism. In the following pages, consequently, no effort has been made to avoid the broader and profounder problems connected with the Christian doctrine of God. A clear understanding of these problems will do much to save religious thought from the confusion in which it at present finds itself.

My friends and colleagues, Dr. Edgar S. Brightman and Dr. Earl Marlatt, who kindly read the manuscripts of my last two books, have also rendered me a similar service in this instance, for which I am again deeply grateful to them. I wish also to express my gratitude to President Daniel L. Marsh for the generous encouragement he has given me in my scholastic and literary work.

ALBERT C. KNUDSON.

# PART I

# INTRODUCTION: THE PROVINCE OF THEOLOGY

## CHAPTER I

## RELIGION AND THEOLOGY

THEOLOGY may be defined as the systematic exposition and rational justification of the intellectual content of religion.

In this definition it is assumed that religion has an intellectual content and it is also assumed that this content is capable of rational justification. Both of these assumptions have been and are called in question, and never more so than at present. It is claimed by some that religion is purely a practical affair and that it has nothing to do with knowledge in the objective and theoretical sense. There is, therefore, no place for theology. Theology is mythology. By others it is admitted that religion has an objective intellectual content, but this content, it is maintained, takes the form of faith and as such is altogether distinct from reasoned knowledge. It stands in its own right and neither needs nor admits of rational justification. It may be systematically expounded, and in this sense we may properly have a theology. But a theology like that of the past, which seeks not only to expound religious belief but to establish its truth, has no legitimate standing. It is "the bastard child of faith and reason."

In view of this skeptical attitude toward theology, as above defined, it is necessary for us to consider at some length the relation of theology to religion, on the one hand and to science and philosophy on the other. Not until we have done so, not until we have differentiated the field of theology and established its legitimacy are we prepared to enter upon our main task, that of expounding and justifying the Christian doctrine of God. We begin, therefore, with an inquiry into the nature of religion and particularly into the question as to whether religion has or can have a distinct and valid intellectual content.

### Illusionism

That religion in its spontaneous and positive forms has always had an intellectual content of some kind would generally be conceded. The history of religion furnishes decisive evidence on this point. No religion has ever taken a subjectivistic view of itself.[1] Every religion has had beliefs of one sort or another, and to these it has always ascribed a measure at least of objective validity. But all these beliefs, it may be argued, have been mistaken. Hence we must conclude either that they form no essential part of religion or that religion itself is an illusion. The latter conclusion is drawn by those who, for one reason or another, reject religion altogether; the former by those who see in religion something of permanent value, but who deny to it any intellectual content or reduce this content to a minimum, to an extreme of vagueness and plasticity. The distinction between these two viewpoints is not always sharply drawn.

[1] To this not even Buddhism is an exception, as will be seen from the later discussion of it.

The difference between them is one only of degree and to a large extent one of words. Both are opposed to religion in its traditional and positive form, regarding it as an illusion. But the opposition is less pronounced in one case than in the other. Then, too, some discard the word "religion" altogether as applied to their own position,[2] while others insist on retaining it and still others vacillate in their use of it. To distinguish between these two tendencies is not, therefore, easy and may in some instances seem arbitrary. But the difference between them is nevertheless clear enough to be worth noting.

The more extreme theory, which seems to regard religion as a complete illusion and to point logically to its eventual extinction from human life, has taken various forms. These may, perhaps, be reduced to three fundamental types, all of which are genetic in character. The first finds the source of religion in some unworthy or pathological or misguided element in human nature. This may be called "psychological" illusionism. The second derives religion from the unjust structure of human society and the evils that result from it. To this type of illusionism the term "sociological" may be applied. The third type is the "intellectualistic." It identifies religion with primitive science or deduces it from some baseless fancy or superstitious belief of early man.

Of these three types of illusionism the first, or psychological type, is represented by such men as Lucretius (99–55 B. C.), Ludwig Feuerbach (1804–72), and Sigmund Freud (1856–1928). Lucretius emphasized

[2] Cf. J. M. Guyau, *The Irreligion of the Future.*

the element of fear in religion, fear of the gods and of death. It was to this fear, he held, that historical religion owed its origin. But fear in both these respects, he argued, was irrational, and with its disappearance religion itself would naturally and logically vanish. This view in more or less modified form has appeared again and again in the history of skeptical thought. It reduces religion to the objectification of our fears, and this stamps it as illusory. It tells us that but for ignorance and timidity there would have been no such thing as religion in the traditional sense of the term.

Feuerbach is the most significant and influential representative of illusionism in the modern world. In his account of the nature of religion special stress was laid upon the objectification of human desire. The driving force that, according to his view, lies back of religion is the instinct of self-preservation, the quest after life, after happiness. "The end of religion," he says, "is the welfare, the salvation, the ultimate felicity of man; the relation of man to God is nothing else than his relation to his own spiritual good; God is the realized salvation of the soul, or the unlimited power of effecting the salvation, the bliss of man." Religion has thus a natural and not unworthy source.[3] But its utilitarian and egoistic aim renders its objective affirmations entirely untrustworthy. In it the wish is father to the thought, and the "thought" is consequently illusory. There is no transcendent Divine Being. God is "nothing else than a product and reflex of the supernatural

---

[3] *The Essence of Christianity*, p. 185.

human mind" and theology is simply "a web of contradiction and delusions."[4] This is a truth which, according to Feuerbach, religion itself ought to recognize. If it did, it would only be opening its own eyes and coming to self-consciousness. To help it to do so was the professed aim that he set himself. There was thus a humanistic sense in which he accepted the truth or validity of religion. But his polemic was directed so sharply and persistently against religion, as commonly understood, that he is properly classed with the more extreme illusionists, despite his occasional protests to the contrary.

Freud and his disciples have, perhaps, given the most systematic and thoroughgoing expression to what is called "medical materialism," the theory that religion and the higher spiritual life of man owe their origin to physical and psychological causes of a pathological nature. More particularly, in their psychoanalysis they have found the roots of religion in perverted sexuality. It was the incestuous desires of primitive men that led to the rise of totemism, and it was the deification of the totem-animal that led to the belief in God. No proof of such a theory is, of course, possible. The whole "Oedipus-complex"—of which we hear so much in psychoanalytic literature—with its incestuous sons and its slain and later mourned and reverenced father, is a fanciful construction that could hardly be taken seriously as a transcript of reality. Yet the idea that religion has some direct connection with sexuality has considerable currency, and still more widespread is the view that it grew up

---

[4] *Ibid.*, pp. xv, x.

out of abnormal mental and physical states. A number of serious attempts have been made to explain Jesus as a psychopath,[5] and similar explanations of other religious geniuses are not uncommon. Such explanations start with the assumption that religion is false and derive whatever plausibility they may have from this assumption. So far as the interpretation of religion as perverted sexuality is concerned, William James[6] is quite right in saying that we might almost as well interpret it as an aberration of the digestive or respiratory function. Conversion, it is true, is most common during the period of adolescence, but so, also, is the awakening of the entire higher mental life; and to ascribe the latter to a perversion of the sexual instinct would be hardly more absurd than to ascribe the religious life to this source. The same may also be said of the supposed connection between religion and abnormality in general. This connection is probably not much closer than that of the other phases of man's higher life with abnormal mental states. In none of these cases is abnormality the determining cause. Pathology can account for theology no better than it can for philosophy and art.

The three methods of discrediting religion that we have thus far considered have been predominantly psychological in nature. They have consisted in deducing religion from fear or from the desire for happiness or from some pathological state such as a per-

[5] See *The Psychic Health of Jesus*, by Walter E. Bundy, for an excellent review and criticism of these theories.

[6] *The Varieties of Religious Experience*, pp. 9-18.

verted sexuality. We now pass to two methods that may be classed as sociological. Of these, the first is the ancient view, revived in the eighteenth century, that religion is a device of state and priestcraft. It was early observed that religion is not infrequently utilized by those in authority to promote their own selfish interests. So this fact was seized upon by unfriendly critics as indicating the very source and essence of religion. It was said that people were deceived into believing in the existence of gods in order that they might be led to accept the existing social and political order as one having divine sanction, no matter how inequitable it might be. In this theory it was assumed that fictitious and purely adventitious ideas might be imposed upon the mind from without in such a way that they would seem to be spontaneous convictions. But this assumption runs counter to all sound psychology. One might as well suppose that a man could be deceived into believing that the wig he wore was his own hair. Settled convictions must have some direct rootage in the human mind and must spring up out of inner need. Insight into this truth has rendered obsolete the theory that religion owed its origin to fraud.

A modification of the theory, however, has arisen which is at present widely held in socialistic circles. The theory in its new form retains the idea that religion was established or "invented" in the interest of the propertied or ruling class, the lords of society. But its establishment was not due to direct deception. No doubt deception was practiced to some extent by the privileged classes; the "laws of thought" were violated. But it was a case of self-deception on the part of the poor quite as much as of deliberate deception on the part of others, and both forms of deception arose more or less naturally out of the social situation. The rich were threatened by the discontent of the poor and so encouraged them to seek satisfaction in a way that would not disturb the existing social order. The poor, on the other hand, in their ignorance saw no other way of attaining happiness than in an imaginary realm of bliss which they mistook for real. It was thus that religion arose, out of dishonest self-interest on the part of the rich and out of a misguided quest after happiness on the part of the poor. At this point the new theory attached itself to Feuerbach, who, as we have seen, found the source of religion in an unwarranted objectification of human desire.

The wide prevalence of the theory is due largely to the influence of Karl Marx, who said of religion that it "is the striving of the people for an imaginary happiness; it springs from a state of society that requires an illusion, but disappears when the recognition of true happiness and the possibility of its realization penetrates the masses." The elaboration of the theory, however, and the most thoroughgoing attempt to ground it historically were the work of Otto Gruppe,[7] a man little known in America and England. Gruppe gives to the theory the name of "adaptionism." According to it the wide dissemination of

---

[7] *Die griechischen Kulte und Mythen in ihren Beziehungen zu den orientalischen Religionen*, 1877; *Griechische Mythologie und Religionsgeschichte*, 1906.

religion is due to the fact that people generally "adapted" themselves to it. It originated as a matter of fact or was "invented" at a definite point of time, and only in one place—probably Western Asia. It did not, then, spring up spontaneously in human life everywhere. Men have no "active impulse" toward religion; they simply have a "passive potency" as over against it, a capacity to receive it from others. There was a time when there was no religion, and there will be a time when this fortunate state will return. It was the strained relation between the rich and the poor that gave rise to religion, and when this strained relation is removed, as it will be in the new communistic social order, religion will vanish from human life. Men will lay it aside as they do an outworn garment.

Unfortunately for this interesting theory, the two main pillars on which it rests are quite insecure. The assumption that men at first had no religion is without adequate warrant. Even if it should be discovered, as it has not been, that there are human tribes without religion of any kind, it would not follow that this was also true of primitive men. It is quite possible, and indeed probable, that they would represent a departure from the normal and original human type. The assumption also that man has a "passive potency" and not an "active impulse" toward religion is entirely arbitrary and a begging of the whole question as to the validity of religion. Apart from an initial anti-religious prejudice it has no standing. History as a whole is against it.

In addition to the "sociological" and "psychological" theories we have briefly outlined, there is, as we have already noted, a third type of illusionism to which the term "intellectualistic" may be applied. Theories of this type differ from those already dealt with in that they lay stress upon the primitive ideas or beliefs underlying religion, rather than upon the psychological or sociological conditions that are supposed to have given rise to it. They, for instance, derive religion from the primitive belief in the animation of all nature or from the still more primitive belief in an impersonal power known as *mana*. Or they interpret it as a primitive method of explaining phenomena by referring them to personal wills. To each of these three theories a brief word may be devoted.

Since the publication of E. B. Tylor's famous work on *Primitive Culture* in 1871, animism has probably been the most widely accepted theory with reference to the origin of religion. It is closely connected with the dream or trance theory and also with the theory of ancestor worship. In its simplest form the theory runs like this: Men, as a result of dreams and trances, came to believe that they had souls distinct from and more or less independent of their bodies. This conception they extended to natural objects in general. They also deduced from it the belief that there are pure spirits or souls, unconnected with bodies, and that the human soul survives death. The result was that there arose a special reverence for the souls of ancestors amounting to deification, and this, together with the personifying tendency of the primitive human mind, led to the belief in gods. Such, in a nutshell, is the animistic account of the origin of religion.

That there is considerable truth in the theory from the historical point of view, is generally conceded, though it is in less favor now than it was some years ago. But what we are here concerned with is its view of the nature and truth of religion. It is possible to allow that dreams, trances, the belief in ghosts, and ancestor-worship played an important part in early religion without allowing that they express the essence of religion or compromise its truth. But animism has not infrequently been interpreted in an illusionistic sense. It has been assumed and maintained that the true essence of religion is to be found in the "primitive philosophy" above outlined and that all religion, consequently, is illusory.

In its earlier form, animism, as an historical theory, did not distinguish clearly between the aliveness or animation of nature and its ensoulment in the stricter sense of the term. Tylor emphasized the latter, and the term "animism" is now often used in that restricted sense. To the theory of a vaguer and more impersonal kind of animation, advocated by Spencer and others, the term "animatism" is applied. Animatism does not exclude animism, but points to an earlier and more rudimentary form of religion, a "preanimistic" stage. The general sense of an all-aliveness of nature, it is claimed, preceded the attribution of souls to things.

But even animatism, it is now maintained, does not go far enough back. Earlier than the belief in the animation of nature was the belief in *mana,* a non-personal but supernatural force, which manifested itself in various objects that, for one reason or another, were supposed to be possessed of an extraordinary power or character. *Mana* stood closely related to *tabu* and may be regarded as its positive counterpart. By Durkheim it is identified with the principle of totemism.[8] Everything sacred had *mana,* and so also every object that might be called "supernatural" in an evil as well as a good sense. *Mana* is itself impersonal, but, according to Durkheim, it was regarded as incarnated in individuals, and in this way the belief in souls arose. The principle of animism was thus secondary to the totemic principle; and the totemic principle, Durkheim holds, is to be identified with society. There is no objective or metaphysical *mana.* The only real *mana* is that embodied in society. It is society that constitutes the true reality of the *mana*-istic or totemistic religion and of all religion. If interpreted in a more-than-human or transcendent sense, *mana* is as fictitious as is the animistic world of souls and spirits. To identify religion with *mana*-ism in this form is, therefore, to reduce religion to an illusion. Such is Durkheim's view; and it may be added that his own sociological theory also deprives religion of any valid intellectual content. But to this we shall recur a little later. *Mana*-ism, as commonly understood, might, of course, be accepted as a valid account of the earliest stage of religion without any reference to the question of the validity of religion in general, and many, no doubt, do so accept it. But not a few regard it as necessarily illusionistic in its implications.

The third form of "intellectualistic" illusionism,

---

[8] *The Elementary Forms of the Religious Life,* pp. 188ff.

above referred to, is represented by Auguste Comte and James G. Frazer. Comte distinguished three stages in man's intellectual development: the theological, the metaphysical, and the positivistic. Religion in its traditional sense he referred to the first stage. Events were then explained by referring them to personal wills—that was the essence of historical religion—but the method was one that is now discredited. Hence, religion in this form has no future. Such, essentially, is also Frazer's view. He holds that religion was preceded by an age of magic and represents a higher standpoint. Magic was based upon the principle of natural causation as understood by the savage mind, but it proved unsuccessful in attaining the practical ends of life. Hence it was superseded by religion which rests on the belief that the course of nature is controlled by personal beings superior to man, who may be entreated on man's behalf. This belief, however, has also proven mistaken, and consequently religion is destined to disappear as did magic. Science has rendered it obsolete.

The forms of illusionism which we have thus far considered I have characterized as extreme because they take a negative attitude toward religion as a whole. Not only theology but religion itself comes under their ban. They hold that it has had its day, and that with the growth of enlightenment and the improvement of social conditions it will vanish from human life. As distinguished from these illusionistic theories, there are others that are more positive in their appraisal of religion. The theologies of the past they emphatically reject and also the theological world-view in general. But religion, they feel, has persisted so long that there must be something of permanent worth in it, and this something they seek to salvage. They reveal, therefore, a more sympathetic attitude toward historical religion than the theories already discussed.

Of these less extreme illusionistic theories perhaps the most interesting is that represented by Emile Durkheim. It is his contention that religion is an essential and permanent aspect of humanity. It is not the outgrowth of social inequality and injustice. It is structural within society itself. No society can exist without ideals, and faith in the ideal is the essence of religion. Without this faith society could neither create nor recreate itself. The idealizing faculty is the very condition of man's existence as a social being. Without it man would not be man. Religion, then, is a human necessity, and in its essence is eternal. Man will never outgrow it.

But this is true of religion only in its essence, and its essence is wholly practical in nature. It helps us to *act,* to *live,* but not to *think.* Thinking is the business of science. Religion, insofar as it has assumed this rôle and has become speculative and dogmatic, has gone astray and become "scarcely more than a fabric of errors." There is no such transcendent order of reality as theology assumes. Viewed as a system of doctrine, religion is an "inexplicable hallucination." But this does not mean that religion in its essential nature is false. All religions are true in the sense that they serve an indispensable practical purpose. They have, however, in their purity no intellectual content, no cognitive function. Their doctrines are mythical objectifications of the tribal or communal sentiment. They represent nothing metaphysically real. A sharp distinction must thus be drawn between religion and theology. The latter is illusion and may be sloughed off without loss, but the former is a necessary and permanent factor of human society. It may later express itself in a new theology, but, if so, the new theology will be no more essential to its nature than the old. Only social or practical religion will abide.

Akin to this form of illusionism is that represented by such neo-Kantians as F. A. Lange[9] and Paul Natorp.[10] Both of these men took a positive and favorable attitude toward religion. Indeed, Natorp before his death set aside his earlier positivistic position and adopted the transcendental or metaphysical standpoint. But he is best known by his earlier view and it is to this that I here refer. He and Lange ascribed permanence to religion, as did Durkheim, but they grounded it somewhat differently. Instead of finding its basis in sociology they found it, rather, in psychology, in the subjective nature of the individual. Religion, according to Natorp, consists in feeling, and feeling is subjective. It cannot transcend the limits of humanity, but within these limits as a bond of union between man and man it is structural in human nature and has an abiding function. Lange likened religion to poetry. As such it has to do with an ideal world, a world that is not metaphysically real, but a

---

[9] *History of Materialism.*

[10] *Religion innerhalb der grenzen der Humanität.*

world nevertheless that stands higher than all objects of scientific knowledge and which is, at the same time, essential to all human progress. The time will, therefore, never come when men will not need and have a religion. But the religion of the future will be a religion of humanity, a religion of pure symbolism, not a theistic religion in the realistic sense of the term.

This conception of a religion without God has, in recent years, come to be known as "Humanism,"[11] and under this name has become the professed creed not only of a considerable number who have broken with organized religion, but also of a few radical spirits occupying pulpits in American churches. These people, especially the latter group, profess with a good deal of unction that they believe in religion. Religion, however, they stoutly insist, does not necessarily involve belief in God. Indeed, the idea of a personal God is their pet hostility. They emphatically reject it and not only it, but also the very word "God," which they think has become contaminated by its personalistic associations in the past. In the place of God they put the idea of "the sacred," and to the sacred they give whatever content happens to satisfy their idealizing mood. Of the world they take a thoroughly naturalistic view, which they confuse with that of current science. Nature for them is entirely impersonal. There is no such thing as Providence.

---

[11] To be distinguished from the literary "Humanism" represented by Paul Elmer More and Irving Babbitt. For a clear exposition of the latter movement in its relation to theology see P. E. More's article on "A Revival of Humanism" in *The Bookman* for March, 1930.

Providentialism, we are told, is the direct antithesis of humanism.[12] What humanism preaches is self-help, not dependence on Providence. "Human control by human effort in accordance with human ideals"—such is the program of the new humanistic religion. God and theology have no place in it.

The foregoing survey of illusionistic theories is not exhaustive, but it is sufficiently comprehensive to give a fairly adequate view of current illusionism. All of these theories agree in denying the objective validity of religious belief, insofar as the latter implies a theistic and in this sense supernatural world-view. In other words, they all rest upon a naturalistic philosophy. This philosophy may be materialistic or positivistic. It may be Epicurean, Humian, or Kantian in its historical affiliations. It may be individualistic or socialistic. It may find its support in anthropology or pathology or sociology or in science in general. In any case, it starts with the assumption that the natural order, whether viewed metaphysically or positivistically, is all that there is, or at least all that can be known. No proof of this assumption is offered, for the very good reason that no such proof is possible. The assumption grows out of crude sense prejudice, and this prejudice is relied upon to be strong enough to float the assumption and any theory

[12] J. S. Huxley, *Religion without Revelation*, p. 18. Among other recent books representative of essentially the same standpoint the following may be mentioned: *Things and Ideals*, by M. C. Otto; *Religion and the Modern World*, by J. H. Randall and J. H. Randall, Jr.; *Religion in an Age of Science*, by Edwin A. Burtt; *A Preface to Morals*, by Walter Lippmann; *The Quest of the Ages*, by A. E. Haydon; *The Twilight of Christianity*, by H. E. Barnes. For a sympathetic criticism of humanism see *Theism and the Modern Mood*, by W. M. Horton.

based upon it.[13] It is here that the fatal logical weakness of all illusionistic theories is to be found. They presuppose what they pretend to prove. They profess to give purely scientific accounts of the origin of religion which exclude its validity. But the illusionistic conclusion is already contained in the naturalistic premise upon which the theories are based, and apart from this premise would be wholly unwarranted. This fact deprives such theories of a genuinely scientific character. For pure science is not "naturalistic." Only a materialistic or positivistic misinterpretation of it makes it such. The illusionistic theories are, then, defective both from a philosophical and a scientific standpoint.

Another criticism to be passed upon them is that they involve a mistaken conception of the nature of religion and of its place in human life. Here, however, the situation is more complex. All the illusionistic theories agree that faith in a superworld is no inherent and essential need of the human mind. This faith, they all hold, is destined to disappear from the world. As such a faith religion is an illusion. It has no future. But they differ on the point as to whether religion is to be identified with faith of this kind. The more extreme illusionistic theories assume that the two are identical, while those which I have classed as less extreme confidently affirm the contrary. The latter have a deeper appreciation of the value of reli-

[13] It is this obscurantist tendency in current naturalistic humanism, this uncritical reliance on sense dogmatism, this failure to justify its own metaphysics, that makes the movement so profoundly unsatisfactory from the intellectual as well as the religious point of view.

gion and its practical significance in human life. They cannot envisage human life without it. For them religion is a human necessity. Men will never outgrow it. But the religion of the future, they maintain, will be a religion without belief in a supernatural and spiritual world, a kind of decapitated religion, which will still manage somehow to keep alive through the beating of the heart.

The less extreme illusionistic theories thus reveal a deeper and truer insight into the essentially religious nature of man than do those that we have termed more extreme. The latter, however, imply a truer grasp of the distinctive nature of religion. Religion is, no doubt, primarily a matter of life, of feeling, of will. In stressing this fact the less extreme illusionistic theories are right. But they are mistaken insofar as they fail to see that the peculiar type of life or feeling or will represented by religion is indissolubly bound up with faith in a superworld. To renounce this faith, to deny the existence of God, or of superterrestrial beings in general, is to renounce religion itself. Philosophical naturalism and religion negate each other. All genuine religion has an intellectual content, a content that lays hold of a supernatural and superhuman reality. Without such a content, without at least an implicit theology, there is no religion. And if this intellectual or theological content is a vain dream, so also is religion. In taking this position, the more extreme illusionistic theories are right. Religion is either "true" in the Platonic sense of the term or it is a complete illusion. To attempt to save religion at the expense of its truth is a hopeless endeavor. Religion without "faith" is a contradiction in terms. There is and can be no such thing as a purely scientific or *this*-worldly religion. A religion of this kind would be such only in name. Belief in a superworld is essential to religion.

### Magic and Mythology

But while this differentiates religion from philosophic naturalism and makes a synthesis of the two impossible, it leaves the relation of religion to magic and mythology undefined. Both magic and mythology imply the existence of supernatural or transcendent powers that affect, if they do not control, human life, and in this respect they resemble religion.[14] But they differ from it in that they are both completely discredited by modern thought. There are no "magical" powers, and "mythological" objects are simply free creations of the fancy. The very words "magic" and "myth" are synonyms for unreality. Religion, on the other hand, still commands to a large extent the assent of men. The objects of its faith are regarded as real and living. Illusionists, it is true, relegate religion in its theistic form to essentially the same level as that of magic and myth. For them theology is mythology, and religion is a modified form of magic. At bottom, the intellectual content of one is no more tenable than that of the other. Men in general, however, take a different view. Religion persists in a way that magic and myth do not. It continues to enjoy the favor of thinking men and women. There must, then,

---

[14] See Georg Wobbermin, *Systematische Theologie*, Bd. II, "Das Wesen der Religion," pp. 327-73.

be an important difference between it and the "magical" or "mythological" types of thought.

Much has been written on this subject, and there are still wide differences of opinion. It is probable that originally there was no clear distinction between religion, magic, and mythology. All mingled together in a more or less indiscriminate whole. There were, however, implicit differences between them, and these gradually began to manifest themselves until eventually a sharp antithesis came to exist between religion and theology on the one hand, and magic and mythology, on the other. One, however, did not supplant the other. Both continued to coexist. This fact alone renders highly improbable Frazer's theory that an age of magic preceded that of religion. History knows no such succession of æons. So far as our knowledge goes, magic and religion have always existed side by side. But time has tended to bring out more and more clearly the contrast between them.

What, then, is the *differentia* of religion? It has been maintained that religion is social, while magic is anti-social. But this is not always the case. Therapeutic magic is not anti-social. Again, it has been held that religion refers extraordinary events to personal wills, while magic attributes them to impersonal powers or spirits. But this also is not true in all cases. Magic does not necessarily exclude the idea of personal powers or spirits back of or in nature. More satisfactory than either of these theories is the one which finds the distinction between magic and religion in the coercive character of the one and the conciliatory character of the other. Magic says, "My will be done." It seeks to compel the supernatural power or spirit to do its bidding. Religion, on the other hand, says, "Thy will be done." It teaches submission, trust, a conciliatory and personal attitude toward the transcendent Being or beings back of nature. Such an attitude would naturally lead to a more personal conception of the supernatural powers dealt with, and would also naturally lead to a more social and ethical relation with one's fellow men. But these are the results of the religious attitude rather than its essence. A submissive, trustful, conciliatory feeling toward the powers-that-be in the universe is primary in religion. And here it is that we have the reason for the survival of religion and the decay of magic. It was not, as Frazer tells us, the failure of magic to provide men with food that led to the rise and growth of religion. In that respect it is doubtful if religion has been more successful than magic. The real reason for the persistence and development of religion is to be found in the sense, that it implies, of friendly communion with the supernatural and in the comfort, strength, and inspiration that this has brought to men. In other words, it was man's capacity for an inward and spiritual experience that led to the triumph of religion over magic. This capacity religion awakened and developed in a way that magic with its coercive method could not. Furthermore, the consciousness of man's imperfection involved in his relation to the divine became a mighty motive power to progress.[15] Religion thus stands for a dis-

[15] See Eric S. Waterhouse, *The Philosophy of Religious Experience*, pp. 51, 58.

tinctly different attitude toward the universe and toward human life from that of magic.

An equally significant difference also exists between religion and mythology. The origin of mythology is commonly traced to the personifying tendency of the human mind, and this, it is said, is also one of the chief factors in the rise of religion. Primitive men, like children, conceive natural objects and events after the analogy of human and animal life. They ascribe to them will and personality. The sun and wind, mountains and springs are represented as living beings. An anthropomorphic or theromorphic view of the world thus arises. This view we call mythology. It grows entirely out of the poetic fancy, and hence has no claim to credence. But between this and the religious view of the world there is an important difference. The personality attributed by mythology to material objects has no ethical or spiritual character. It is itself in a sense a thing of nature, something purely metaphysical. The personified objects of mythology do not evoke the feelings of dependence, of hope and trust. They are merely existential facts, variable in value. In a word, they lack religious quality, they do not call forth faith. What differentiates religion from mythology is the fact that the personal Power or powers which it finds operative in the world are powers that can be trusted. They have character; and this means that the world at bottom is an ethical, a rational world. It has meaning, a purpose. There may be mythological elements in the religious world-view; there usually are. But religion is religion only insofar as it transcends mythology, only insofar as it ascribes to the Personality or personalities regnant in the world a rational and moral nature and so makes them objects of a living human faith.

Magic and mythology may prepare the ground for religion. By assuming the reality of a superworld, personal or impersonal, they may make religious faith easier. But they are not themselves religion. They sustain logically about the same relation to religion that alchemy does to chemistry, or astrology to astronomy. Between magic and mythology on the one hand, and the essence of religion on the other, there is all the difference that there is between irrationality and rationality. Religion in its essential nature means faith in the rationality and purposiveness of the world. It thus stands heaven-high above magic and mythology; and no attempt to reduce it to the plane of the latter can succeed. In its inmost nature it differs radically from them, and occupies a place by itself.

The view is not infrequently expressed that religion owes its uniqueness to the fact that it is a fusion of mythology with morality.[16] In this view it is assumed that religion becomes purer the more dominant the ethical element becomes and the more completely the mythological element is sloughed off. It is in its ethical content, we are told, that the true nature of religion is to be found. But what, then, becomes of its uniqueness? If pure religion is identical with morality, it manifestly has no distinctive character of

[16] See Paul Deussen, *Allgemeine Geschichte der Philosophie. Mit besonderer Berücksichtigung der Religionen.*

its own, and the very theory that its essence consists in its being a synthesis of morality and mythology, lapses. The view under consideration thus turns out to be self-contradictory. Nevertheless, it is widely held. Indeed, it is in principle essentially the same as that represented by the less extreme illusionistic theories above discussed. The assumption underlying it is that religion, in its traditional form, is mythology, but that it has in it an ethical kernel which is of permanent worth and that this kernel will constitute the religion of the future, a religion devoid of faith in a superworld. Such a view, however, misses the true genius of religion. Religion is not identical with either mythology or morality. It never has been and never will be. In its essential nature it is unique, and this uniqueness consists in a personal relationship to the Divine, a vital experience which links the believer to the higher realm of spirit.

Our study thus far has brought out the unsatisfactory character of all illusionistic theories. These theories have a double defect. They are based both upon a mistaken philosophy and upon a mistaken conception of the nature of religion. The philosophy is naturalism, a type of thought that is peculiarly vulnerable to criticism, but one which, in this instance, seems to be accepted as self-evident. This philosophy involves the conclusion which the illusionistic theories seek to establish. It is the major premise of one and all of them. Without it their argument would have no cogency, and with it the argument is a *petitio principii*. The idea that these theories offer a scientific proof of the illusory character of religion is itself an illusion.

The other defect in them appears most clearly in those theories that I have classed as less extreme. Here the attempt is made to salvage religion by redefining it. All relation to God and a supernatural world is eliminated and what is left is a religion without Providence and without a deep and permanent hope. But such a religion is unworthy of the name. It is really an effort to get the ethical benefits of religion without religion. The more extreme illusionists see this and so reject religion altogether. They recognize the fact that religion implies belief in a higher world of spirit, but they make the mistake of supposing that this belief belongs to the same level as that of magic and mythology. They fail to recognize the unique ethical and rational elements that are involved in religious experience and in the religious world-view. Religion affirms a superworld, but it does so in response to the deepest emotional, moral, and intellectual needs of the soul, and not as a mere play of fancy.

Accepting this view of religion we are warranted in saying that it contains in its essential nature a unique intellectual content and that this content furnishes a valid basis for theology. But in order to understand adequately the relation of theology and religion to each other, there are several other phases of the subject that need to be considered more fully. We need to analyze and define more precisely the nature of religion; we need to determine more exactly what is involved in the superworld affirmed by religion; and we need to bring out more clearly the practical function of theology in the field of religion.

## The Nature of Religion

One significant point with reference to the nature of religion has thus far been established. It is that religion is not purely subjective; it involves a personal attitude toward an objective realm of values. But this personal attitude is complex. There are in it at least three essential elements. One is that of trustful dependence upon a Higher Power. We might, with Schleiermacher, call it the feeling of absolute dependence. But the term "absolute" is not altogether satisfactory. It differentiates religion from the ordinary limited feelings of dependence with which our secular life is filled, but it does not bring out what is unique and distinctive within religion itself. Indeed, "absolute dependence," taken strictly, suggests fatalism rather than religion. The feeling of dependence becomes truly religious only when the element of trust is included. The same may also be said of the consciousness of being "in relation with God" which Schleiermacher adds as the equivalent of the feeling of absolute dependence. Conscious relation to God is religious only in case the relation is one of trust. This also applies to the "creature-feeling" which Rudolf Otto substitutes for that of absolute dependence.[17] The mere feeling of creatureliness, of self-abasement, of awe, of stupefying fear before the "Wholly Other" is not religion, unless it implies that the Wholly Other is a Being which, despite its unapproachableness and overpowering might, is one that in its essential nature can be trusted. Trust,

---

[17] *The Idea of the Holy*, pp. 10ff.

or, in other words, the belief in Providence, is inherent in religion. To eliminate it and to stigmatize providentialism as a "vice," as some of our neo-religionists do,[18] is to mutilate religion and to deprive it of its most fundamental characteristic.

Another essential element in religion is the longing after life or redemption. This longing stands closely related to the feeling of trustful dependence, but it has a more specific object in view. It looks to the goal of life rather than to its ordinary experiences. Its keynote is consequently hope, but hope based upon faith in some superhuman power or order. Mere hope or a mere longing after something better is not religious. It becomes such only through faith. And faith is to be viewed as something more than a mere product of unsatisfied desire. It is not simply man's inability to carry to a successful conclusion his quest after life that leads to the belief in a superworld. No doubt this inability has accentuated and strengthened the belief. But the belief itself is something deeper and more immediate than such an inferential process. It is rooted in elementary experience and in the very structure of reason. There is such a thing as a religious *apriori,*[19] and there is such a thing as a "numinous" experience, a direct awareness of the Divine, both of which antedate the inference from human defeat to supernatural aid. It was not simply the quest after happiness that led to the assumption of a more-than-human power or world-order. Religion is some-

---

[18] J. S. Huxley, *Religion Without Revelation*, p. 18.

[19] See my article on "Religious Apriorism" in *Studies in Philosophy and Theology*, edited by E. C. Wilm.

thing more than the valid or invalid objectification of desire.[20] But desire nevertheless plays an essential part in it. Without the longing for salvation or for a larger and fuller life, there would hardly be such a thing as religion. It is in this longing that religion comes to its sharpest focus.

A third characteristic of religion is its implicit alliance with the moral ideal. Much has been written on the relation of morality and religion to each other. Some have argued that morality is independent of religion, others that religion is independent of morality, and still others that one is dependent upon the other. The fact, of course, is that historically the two have stood in a close relation to each other. Religion has inspired morality, and morality has humanized religion. Yet each has its own specific character and stands in its own right so that it is possible to define one without taking account of the other. But such a definition, at least in the case of religion, would give us an abstraction rather than concrete experience. For if religion involves trust, it is evident that the object of its trust must be regarded as having something akin to an ethical character. And if religion is a yearning after a redeemed life, this life must be conceived of as including more or less of the ethical. Then, too, both religious trust and the quest

---

[20] The classic expositions of this theory of religion are to be found, from the standpoint of belief, in J. Kaftan's *Das Wesen der Christlichen Religion*, and from the unbelieving standpoint, in L. Feuerbach's *The Essence of Christianity*. The fact would seem to be that religion is primarily an experience of the divine, an experience, however, that stands in the relation both of cause and effect to man's persistent quest after life. It is not a wish-philosophy, but an ought-philosophy that grounds religion.

after life imply that certain conditions must be met if divine aid is to be secured. In other words, they involve the sense of obligation.

Furthermore, the sense of obligation inherent in religion is not exhausted in the saying of prayers and the offering of sacrifices—duties that have to do directly with the superworld. It extends also to duties to our fellow men. Here, however, the relationship has not always been so self-evident, and hence there has at times been an apparent divorce between religion and morality in the purely human sense of the term. The former has seemed to exist without the latter. But when once the inclusiveness of the religious obligation has been pointed out, it has presented itself to the human mind as a self-evident truth. The recognition of it has been immediate and imperative, so much so that Rudolf Otto asserts an *apriori* relation between religion and morality.[21] Duty to God involves duty to man. There is no escaping this interlocking of obligation on the part of the religious conscience. When the prophetic word of moral obedience is spoken, it carries conviction within itself. The religious believer instinctively recognizes its binding authority. Between religion and morality there is, therefore, an alliance which religion at least cannot break without renouncing its own true nature.

The foregoing analysis has brought out what seem to me the fundamental and indispensable elements in the religious attitude toward the superworld. They are the feeling of trustful dependence, the longing

---

[21] *The Idea of the Holy*, pp. 140f.

after salvation and the sense of obligation to man as well as God. These elements correspond roughly to the faith, hope, and love which Paul singled out as the things in religion that abide. They appear in different degrees and different forms in different religions. But there is no religion worthy of the name in which they do not manifest themselves to some extent.

Buddhism is the classical illustration of a religion defying the ordinary notions of what a religion should be, and it is not infrequently cited as evidence that the feeling of trustful dependence is no essential ingredient of religious experience. But this appeal to Buddhism is of doubtful validity. For one thing, it is a question whether original or *Hinayana* Buddhism was a religion in the strict sense of the term. Much could be said in favor of its being rather a philosophy. Certainly, it was predominantly theoretical in character—a school rather than a church. And the fact that in the process of becoming a popular faith it was transformed into a polytheistic system is a strong indication that in its earlier form it was at least defective as a religion. Furthermore, even in that earlier form the element of dependence and of trust was not altogether lacking. "I take refuge in the Buddha," ran the ancient confession of faith, "I take refuge in the Doctrine, I take refuge in the Order."[22] Here the feeling of trustful dependence is emphatically expressed, only it is directed toward a human object, and hence was not truly religious. Beyond the Buddha and his doctrine, however, there was a supernatural world-order, which conditioned the ap-

[22] See G. F. Moore, *History of Religions*, I, p. 297.

pearance of the Buddha and also conditioned the attainment of Nirvana. In this superworld the Buddhist from the beginning had an implicit faith. He did not dwell much upon it nor did he worship it, but it was nevertheless the presupposition of the whole system, and in this indirect way might be said to be an object of trust. The feeling of absolute dependence was not, then, entirely absent from early Buddhism; but even if it were, this fact would not require a change in our definition or analysis of religion.

Wherever religion manifests itself spontaneously and vigorously, it does so in the threefold way above described. These manifestations are subjective in the sense that they are states of the mind, attitudes of the soul. But they have an objective reference, they imply belief in a superworld. This belief religion shares with magic, mythology, and certain philosophies, but it holds it in a unique form. It conceives the superworld in a distinctive way and has its own unique responses to it. These responses are matters of feeling and will. They are the "first" things in our religious consciousness and with them an empirical theology naturally takes its start. Doctrines are secondary; they are, as Schleiermacher says, "accounts of the religious affections set forth in speech."[23] But they are not arbitrary additions to them nor are they mere descriptions of them. The religious affections have a doctrinal content, they profess to grasp an objective reality, and their very character and worth are determined by their upward reach. In and of

[23] *Der Christliche Glaube*, Par. 15.

themselves they are of little consequence. It is what they apprehend that gives them their significance. The psychologist may be interested in them merely as facts of experience, but not so the theologian and religious believer. What interests them is the *truth* of religious experience. They are concerned with God and the superworld, not with religion as a purely human phenomenon.

From the study of the subjective nature of religion we turn, then, to its objective content. We have already seen that religion differs from magic and mythology in that it ascribes to the world of spirit more or less of a rational and ethical character. It also differs from them and from speculative philosophy in that it holds that the spiritual world can be truly grasped only by one who stands in a living personal relationship to it. In other words, it maintains that faith, hope, and love are themselves conditions of religious knowledge. But while religion thus has its own unique approach to the problem of the superworld and a more or less distinctive conception of its nature, it leaves us in uncertainty at one very important point. It is unequivocal in attributing supreme worth to the spiritual realm, but whether the transcendent Reality is to be conceived as personal or not is left undecided. Opinions on the subject are numerous and definite, but they contradict each other so that one is not warranted in saying offhand that the cause of religion requires one view rather than the other. A deep cleavage here runs through the religious world. Most people perhaps would subscribe to a personalistic theism, but many lean toward an impersonal pantheism. The question as to which of the two is right is the profoundest problem of religious thought. There is only one other comparable in significance to it, and that is the question whether both may not be wrong. The latter is the question of illusionism which we have already considered.

One need but read the history of religion in order to realize how ancient and deep-seated is the cleavage between the theistic and the pantheistic types of thought. We can trace it back almost to the beginnings of religion. If we accept the interesting and impressive theory outlined by Archbishop Söderblom,[24] the belief in God had its source in three primitive and originally independent ideas: the idea of *mana,* the idea of soul or spirit, and the idea of creators or "high gods," as Andrew Lang termed them.[25] Each of these ideas has been treated by different anthropologists as the sole original source of religion, but the resulting theories have been one-sided. All three probably co-operated in the production of the idea of God. The first contributed the sense of a supernatural power, the second the idea of personal will, and the third the thought of creatorship; and together they thus gave rise to the belief in a supreme and transcendent spiritual Being.[26]

What we are particularly concerned with here, however, is the relation of these primitive ideas to that of personality. *Mana* was thought of as impersonal, souls or spirits as personal, and the creators or

---

[24] *Das Werden des Gottesglaubens,* 1916.

[25] *The Making of Religion,* 1898; *Myth, Ritual and Religion,* 1906.

[26] N. Söderblom *ibid.,* pp. 190, 318.

"high gods" probably also as personal though less clearly and definitely so. Primitive thought thus anticipated some of the important differences found in the later historical religions. Indeed, it may be said to have projected itself into them. Söderblom, for instance, points out that the *mana*-idea has been dominant in India, the "creator"-idea in China, and the animistic or soul-idea in the Western world. In India the most characteristic religious term is *Brahman.* It denoted originally a power akin to that of *mana* and later was used to designate the fundamental reality of the universe, a kind of impersonal power-substance, that manifests itself in the multitudinous forms of the phenomenal order. In Chinese culture the outstanding and most significant divine figure is *Shang-ti,* "Heaven" or "Supreme Ruler," who has usually been conceived of as a personal but distant deity. In the Western world the personality of God under Christian influence has as a rule been clearly defined and accentuated. But in none of these geographical divisions has there been complete unity and uniformity of belief. In India personal conceptions of the Brahman have struggled against the impersonal, in China there have been impersonal as well as personal interpretations of Shang-ti, and the same holds also, though in a less pronounced degree, of Western thought relative to the Deity.

The long continuance and wide prevalence of this conflict between the personal and the impersonal or agnostic points of view suggests that we have here to do not simply with a speculative or theological difference, but with a deep-seated difference in religious experience itself. The general marks or tests of religion we have already pointed out, but within the circle of these marks or tests there are important differences, and of these differences the most fundamental is that between the mystical and the prophetic type of piety. These two do not necessarily exclude each other, but they represent distinct tendencies, and when developed in a thoroughgoing way they naturally lead to or ally themselves with different conceptions of the Deity.[27]

### Mystical and Prophetic Types of Piety

The mystical[28] type of piety seeks immediate union with its transcendent object, and this it professes to achieve through ecstasy or some other form of ineffable experience. The result is that the object comes to partake of the vagueness and indefiniteness of the experience by means of which it is apprehended. It is defined as the One that transcends all the multiplicity of finite existence. It is the ultimate reality that has no analogue in the world of phenomena. No definite character can, therefore, be ascribed to it. It is pure negativity; its essential nature is completely hidden from us. Yet it is of infinite worth. In it the soul finds its deepest satisfaction.

But the satisfaction thus attained is entirely different from that which the world yields. Indeed, it is

---

[27] See W. P. Paterson, *The Nature of Religion*, pp. 54-56; Friedrich Heiler, *Das Gebet*, pp. 248-83.

[28] The term "mystical" is here used in its more extreme and abstract sense as antithetical to "prophetic." There is also a prophetic type of mysticism, of which account will be taken in the next chapter.

the very negation of all worldly satisfaction. From the standpoint of the Infinite, both the world and the self are condemned to the phenomenal plane. They have no abiding being and no abiding worth. The soul is destined to be absorbed in the Infinite. This is at once its goal and its glory. For it to desire to continue its existence as a separate entity is to remain in sin and to close the door to its own highest good. Nothing of real or permanent value is to be found in the realm of the finite. Man's only hope lies in release from the finitude both of the world and of his own individual existence. A world-denying and a soul-denying pessimism thus is associated with the mystical quest after oneness with the Infinite. The great historical representatives of this type of piety are the religion of the Upanishads in India, to which the Buddhistic type of piety stands related, Taoism in China, and Neoplatonism in the Græco-Roman world.

Over against this form of religious experience we have the prophetic type, represented chiefly by Zoroastrianism, Mosaism, Christianity and Mohammedanism. Here stress is laid upon the personality both of God and man and upon the eternal distinction between them. Not absorption in God, but loving fellowship with him is man's goal. Not ecstasy, not *Nirvana,* not monastic flight from the world, but faith, activity, the transformation of the world are the ends toward which men should struggle. For the knowledge of God we must turn, not to passive contemplation or to a vague mystical feeling, but to history, to revelation, and to that illumination which comes through moral obedience. Not the extinction of self, but its redemption and permanent preservation is man's hope, and no basis for this hope can be found except in the personality, the concrete, individual will of the Infinite. With such a conception of God the prophetic type of piety both begins and ends.

Between these two types of religious life and thought, there are many of a mediating character. Mysticism is not infrequently associated with a more or less personal view of God, and prophetism with a more or less agnostic philosophy or theology. But these are composite forms that fail to carry out in a consequential way the inner logic of either of the two fundamental types. They do, however, testify to this important fact that religion embraces both types, and that these types, while they represent opposite poles of the religious life, nevertheless have a positive attraction for each other. Mysticism has an affection for prophetism and prophetism for mysticism. Between the two there is an underlying kinship. But the differences that we have pointed out between them are still so deep that if we are to have unity in our religious life and thought, one must be subordinated to the other. Either the personal or the impersonal point of view must be made controlling. And when both of these are tried out, a considerable advantage is seen to attach to the personalistic or prophetic viewpoint.

There is, first, a practical advantage. The prophetic type of experience is more "healthy minded" than the mystical. It stands closer to the normal life of men.

It is optimistic. It finds value and the possibility of increasing value in the world and in human life as a whole. Not negation, but affirmation is its watchword. What it aims at is not the extinction of the natural, but its transfiguration. It thus takes its stand on the common ground of human need and human hope. It links itself up with the instinctive quest after life and thus has a universality of appeal which would hardly be possible to mysticism with its pessimistic, transcendental, and ecstatic type of experience. The latter may serve as a valuable supplement to prophetism, as a purging or sublimating factor in it; but made central and controlling it upsets the balance of human life and leads to asceticism and monasticism with their inner contradictions. Only a religious life, unified by an ethical and prophetic outlook, can meet the practical needs of mankind as a whole.

It is but another phase of the same general idea when, in the next place, we point out that the fundamental and distinctive elements in religion come to a clearer and more consistent expression in personalistic prophetism than in an impersonal mysticism. Both types of piety imply trustful dependence, the yearning after redemption, and more or less of ethical idealism. But the first and last do not receive adequate expression in mysticism. Interest there centers in the second, in the quest after salvation, and this takes on an almost unhuman form so that it runs counter to rational trust and obedience. The fundamental pathos of mysticism is wonder, awe, mystery, and these emotions belong to the threshold of religion rather than to religion itself. Mystical religion is, then, undeveloped and onesided. Only in prophetic religion do the elementary religious interests come to a well-rounded and complete fruition.

A further advantage in the prophetic type of religion is its clearer, more adequate and more rational conception of Deity. A personal God in the plenitude of his perfections is a Being whom we at least in principle understand. He stands related to the selves that we experience. He is no airy abstraction, but a concrete individual. He performs an intelligible function in the universe. He fits into a rational view of the world. And he furnishes an adequate ground for religious faith. In him both trust and hope can repose with perfect security. Not so, however, the impersonal Being of pantheistic mysticism. Its nature is both unknown and unknowable. We can form no clear or rational conception of it. It is itself superrational or irrational and ineffable. The only proper attitude toward it is one of silence. If faith be extended to it, there is no rational warrant for so doing. It is all a matter of feeling, and feeling that soars above the plane of reason into the realm of ecstasy. Such a vague and agnostic view of the ultimate reality may have its value in certain esoteric circles, but history offers convincing evidence that it cannot be made the basis of a popular and vital religious faith.

In recent years the feeling seems to have arisen that the mystical world-view is more consonant with modern science than the prophetic, and hence the effort is being made to detach religion from its theistic basis. The idea is that if religion would only renounce its personalism and consent to be reduced to a sense of awe or to reverence for the "sacred," whatever that may be, it would be more acceptable to the modern mind. One could in that case accept the current philosophical naturalism and yet be religious. For religion in its mystical form does not require faith in a personal God. Its world-view is impersonal and agnostic, as is that of naturalistic science. A fusion of the two is, therefore, possible, and when this is accomplished we may expect that the modern world will again become religious. But this is a delusive hope. No real synthesis of mysticism and philosophic naturalism is possible.

For one thing, the mystical Absolute is a very different Being from the naturalistic absolute. The latter offers no basis for faith and hope and no incentive to idealism. The former, on the other hand, is enshrouded in a veil of sanctity. Though unknowable in its inmost being, it is an object of veneration and of trust as no naturalistic absolute could be. Again, the spirit of modern naturalism is entirely different from that of mysticism. The latter is pessimistic and other-worldly, the former optimistic and secular. One is idealistic, the other realistic; one aims at the suppression of desire, the other at its gratification. The two in spirit run directly counter to each other. No real union of the two can be effected. Indeed, the realism and optimism of modern naturalism stand closer to the prophetic than the mystical type of religion. If religion in any form is to persist in the modern world, it must be of the prophetic type. Theistic personalism, and it alone, makes possible a spiritual interpretation of the universe which conserves the truth both of religion and of science. To renounce the personality of God is to deprive religion of its rational basis and transform it into a vague and futile mysticism; on the other hand, to make the still further renunciation that philosophic naturalism would require of us, would be to reduce religion to a vacuous ejaculation of wonder.

Our argument in this chapter has in the main consisted in showing, first, that religion implies vital faith in a superworld and, secondly, that while its view of the superworld may be either personal or impersonal, the former is the one in which it comes to its highest and truest expression. If there is no superworld, religion has no valid intellectual content; its theology is mythology. As such it might be treated as a kind of symbolic sociology or as a poetic interpretation of nature,[29] but it would have no scientific standing. If religion under these circumstances should continue to exist, it would be as a purely practical affair without any cognitive significance. It would be regarded as throwing no light whatsoever upon the structure of the universe and hence would have no power from above either to command the conscience or to console the heart. It would be a religion without faith, and a faithless religion is a contradiction in terms.

---

[29] See Emile Durkheim, *The Elementary Forms of the Religious Life,* and J. S. Huxley, *Religion Without Revelation,* pp. 61ff. Compare the "civil theology" and the "poetic theology" of Varro.

Assuming that this is so, that faith is indispensable to religion and that it is also valid so far as its affirmation of a superworld is concerned, we have a basis for theology as well as for religion. But the nature of our theology will vary greatly according to the view we have of the superworld. If we, in mystical fashion, regard it as essentially impersonal and unknowable, our theology will be largely negative in character. It will take the form of an attempt to show that ultimate reality transcends human knowledge and that it is only as the antithesis or negation of the sensible world that we can be said to know it. Indeed, it presents itself to us as hardly more than a deification of the word "not." What it is in any positive sense lies completely beyond us. There is no divine revelation upon which we can draw for knowledge. The only way that any positive insight can come to us is through a mystical or ecstatic experience. And this experience is of an ineffable nature so that its content cannot be communicated to others and hence cannot become the subject matter of theology. It may give to him who has the experience, the assurance *that* God is, but *what* he is remains a mystery. All that theology can do as over against such an experience is to try to provide a place for it and, if possible, to validate it. No positive theological material can be drawn from it. Theology from this point of view exhausts itself in a largely negative metaphysics and epistemology.

One may, it is true, from the mystical standpoint, have what might be called a secondary theology, a theology dealing with the gods of the popular religions. But such a theology would be mythology. At the best, it would be a symbolical or allegorical expression of truths contained in the higher negative theology. In itself it would represent nothing final. It would assume that the truth of polytheism is to be found in pantheism.

Pantheistic mysticism is, in one way, more favorable to theological development than theistic prophetism, but in another way less so. It is more favorable insofar as its world-view involves a more radical reconstruction of common-sense experience. Prophetism is compatible with ordinary dualism, and with more or less of secular optimism. But mysticism is monistic and pessimistic. It holds to the phenomenality of the world both in the metaphysical and the valuational sense of the term. And this viewpoint is one that cannot be attained without considerable intellectual effort. Profound reflection is necessary to make it one's own. Philosophy and theology would thus seem to inhere in the very blood of mysticism. And to a large extent this is true. Mysticism is rationalistic and theological. It moves on a different plane from that of ordinary experience.

But, on the other hand, mysticism tends also to restrict theological activity. It does so by ascribing to theology a function that is largely negative and by emphasizing ecstasy as the one great source of religious illumination. If the ecstatic experience were itself capable of theological explication, we might have in it an additional and fruitful source of theological development. But, according to mysticism, this is not the case. The ecstatic state has no communicable content and hence is theologically sterile. Furthermore, rational theology yields no insight into ultimate reality. It affirms a transcendent Being, but enshrouds him or it in an impenetrable veil so that a positive or constructive theology is hardly possible.

For the most fruitful development of theology we must, therefore, turn to the prophetic type of religion. Religion in this form does not require such a radical intellectual reconstruction of our common experience as does mysticism. It stands closer to the ordinary life and thought of men, and in this sense is less intellectualistic. But in contrast with mysticism, it finds both in reason and in revelation or religious experience positive sources of religious knowledge, and hence gives to theological activity an encouragement that it could not otherwise have. The result is that theology has received on prophetic soil a development far transcending in significance that which it has received at the hands of mystics.

This development has not been without its peril to religion. There has always been a danger that theology might become the master of religion rather than its servant. And whenever this has occurred, religion has lost its pristine power, it has become a doctrine instead of a life. This is the error or evil in scholasticism. What theology needs to learn is that its function is regulative, not creative. The religious impulse is native to man. It springs up spontaneously in human life. It is not created by theological reflection nor, as a rule, even evoked by it. Religion is something other and deeper than a doctrinal system. It is a profound personal attitude, a vital experience. It was this fact that Schleiermacher brought out in his famous definition of religion as "the feeling of absolute dependence." This feeling is prior to conceptual knowledge, but it does not exclude it. Indeed, it has in its simplest form an implicit intellectual content. And the function of theology is to clarify, systematize, and logically justify this content. The content itself is ultimate and, in a sense, self-justifying, but imperfectly self-conscious and self-directive. What theology has to do is to bring it to self-consciousness, to guide it and to supplement it with rational grounds of belief. Its task is thus regulative, not constitutive.

But while we need to recognize the subordinate and instrumental relation of theology to religion, we need also to recognize the importance of the service it renders. The religious instinct easily goes astray both in the field of thought and practice. Superstition and mythology have dogged its steps from the beginning and have often made of primitive and historical religion a scandal alike to reason and conscience. To remove these excrescences is, then, a task of the utmost significance; and this is the chief function of theology. Its duty is to define the nature of true religion, to eliminate what is out of harmony with it, to systematize its teaching, and to present it to the world in a way that will appeal to the common intelligence. Such a task as this is manifestly integral to religion itself. Without it, without a theology, religion would not rise above the blind, instinctive stage.

## CHAPTER II

## THE CHRISTIAN FAITH AND THEOLOGY

THEOLOGY has its roots in the objective reference of religious experience. If religion had no such reference, if it were purely subjective, there would be no theology. In that case religion would have no intellectual content. But that it does have such a content has been made evident in the preceding chapter. Religion by its very nature refers to a Divine Object, it looks beyond the visible to the invisible, it has transcendental implications. These implications, however, are at first vague and ill-defined. They call for clarification, for systematic exposition, for rational justification. This it is that gives rise to theology.

There are, as we have seen, two main types of religion: the mystical with its leaning toward impersonalism and pessimism, and the prophetic with its stress on personality and hope. Of the latter type, Christianity is the chief representative. As such it stands for a definite theistic world-view. But there is a question as to whether this world-view is exclusively a matter of revelation or whether it is also grounded in reason. If we take the former view, Christian theology has merely the task of systematically expounding the Christian faith; if we take the latter view, it has the additional task of seeking rationally to justify it. On this point there has been a long-standing debate.

There has also in this connection been a question as to whether in addition to faith and reason there is not another more direct and immediate source of religious knowledge. Some have maintained that there is, that the soul is capable of a direct and intuitive apprehension of the Divine. In this way mysticism has been introduced into Christian theology and has played a considerable rôle in it. Whether it is, however, congenial to the true nature of Christianity, is a question on which there has been and is wide difference of opinion. Many regard it as an exotic, as an alien and disturbing influence.

Then, too, Christianity has brought into theology a new and distinctive problem. Like other religions it is at bottom concerned with the superworld, with the question of its reality, its nature, and its relation to human life. But all these problems in the Christian system come to a focus in the person and work of Christ. In him Christianity claims to have a unique and absolute revelation of God. A new problem, consequently, arises as to how this could be and how it is to be conceived—the problem of Christology. The details of this problem will come up for discussion in a later volume, but in a preliminary way some account needs here to be taken of it insofar as it implies the absoluteness of Christianity.

The particular topics, then, to be discussed in the present chapter are the relation of the Christian faith to reason or knowledge, its relation to mysticism, and its claim to be the absolute religion.

### Faith and Reason

The relation of faith and reason to each other is one of the most complex problems that has arisen in the history of Christian thought and one with reference to which there has been the widest diversity of opinion. We may distinguish two main tendencies. Some have held that faith and reason are mutually antithetical, and hence have either tried to destroy one in the interest of the other or have held to a "double truth." Others have maintained that there is a kinship between them, but have interpreted this kinship in different ways, either subordinating one to the other or holding that they in some sense imply or supplement each other. Both of these tendencies have been widely represented in the history of Christian theology.

The first received occasional expression in the early church, as, for instance, by Tertullian, and has perhaps never been without its representatives. But there are two periods, at which it became acute, if not dominant. One was the close of the Middle Ages and the other the past fifty years or so. Professor W. P. Paterson has pointed out that in its attitude toward religious knowledge Christian thought has twice traversed "the cycle of appreciation, exaggeration and depreciation."[1] The first cycle extended from the Apostolic Age to the Reformation, and the second from the Reformation to modern times. We to-day represent about the same depreciatory attitude toward religious knowledge that we find at the close of the medieval period.

---

[1] *The Nature of Religion*, pp. 324-36.

The causes of this attitude are various, but we need not here inquire into them in detail. We should, however, distinguish between a vigorous and triumphant faith which opposes itself to knowledge and a weak and halting faith which lives only by renouncing the claim to knowledge. The latter is a sign of spiritual decay and may be regarded as owing its origin to a pathological state of the religious consciousness. The former has its source in religious and practical motives and in a more or less dualistic and agnostic type of philosophy. The chief source is the religious feeling or conviction that reason is a purely human faculty and that the knowledge it acquires is also purely human. It cannot, therefore, be of any positive value in the field of religious belief. For the one source and object of faith is God. He alone redeems us and gives us a saving knowledge of himself. Human reason itself can do nothing toward that end. There is, consequently, a necessary antithesis between faith, on the one hand, and reason or knowledge, on the other, since the former is divinely imparted to us, while the latter is a human endowment or attainment.

This dualistic view has often been strengthened by practical exigencies. The church has been under the necessity of defending itself against the encroachment of heresy, and in so doing has not infrequently found it more convenient and effective to appeal to the authority of its own faith than to the common reason. Reason has been declared to be incompetent to deal with religious beliefs, and to be, when so used, an inevitable source of error. The dualism of faith and reason has thus served the purposes of ecclesiastical authoritarianism and has to some degree been the result of it. It has also naturally been linked up with a more or less agnostic tendency in philosophy. Indeed, philosophical agnosticism may be said to be the logical correlate of the antithesis of faith and reason. If faith is the sole source and ground of religious conviction, it follows necessarily that reason is metaphysically incompetent.

In the long discussion connected with this dualistic view there has been much unclearness and confusion of thought with reference to the meaning of "faith," "reason," and "knowledge." "Faith" has generally been interpreted as implying an objective and authoritative revelation. But the content of revelation and the nature of its authority have been very differently conceived. There has also been wide difference of opinion as to the nature of faith, whether it should be regarded as primarily volitional or intellectual and whether it should be viewed as exclusively the work of the Divine Spirit or as at least partly human. Then, too, there has been no agreement as to the exact nature and limits either of reason or knowledge. A certain antithesis to "faith" has been affirmed, but the line of demarcation between reason or knowledge, on the one hand, and faith, on the other, has never been defined in such a way as to command general assent. Schleiermacher and Kant, no doubt, made important contributions to the problem, so that there is some warrant for holding that they mark a new era in the history of Apologetics.[2] But the history of thought

[2] So Theodore Haering, *The Christian Faith*, I, p. 103.

since their day offers little justification for the view that they solved the problem.

Both Schleiermacher and Kant rejected the older theistic proofs, and the former sought to build up a theology based exclusively on the Christian consciousness. In so doing he fell in line with those theologians who in the past had opposed faith to reason. He disagreed with them in their depreciation of reason and in their authoritarian conception of revelation, but he agreed with them in asserting the independence of the Christian faith and in limiting theology to a systematic exposition of it. The "rational" justification of Christianity he regarded both as unnecessary and as impossible, at least in the older apologetic sense of the term. And this has perhaps been the prevailing view in Protestant theology since his time. It was adopted by Albrecht Ritschl and his followers, and to-day Karl Barth in a quite different manner and spirit is advocating it.

With the claim to independence on the part of faith no fault need be found. Religion does not and could not live from the crumbs that fall from the table of philosophy or ethics. It stands in its own right. But from this it does not follow that faith and reason are irreconcilable or that they are entirely disparate activities so that faith can receive no support from reason. Whatever may be said of the value of the theistic arguments, faith cannot completely divorce itself from reason. It is reason that makes faith articulate, it is reason that systematizes faith, it is reason that helps ward off heresy, it is reason that commends faith to the unbelieving world. Without reason faith would be an inchoate emotion or an erratic bowlder in the life of man. It is reason that weaves faith into the warp and woof of our common experience. No doubt it may also serve the interests of unbelief or be so construed as to lead to a state of suspense with reference to the ultimate objects of faith. But this negative relation to religion does not inhere in the nature of reason as such. There is nothing in reason that necessarily puts it in antagonism to faith; one is not purely human and the other purely divine. Nor is there any valid ground for holding that reason may be used to systematize the intellectual content of faith, but not used to establish its truth. The process of systematizing calls for a certain amount of rational evaluation just as truly as a formal defense does. Between the systematic exposition and rational justification of religion there is no sharp line of demarcation. The latter is a natural supplement to the first. We conclude, then, that the dualistic view of faith and reason had its origin in a mistaken supernaturalism and cannot be consistently carried through.[3]

The currency which this type of thought at present has and which it had toward the close of the medieval period must be regarded as the outcome of a transient mood. It does not express the settled conviction of the church. Theology cannot be permanently based upon such a dualism. The normal and representative view is that which holds to the kinship of faith and

---

[3] "He that takes away reason," said John Locke, "to make way for revelation, puts out the light of both." *An Essay Concerning Human Understanding*, IV, XIX, 4.

reason. This is the view that has prevailed during most of the church's history.

The kinship of faith and reason, however, has been differently conceived. We may perhaps distinguish three historic views: the Augustinian or Platonic, the Thomistic or Aristotelian, and the Hegelian. All of these assumed a fundamental accord between faith and reason, but the actual human relationship of the two to each other they conceived differently.

The Augustinian view recognized two sources of knowledge, Authority and Reason, and subordinated the latter to the former. "Nothing," said Augustine, "is to be accepted save on the authority of Scripture, since greater is that authority than all the powers of the human mind." But he did not oppose the human and the divine sources of knowledge sharply to each other. He regarded every act of knowing as due in part at least to divine illumination. The human mind, he said, cannot be its own light. In knowing it is bathed in an atmosphere of incorporeal or uncreated light. There is, he held, a light of eternal reason by which all men are illuminated and to which all knowledge is in some measure due. Human reason does not, therefore, even in its present estate, stand directly opposed to divine illumination; it rather presupposes it. And so it is also with its relation to faith. "Understand," said Augustine, "that thou mayest believe, believe that thou mayest understand."[4] "For we could not believe at all unless we were rational beings."[5] Believing implies an under-

[4] *Sermo* XLIII, p. 9.
[5] *Epistle* CXX, 3.

standing of what is believed; and understanding in turn implies belief. The latter point was especially emphasized by Anselm. "I do not seek," he said, "to understand that I may believe, but I believe in order to understand. For this also I believe—that unless I believed, I should not understand."[6] Belief, in other words, while not produced by the understanding, is not a blind act. It both leads to knowledge, and in its inception, as Augustine pointed out, is guided by it. Faith thus implies reason and reason faith. One cannot exist without the other.

This, however, does not mean that faith has no mysteries or that its mysteries are all open to reason. Human knowledge has its limits. But these limits are not arbitrarily fixed by the nature either of faith or reason. Faith is not a barrier, but a challenge to reason. It invites rational investigation, reflection, justification. It does not spurn reason, but seeks cooperation with it. And so we find Anselm developing his famous ontological argument for the existence of God and his almost equally famous theory of the atonement. We likewise find Augustine seeking to throw light upon the Trinity and other mysteries of the Christian faith. Such intellectual ventures as these could not be entirely successful, nor were they intended to be. But they did establish a liaison between faith and reason, and thus prepared the way for a rational theology—a theology that sought not only to expound, but also to justify the intellectual content of religion.

The Thomistic conception of faith and reason,

---

[6] *Proslogium*, Chap. I.

which superseded the Augustinian in the thirteenth century, was based upon the Aristotelian philosophy. Platonism was aprioristic and mystical in its theory of knowledge. This gave to the human intellect an indefinite reach and led to a mingling of natural and supernatural knowledge which prevented a sharp line of demarcation between them. It also tended to release human thought from its bondage to sense and to encompass it with a divine light that afforded it direct glimpses of the superworld. Aristotelianism, on the other hand, was empiricistic and naturalistic. It restricted knowledge to sense experience and to what could be legitimately extracted from it. There was, consequently, no place left for the ontological argument or for direct divine illumination. The existence of God might be inferred from the existence of the world, but no direct insight into the necessity or actuality of his being was possible. The inference to his existence was by its very nature indirect and was effected solely by the natural reason, leading only to such a conception of his nature as was warranted by sense experience. Whatever lay beyond this conception in the Christian view of God was due to revelation and was beyond the power of the human mind to substantiate. It was wholly mysterious in character and could be accepted only on authority.

The abstract Augustinian antithesis between authority and reason was thus translated into a strict epistemological dualism, and a sharp distinction drawn for the first time between natural and revealed theology. The latter was based upon the authority of revelation and had to do with the distinctive doctrines of the Christian faith such as the Trinity and the Incarnation. These doctrines were regarded as transcending human reason. No proof of them was possible. All that the theologian could do was to expound them and to show that they are not self-contradictory or contrary to reason. For however much these doctrines might transcend human reason, they were not regarded as irrational. They, rather, represented a profounder type of reason which the human mind could not fathom, but between which and the human reason there was no essential contradiction. Their validity, however, depended not upon their inherent rationality, but upon the divine authority from which they proceeded. It was revelation, not reason, that guaranteed their truth.

Natural theology, on the other hand, was concerned with such doctrines as are accessible to the unaided reason, doctrines that are not peculiar to Christianity, as, for instance, the belief in God and immortality. These doctrines might not be capable of absolute demonstration, but rational grounds could be offered in support of them which put them on the same level as other conclusions reached by philosophy and science, and in this general sense they might be said to be demonstrable.

Religious truth, or theology, was thus divided into two parts, one based on natural reason and the other on divine revelation. Strictly speaking only the latter called for faith. For faith as distinguished from reason could exist only where the light of reason failed. But here a double difficulty arose. It was by no means certain just where the line between faith and reason should be drawn; and it was also not clear to which the greater degree of certainty should be attached. From one point of view faith seemed less certain than reason, for reason yields knowledge, and knowledge by its very nature carries with it a greater degree of certitude than faith. But from another point of view faith seemed more certain than reason, for it is based upon divine authority and in comparison with it human reason is weak and errant. Then, too, the content of faith was not clearly fixed. The truth revealed in Scripture manifestly included not only the distinctive doctrines of Christianity, but also such general religious doctrines as those relative to God and immortality for which there was supposed to be a basis in reason. The provinces of faith and reason thus seemed to overlap each other, and it would also seem that there were two different kinds of faith, one supported by reason and the other transcending it. The tendency, however, was to emphasize the latter and yet to insist that there could be no fundamental conflict between faith and reason. Such was the view of Thomas Aquinas and Duns Scotus,[7] and such is still the official teaching of the Roman Catholic Church. It was also the view that prevailed in orthodox Protestant circles down to a century or so ago.

Augustinianism and Thomism both subordinated reason to faith. They differed chiefly in the fact that Thomism distinguished more sharply than Augustin-

[7] For an excellent exposition of the medieval conception of the relation of faith and reason or philosophy and theology to each other, see *Duns Scotus*, by C. P. S. Harris (1927), especially Vol. I.

ianism between natural and supernatural knowledge and based theology more exclusively upon the latter. The effort was made, but with rather indifferent success, as we have seen, to draw a hard-and-fast line between the truths of reason and those of revelation, while it was still maintained that the two were in fundamental accord with each other. In the case of any apparent conflict between them reason must yield to revelation. That seemed the logical procedure, and it was furthermore the line of action naturally required by the recognized authority of the church. But with the modern decline of ecclesiastical authority there was a tendency for reason not only to assert its independence, but to assume the hegemony. Instead of allowing itself to be subordinated to faith it now subordinated faith to itself, and that, too, with the conviction that rightly understood there is a fundamental harmony between them. In bringing about this harmony there are two methods possible. One may cut down faith to fit reason, or one may enlarge reason so as to make it fit faith. The first method was adopted by the "deistic" movement and the result was such a cramping of faith that eventually "deism" became practically synonymous with atheism. The other method was adopted by Hegel, who found in reason a basis not only for faith in the transcendent reality of spirit, but for faith in the Christian doctrines of the Trinity and Incarnation. By developing this position and sustaining it with all the resources of genius he rendered for a time a very considerable service to the historic Christian faith. He gave to it an intellectual standing that it seemed to have permanently lost under the disintegrating influence of eighteenth-century rationalism. But in doing so he transformed its true nature by subordinating it to a more or less alien "reason" and by giving to it a new symbolical interpretation.

To the symbolic theory of religious belief as such no objection need be raised. Symbolic truth is no doubt better than no truth at all. But when the truth supposed to be symbolized turns out to be radically different from that which the symbol originally denoted, there is a question whether the symbolic interpretation renders a permanent service to the cause either of faith or reason. And this question may legitimately be raised with reference to the Hegelian interpretation of religion and particularly of Christianity. Its distinction between truth in the form of *Vorstellung* (imaginative representation) and truth in the form of *Begriff* (concept) is suggestive and describes fairly well the difference between religion or theology, on the one hand, and much philosophy, on the other. But when it is maintained that the *Vorstellung* of theistic religious faith has only a temporary validity, that it is merely preliminary in character and that it is destined eventually to give way to the *Begriff* of a pantheistic absolute idealism,[8] it is evident that we have to do with a viewpoint that involves a fundamental reconstruction of the Christian faith. Faith now becomes a pale reflection or vague anticipation of reason and derives its entire justifi-

[8] Hegel himself, it is true, objected to being called a pantheist, but in the sense that he did not allow a place for the free relation of God to the world his system would generally be admitted to be pantheistic.

cation from that relationship. In and of itself as a unique body of belief it has no ultimate validity. Its truth is to be found not in itself, but in the idealistic and pantheistic philosophy which it is supposed to adumbrate. In other words the truth of faith is reason.

This Hegelian view of the relation of faith and reason to each other is manifestly unsatisfactory from the standpoint of faith; and the same may be said of the Platonic and Aristotelian views from the standpoint of reason. Hegelianism denies to faith its uniqueness and absoluteness and intellectualizes it too much. Augustinian Platonism and scholastic Aristotelianism, on the other hand, did not allow reason to come to its full rights. They subordinated it to faith in the case of a conflict between the two, and failed to define satisfactorily the nature of each. They linked up faith too closely with ecclesiastical authority and, at the same time, gave to it too intellectualistic a cast. Augustinianism, furthermore, did not distinguish clearly between human reason and divine illumination, while Thomism distinguished too sharply between them and tried to draw a fixed dividing line between the realm of reason and that of faith, assigning the first to natural theology and the latter to revealed theology. This Thomistic solution of the problem of faith and reason has had great historical influence and is not yet obsolete, but its persistence is due to its practical utility in conserving the idea of an objective religious authority rather than to its own adequacy in dealing with the complex data involved in the problem.

Modern thought has made three important contributions toward a more satisfactory determination of the relation of faith and reason to each other. It has released faith from its traditional connection with an external and more or less coercive authority, and has given to it as well as to reason an autonomous position in human life. It has, in the next place, interpreted faith in a more voluntaristic sense than heretofore and has shown that in this respect it is a permanent presupposition of reason rather than a temporary adumbration of it or a transitory stage in its development. In the third place, it has defined reason more precisely and shown from what points of view it is and from what points of view it is not an ally of faith.

It was Schleiermacher who first clearly and emphatically grounded religious faith in the human soul itself and gave to it a place co-ordinate with if not superordinate to the intellect and the moral nature. Faith, as thus understood, did not, it is true, necessarily include the full Christian faith. But insofar as the latter represents religion in its highest and purest form, it is entitled in a pre-eminent degree to whatever logical cogency or apologetic value attaches to Schleiermacher's contention that autonomous validity is to be ascribed to man's religious nature. Such a grounding of faith dispenses with the idea of an external and absolute authority. To some minds this may seem a loss. But whatever loss is sustained at that point is more than recouped by the new independence that releases it from bondage alike to tradition and to reason and enables it to stand in its own right. We have here a kind of naturalistic justification of faith taking the place of the older supernaturalistic and authoritarian apologetic.

The second contribution made by modern thought to the solution of our problem takes us a step further. It not only asserts that religious faith is co-ordinate with reason in the sense that it is autonomously valid, but shows us why it may properly be regarded as such. The older religious thought took little account of the presuppositions of knowledge. Our ordinary knowledge, mediated through sense and intellect, was rather taken for granted as self-evident and as manifestly valid, at least within certain prescribed limits. That such knowledge involves practical interests and ideals and is conditioned by them, received scant attention. Certainly, no special significance was attached to the fact. But since the enunciation of the Kantian doctrine of the primacy of the practical reason increasing stress has been placed upon the volitional and vital factors that condition our common knowledge or supposed knowledge. This emphasis has been carried to an irrational extreme by pragmatists and instrumentalists, but the basal fact, that knowledge is rooted in our practical nature, in our interests and ideals, is not discredited thereby. Take, for instance, our natural sciences. They assume that the world is intelligible and that we are able to understand it. Neither of these assumptions can be demonstrated. They rest upon an instinctive faith in reason and in the validity of our cognitive ideal. If it were necessary to demonstrate their truth in advance, the natural sciences would never get under way. They owe their entire development to faith. Indeed, without faith there could be no knowledge. In a profounder and more universal sense than either Augustine or Anselm realized, we must believe in order that we may know.

The faith that underlies scientific knowledge is not, it is true, religious faith. But from the epistemological point of view the two kinds of faith are in principle alike, since both consist in assuming the objective reality of ideals whose existence cannot be demonstrated. The ideal in one case is cognitive and in the other ethical. But both are assumed to be real. And the fact that this assumptive element underlies both science and religion, constituting, as it were, their common denominator, is a fact of profound significance. For if the assumption of the reality of an ideal is legitimate and valid in one case, there is no good reason why it should not be in the other. Logically faith in its religious form has as sound a basis as has faith in its scientific form. And since the latter is commonly accepted, no valid objection can be raised in principle to the former. There is, therefore, no antithesis between faith and reason. Rather does reason presuppose faith; it will never supersede it.

This, however, is true of reason and faith only in their more general aspects. It is possible to construe reason in such a way as to make it antithetical in content, if not in principle, to religious faith. And here it is that modern thought has made its third contribution to our problem. It has defined reason more precisely and thus clarified its relation to religious belief. But this does not mean that any one definition of reason or of knowledge has been agreed upon. There are three such definitions and each implies a different attitude toward the Christian faith. One may be called the necessitarian or deterministic, another the positivistic or agnostic, and the third the teleological. None of these is modern in the sense that it was unknown to earlier times, but all three have in modern thought been more clearly formulated and more sharply differentiated from each other.

The deterministic conception of reason received its most thoroughgoing expression from Spinoza and gained wide currency through the influence of a materialistic interpretation of science. Such a view is manifestly out of harmony with the Christian faith and, when logically carried out, excludes it altogether. The positivistic or agnostic conception of knowledge owes its present vogue largely to Hume, Kant, and the empirical sciences in general. Theoretically, this view leaves the door open to faith, and some theologians, as we have seen, have sought to establish an alliance between the two. But no such alliance can endure. The prevailing tone and temper of positivism is naturalistic, and for Christian theology to be linked up with it is for it to be unequally yoked with unbelief. A reason that denies all knowledge of the superworld will end by suppressing faith also.

We are then left with the teleological conception of reason as the only one consistent with the Christian faith. And it may be added that it is also the only one that is consistent with itself. A positivistic reason that denies the categories of substance and cause never succeeds in dispensing with them. In one way or another it surreptitiously introduces them into its own operations and thus negates its own fundamental principle. On the other hand, a reason that sees in the world an absolutely necessitated system, either logical or mechanical, destroys itself. For only a free intelligence can distinguish between truth and error and thus make knowledge possible. If reason, then, is to escape self-contradiction and self-destruction, it must rise above the positivistic and also the necessitarian plane and be conceived of as free and purposive. Such a reason will not only be consistent with itself, but it will give us a view of the universe that is consistent with religious belief. It will find purpose not only in itself but in the world, it will show us that personality is the only satisfactory key to ultimate reality, and will thus furnish a sound basis for Christian faith.

Reason, so conceived, stands in its own right, but it is nevertheless an ally of faith, and faith in its turn is an ally of reason. The two belong together. There is no reason without a measure of faith, and there is no self-consistent reason without more or less of religious faith. On the other hand, there is no faith without some reason, and there certainly is no self-consistent faith without a very considerable admixture of reason. Knowledge is not a biarchy in which reason and faith hold separate rule over independent provinces. It is a monarchy governed by rational faith or by believing reason. In some instances or in certain respects the rational factor may be dominant and in others the believing factor. But the two cannot be completely separated. Only an illicit abstraction can divorce them. No sharp line can, therefore, be drawn between the theology of reason and that of revelation. One involves the other, and no theology is complete without both. "Revealed theology" is grounded in "natural theology," and natural theology derives its dynamic and living content from revealed theology. It is, then, a mistake to try to limit theology to an *exposition* of the Christian faith. An adequate theology must seek also a rational justification of it. But "rational" in this connection must be understood in the broader teleological sense of "reasonable." A purely logistic or empiricistic rationalism can furnish no basis for religious faith. Such a basis can be found only in a rationalism that recognizes purpose as a fundamental category of thought.

## Faith and Mysticism

In addition to reason there is another source of religious knowledge to which both Christian and non-Christian have appealed. Reference has already been made to it. It is mystical experience, the direct apprehension of the Divine through a supersensuous and superrational act or state of the soul.

The term "superrational," as employed in this connection, is not altogether free from ambiguity. It may denote superiority merely to the formal or discursive reason or it may denote superiority to all reason. The latter view has been held by many mystics and those among the most influential. They have ascribed to man a faculty altogether distinct from reason by means of which he may enter into union with God and acquire an "experimental perception" of his presence. This faculty has been variously designated as the spark of the soul, its essence, its center, its apex, its ground, its virginal portion, as the fund of the spirit, the summit of the mind, and the *synteresis*. But whatever name may be applied to it, it is that capacity, which the soul is supposed to have, of directly contemplating and embracing the Infinite. This "contemplation" has a specific character. In its highest and purest form it manifests itself as ecstasy, a state of mind in which the subject becomes one with its Divine Object. "The eye with which I see God," said Meister Eckhart, "is the *same* eye with which he sees me."[9] In order to know him, "I must become completely he and he I; so that this he and this I become and are one I."[10] Such a unitive experience as this may with Plotinus rightly be said to be "reason no longer, but more than reason, and before reason, and after reason."[11]

By excluding all differentiation and otherness ecstatic contemplation transcends not only discursive thought, but articulate thought itself and becomes in its very nature ineffable. Much may be said with reference to it. It may be analyzed and systematized into a kind of science, as mystics since the time of Hugh and Richard of Saint Victor have sought to do; and from this point of view one might with

---

[9] See *Studies in Mystical Religion*, p. 231, by Rufus M. Jones.

[10] See *Mysticism*, p. 502, by Evelyn Underhill.

[11] *Ennead* VI, 9, 10.

Harnack define mysticism as "rationalism applied to a sphere above reason," and say with Goethe that it is "the scholastic of the heart, the dialectic of the feelings"; but in its essence the contemplative or mystical experience is something apart from reason, unique and independent, if not antithetical to it. Such is the sense in which its superrationality is perhaps most commonly understood.

There are, however, those who seek to bring reason and the mystical experience into closer relation to each other and who hold that the latter is to be regarded as superrational only in the sense that it transcends the discursive reason. If reason be interpreted as "the logic of the whole personality," as it ought to be, the mystic, we are told, would have no interest in appealing to a faculty above reason. He might regard his own unique experience as "the very pinnacle of rationality."[12] Instead, then, of accepting Harnack's definition of mysticism, as above given, we might with Dean Inge invert it, and say that mysticism is "reason applied to a sphere above rationalism."[13] This interpretation of the relation of the mystical and the rational to each other is entirely tenable, provided we understand by the "mystical" the more moderate form of that type of experience.

But what we are here concerned with is not the relation of mysticism to reason, but its relation to faith. The problem of faith and mysticism has never been so acute as that of faith and reason. Mystical experience has been less of a disturbing factor in Christian

---

[12] *Studies in Mystical Religion*, p. xxi, by Rufus M. Jones.
[13] *Christian Mysticism*, p. 21.

thought than the natural reason. There has been a "mystical" as well as a "natural" or rationalistic theology, but it has had a much more limited influence, and has affected "dogmatic" theology much less seriously. The principle at issue, however, in the two cases has been substantially the same. Mystical experience and reason both belong to the "natural" man in the sense that they both have had a recognized place in the so-called "natural" religions, and hence the question has arisen as to the relation which they sustain or ought to sustain to the "revealed" Christian faith. This question, so far as it has to do with reason, we have considered at length. It is now our task to deal with it insofar as it is concerned with mysticism. In the preceding chapter we distinguished the mystical type of piety as embodied in various non-Christian religions from the prophetic type embodied in Christianity, and pointed out certain fundamental differences between them. But here we have to do with a modified form of mysticism, with mysticism within the Christian Church, and the problem of its relation to faith is quite different from the general problem of the relation of the mystical and prophetic types of piety to each other.

As the attempt has been made to establish an antithesis between faith and reason, so a similar attempt has been made in the case of faith and mysticism. But the approach to the problem has been somewhat different. It has, for instance, been argued by Ritschl and some of his followers that mysticism is the characteristic form of Catholic piety, and that it has no place in the true Christian faith as exemplified in

Protestantism. Again, it is maintained by Emil Brunner and other representatives of the so-called "crisis" or "dialectic" theology that there is a Protestant as well as a Catholic mysticism, and that the former as well as the latter stands opposed to the true Pauline and Reformation "faith." With these two conceptions of mysticism and its relation to faith we shall deal briefly.

The Ritschlian view has been expressed most vigorously by Wilhelm Herrmann.[14] He understands by mysticism the Neoplatonic type of piety, "a piety which feels that which is historical in positive religions to be burdensome and so rejects it." This piety is purely subjective, based on feeling, and leads to a vague and empty conception of Deity: God is the mere negation of the world. Such a religious experience as this, we are told, belongs "outside of Christianity." There it will everywhere arise "as the very flower of the religious development." But the Christian must declare it to be a "delusion." For what makes us Christians is this, that "in the person of Jesus we have struck upon a fact that is incomparably richer in content than any feelings that arise within ourselves, and that makes us so certain of God that our conviction of being in communion with him is able to justify itself before the bar of reason and of conscience."[15] The trouble with mysticism, according to Herrmann, is its subjectivity and its consequent emptiness and lack of certainty. It fails to give an adequate place to Christ either in our religious expe-

---

[14] *The Communion of the Christian With God*, pp. 19-56.
[15] *Ibid.*, German edition, 1892, pp. 27f.

rience or in our conception of God. It no doubt may look upon him as the way to God, but it thinks of communion with God as possible beyond him and without him. And this Herrmann regards as "unchristian." The Christian does not "merely come through Christ to God," he finds "in God nothing but Christ." In the personal life of Jesus Christ he has a positive vision of God, and this vision is final and absolute; it dominates his entire religious experience. This is the distinctive position of Protestantism, and hence it has no place for mysticism with its Neoplatonic presuppositions. "It will never be possible," says Harnack, "to make mysticism Protestant without flying in the face of history and Catholicism. . . . A mystic who does not become a Catholic is a dilettante."[16]

By way of response to this Ritschlian teaching it may be urged that mysticism is not to be identified with its Neoplatonic form. The essential thing in it is the "direct and immediate consciousness of the Divine Presence," and this is something quite independent of the particular type of philosophy one holds. It is an elementary religious fact, "common to all religion." There are in religion three fundamental elements: the historical or institutional, the intellectual or speculative, and the mystical or experimental.[17] One of these may be emphasized more than the other and in this way different types of religion may arise. But each has its place in every concrete or positive religion, and the differentia of mysticism is to be

[16] Quoted by W. R. Inge in *Christian Mysticism*, p. 345.

[17] See Baron von Hügel, *The Mystical Element in Religion*, I, pp. 50-82.

found not in any novel element that it contains, but in the special stress that it places upon the subjective or experiential factor in religion. This factor may undergo a unique development under the fostering influence of some particular philosophy or theology such as the Neoplatonic, but what constitutes mysticism is not this unique development, but the common religious experience upon which it is based. Wherever we have the sense of direct communion with God, there we have a mystical experience. Mysticism is not, then, "a particular species of religion," as Herrmann insists, but, rather, one aspect of universal religion or a special emphasis within it. And from this point of view Herrmann was himself a mystic. He felt himself "inwardly grasped of God" and insisted that he differed from the Neoplatonic mystic solely in the way in which he became aware that God was touching him.[18] The divine touch, however, as he experienced it, he refused to call "mystical"; but the difference between him and others at this point was hardly more than verbal.

More important was his onesided stress on the ethical element in Christianity. No doubt this was the major emphasis in the teaching of Jesus and the prophets. They appealed to the absoluteness of the Moral Law, to the categorical imperative, as the means of awakening within men the sense of the Eternal. But in addition to Goodness there are other ideals that reveal the Divine to us, the ideals of Beauty and Truth. And in any comprehensive religion these too must receive recognition. There is a

[18] *The Communion of the Christian With God*, p. 196.

danger, it is true, that under the influence of the æsthetic and the intellectual ideal religion may degenerate into a vague sentimentalism or a lifeless dogmatism; and for that reason there will always be need of the ethical or prophetic emphasis in religion. But this emphasis may become one-sided, and in that case religion may degenerate into a dry and shallow moralism. We need a religion for the whole life; and this means that Truth and Beauty as well as Goodness must be regarded as avenues of approach to the Eternal, and it also means that the mystic sense will be associated with every revelation of the ideal. The Ritschlian conception of "faith" is too narrow, too exclusively ethical.

Again, Ritschl and Herrmann, by way of reaction against the subjectivity of mysticism, sought to establish an impossible historical objectivity. They pointed to the solid fact of Christ as over against the shifting sands of feeling. Here, we were told, is an historical datum that remains the same from age to age. And not only is it more secure than our mystical feelings; it is incomparably richer in content. In Christ we have a wealth of religious truth that sets him apart from every other religious teacher and that gives to him an altogether unique place in human history. Through him, and through him alone, we come to God. There is none other name given among men whereby we may be saved.

In the Ritschlian insistence on this point we have, it is evident, a genuine Christian note; but it is equally evident that this Christian note does not warrant us in condemning the religious life of the non-

Christian or sub-Christian world as worthless. If it were not for a native human capacity for God, there would be no appreciation of the life of Christ and no unique worth would be attributed to him. Indeed, the very conception of Christianity as the crown and apex of man's religious development presupposes something beneath it of which it is the crown and apex. The vague and diffused religiosity of the natural man is the foundation on which the concentrated and truly spiritual life of the Christian is reared. Between the two there is no fundamental antithesis; rather do they involve each other. For there can be no true subjectivity without more or less objectivity, and there can be no true objectivity without more or less subjectivity. The subjective mysticism of the natural man can find its completion only in the objectivity of Christian faith, and the objective fact of Christ presupposes the inner native yearnings of the human soul. One may, out of regard for the absolutist claim of Christianity, say with a measure of justification that it is Christ, and he alone, who gives to other religions whatever permanent truth and worth they have; but, on the other hand, it may also be said with equal truth, that it is the native religious needs and insights of men that alone make possible the appreciation and recognition of the unique dignity of Christ.

The attempt of the Ritschlian school to draw a sharp line of demarcation between faith and mysticism must, then, be pronounced a failure. There is an exclusive mysticism which is to be rejected as non-Christian. But in his reaction against it Herrmann fell into an "excessive Christocentrism," a kind of "*Panchristism,*" and developed a view of the Christian faith which Von Hügel has rather aptly described as "an exclusive amalgam of moralism and history."[19] Such a conception of "faith" may serve the purposes of a partisan Protestantism by differentiating it sharply from Catholicism, but in doing so it narrows Protestantism and tends to eliminate from it one of the most vigorous and wholesome forces that has appeared in its entire history. I refer to pietism in its various German and English forms. During the latter part of his life Ritschl devoted ten years to the writing of a great three-volume work on the History of Pietism, in which he contended that pietism was not a return to the teaching of Luther, nor an advance beyond it, but a reversion to the mystical type of piety current in medieval Catholicism. Even Harnack condemned this attack upon pietism as "one-sided, narrow, and partisan." There is, it is true, a certain kinship between pietism and mysticism; both stress the subjective or emotional element in religion. But this common element, they would both insist, goes back not simply to the Middle Ages, but to the teaching of Paul and John. In the New Testament there is no antithesis between "faith" and mystical experience.[20]

More recently Emil Brunner and other representatives of the "crisis" theology have sought to establish a still more radical distinction between faith and

---

[19] *The Mystical Element of Religion*, II, pp. 263-69, 332f.

[20] For a well-balanced statement of the relation of mysticism to the Christian life see *Humanism and Christianity*, by Bishop Francis J. McConnell, pp. 96-124.

mysticism than that advocated by the Ritschlian school. Not only do they repudiate mysticism in its more extreme form, they reject the experiential principle upon which all mysticism rests. What they primarily object to in mysticism is not its extreme doctrine of divine transcendence, nor its indifference to history, but its doctrine of the divine immanence, its conviction that God manifests himself in human experience, and that through feeling or some other form of psychical activity man is able to lay hold of the Divine. Taking their cue from Sören Kierkegaard (1813–1855), whom they regard as "the greatest Christian thinker of the past century,"[21] they insist that there is an "endless qualitative difference between time and eternity," and thus by one fell stroke they cut the ground not only from under all mysticism, but from under all rationalism and all moralism. Neither in the human will nor the human reason nor human feeling can God be found. He is the antithesis of everything human. The whole adventure of mysticism is, therefore, a mistake, yes, more than a mistake, an "impious presumption." It assumes that through our own experience we can lay hold of God, that men can really build a tower high enough to reach to heaven.

This assumption, according to Brunner and Barth, is the very negation of everything distinctively Christian. What Christianity emphasizes is "revelation" and "faith," and these are diametrically opposed to the "union-intuition" of mysticism and to every attempt to bridge the gulf between the human

---

[21] E. Brunner, *Die Mystik und das Wort*, p. 99.

and the divine from the manward side. Religious experience either with or without its intuitions and ecstasies cannot get us away from the human shore. Only revelation and faith can, and both of these come from God. They form no part of human experience. "Believing God is the antithesis of experiencing God. . . . Our faith stands opposed *to all experience* just as it stands opposed to death and the Devil."[22] We believe in spite of the contradiction of experience. Indeed, it is the contradictory character of experience that makes faith necessary; and for that reason faith is itself superempirical, superhuman, so much so that we do not know when we have it; we can only "believe *that* we believe."[23] There is no way, therefore, of bringing faith into alliance with mystical experience or with experience of any kind. In faith and mysticism we have two distinct types of relation to God. One is Christian, the other heathen; and the two logically exclude each other. No real compromise between them is possible. Faith cannot be translated into religious experience without being distorted. Hence Christian mysticism so called is a hybrid. It is "a mixture of faith and mysticism, of heathenism and Christianity, just as Catholicism as a whole is. This holds also of the religion of Schleiermacher,"[24] and of "modern" piety in general. The great need of our day, consequently, is to disentangle the two and establish their essential antithesis.

Such is the program of the Barthian theology.

---

[22] E. Brunner, *ibid.*, p. 188.
[23] K. Barth, *Römerbrief*, p. 128.
[24] E. Brunner, *Die Mystik und das Wort*, p. 388.

That it has a considerable value as a reaction against a one-sided stress on the divine immanence and as a reaction against the easy-going humanism of our time, is not to be denied. But the attempt to establish a sharp antithesis not only between faith and mysticism, but between faith and religious experience as a whole must be set down as a theological misadventure. For one thing, the supposed or, rather, presupposed "endless qualitative difference between time and eternity" is an arbitrary assumption. Religion no doubt requires a contrast between the human and the divine, but it also requires a kinship between them, if our needs are to be fully met. To insist on the contrast at the expense of the kinship is to do violence to faith and reason alike. Furthermore, "revelation" and "faith" have their proper place and find their true meaning only within religious experience. To detach them from it and even oppose them to it is to reduce them to empty abstractions. And if we then seek to give them content and reality by importing them in some miraculous way into the stream of history or of human consciousness, we have no means of distinguishing them from their immediate human environment except by appealing to some human standard, objective or subjective. To make them the tests of their own divine character is to leave them still in a superhuman isolation. The fact is that there is no way of drawing a hard-and-fast line between the human and the divine. To oppose faith to mystical experience on the ground that one is divine and the other human is to fall into an obsolete supernaturalism.

As in the case of faith and reason, so in the case of faith and mysticism, we must, then, affirm a kinship. But as we found it necessary to distinguish different kinds of "reason," so it is necessary to distinguish different kinds of mysticism, and particularly two, a more extreme and a more moderate type. The more extreme type was introduced into Christianity largely through the influence of pseudo-Dionysius, whose writings date from the early sixth century. They were translated into Latin in the ninth century by John Scotus Erigena, but did not apparently come into general vogue until the twelfth century. From that time on they became the great source of the mystical theology.[25] Their essential teaching has been described as that of "the Neoplatonic philosophy slightly sprinkled with baptismal water from a Christian font." What they especially emphasized was the extreme transcendence of the Ultimate Reality. Language was almost exhausted in the effort to bring out its ineffable character. Only in negative terms could it be described, and yet it was said to transcend all human thought in worth as well as being. The assumption was that the highest degree of universality and also the highest degree of worth correspond with the highest degree of reality. But the ruling notion in the conception of ultimate reality was that of absolute universality, a concept devoid of positive content and identical with bare unity. Now, such a negative and abstract Reality as this, even though capitalized, could hardly fulfill the function of the Christian Deity, and so we find Meister Eck-

[25] See Dom Cuthbert Butler, *Western Mysticism*, pp. 180f.

hart distinguishing between the Godhead and God. This became a popular idea in mystical circles.[26] God was regarded as the personalization of the Godhead, its manifestation and self-realization, and hence as a derived or secondary Being. Among mystics, consequently, the Christian thought of God was shadowed by the thought of a Reality more ultimate, and, therefore, superior to him.

Under the influence of this pantheistic conception, inherent in the philosophic and more extreme form of mysticism, there arose a tendency to ascribe to dogmatic theology a purely symbolical character and to treat its strict theism as essentially metaphorical. An indifference to biblical history also grew up as a result of the immediacy of the mystic's experience. If God was directly and immediately apprehended by the intuition of the mystic, what need was there of an historical revelation? The important thing is to know God and be sure of him, and if this can be attained through mystical vision and ecstasy, why should we trouble ourselves about the facts of history? Such a line of reasoning as this was an almost inevitable accompaniment of the mystical movement, and hence there arose a distinct divergence between it and historical Christianity. The latter made the person of Christ and the personality of God central in its teaching, while the former, under the influence of Neoplatonism, tended to obscure both.

---

[26] Compare *Theologia Germanica*, Chap. XXXI: "To God, as Godhead, appertain neither will, nor knowledge, nor manifestation, nor anything that we can name, or say, or conceive. But to God as God, it belongeth to express himself, and know and love himself, and to reveal himself to himself."

It was, however, mysticism only in its more negative and abstract form that developed in this way a parallax with the Christian faith. The milder and more common form of mysticism had no conscious connection with Neoplatonic metaphysics. It appeared, as we have seen, in the teaching of Paul and John, and throughout Christian history has usually stood close to the traditional teaching of the church. This teaching it has sought to vitalize. It has stressed the importance of religious experience, an experience that actually grips God. Now, such an experience involves no break with the past, nor does it involve an ecstatic union with a "superessential" Reality. It is linked up with faith in the historic Jesus and in the God of Jesus. Instead of being independent of this faith it presupposes it. And in this connection it may be pointed out that all mystical experience implies faith of some kind. The more extreme type of Christian mysticism is based on faith in the Neoplatonic philosophy, and the milder type upon our traditional Christian faith. But it is faith in both cases that gives rise to the experience. Mysticism and faith do not, then, exclude each other, nor are they independent of each other. Without faith there could be no mystical or truly religious experience, and without such experience faith would have no vitality. Faith produces mystical experience, and mystical experience in turn vitalizes faith. This holds true both of the Christian and the Neoplatonic faith.

But what we are here chiefly concerned about is the question as to whether mystical experiences may be regarded as supplementing the Christian faith either in the way of validating it or of adding to its content. The latter kind of supplement is no doubt theoretically possible, but in view of the preceding discussion we should hardly expect positive additions to the content of faith from the experiences of the mystics. Such experiences, as we have seen, are constituted by faith, and hence would naturally reflect it rather than make additions to it. And this, on the whole, is what has actually taken place in the history of Christian mysticism. Here and there mystics have departed from the traditional faith, but they have not done so because of any new revelations of truth made to them in their mystical experiences. They have done so because they had an implicit faith in some non-Christian philosophy such as Neoplatonism, and because this faith molded their experiences into conformity with certain conceptions of God and of the spiritual life different from those sponsored by Christian tradition. In general, however, this deflection from the Christian faith on the part of mystics has been largely negative in character. It has consisted in blurring the positive outlines of Christian belief rather than in substituting anything definite in its stead. Mystics as a rule have been agreed in saying that as a result of their experiences they were sure *that* God is, but *what* he is they did not know. From them we would not, therefore, naturally expect any positive additions to the content of the Christian faith. It is not particular or new truths that they have sought to impart to us.[27]

---

[27] See *A Philosophical Study of Mysticism*, pp. 70-82, by Charles A. Bennett.

What mysticism has primarily aimed to do has been to validate faith, to furnish an experimental verification of it. "Contemplation," said Bernard, "is concerned with the certainty of things."[28] And that it has attained this end in the case of multitudes is evident. But has the supposed verification been trustworthy? Do mystical experiences actually apprehend an objective reality and thus supply us with a kind of perceptual evidence of the truth of religion? Or is the objectivity of religious experience merely an illusory projection into reality of what is given in faith itself? At this point there is much confusion of thought, due to the failure to bear in mind the fact that faith and mystical experience involve each other. There is no such direct and unmediated apprehension of God as some mystics have claimed. But there is also no such apprehension of any objective reality whatsoever. All perceptual experience is interpreted experience; it is conditioned by the apprehending mind. Nowhere do we have pure, unmediated objectivity. Without the categories of thought we could have no knowledge of the external world, and without faith we could have no knowledge of God. Our mystical experience is conditioned by faith in about the same way that our sense experience is conditioned by the categories. But in neither case is the validity of the experience rendered dubious because of the condition on which it rests. All experience and all knowledge necessarily have their conditioning factors. There is, then, no inherent reason

---

[28] *De Consid.* II, 5, translated by G. Lewis.

why mystical experience should not be objectively valid.

Such experience, however, can hardly be regarded as an independent validation of faith. It is, rather, a self-validation on the part of faith itself. What mystical experience does is to give such vividness and richness of emotional content to faith that its objectivity becomes akin to that of vision. It imparts to faith a self-certainty which approaches that of sight. But in doing so it does not so much add anything to faith as evoke from faith what is already contained in it. In other words, what we have in mystical experience is not so much an extra-fiducial justification of faith as the self-evidencing power of faith itself. And in this connection it is important to note that faith justifies itself in *experience*. The effort has repeatedly been made to find a purely objective basis for faith. This motive underlay the old doctrine of biblical infallibility, and has recently reappeared in the Barthian contention that revelation is an ultimate and self-grounding fact and that faith is a divinely produced response to it. Faith does not belong to our experience, nor is it justified by it. It is superempirical and finds its justification or self-justification solely in the *Deus dixit* of Scripture. Beyond that we are told we cannot go.

In this view we have a highly rarefied conception of faith, one that seeks to gain pure objectivity by eliminating all human alloy. The conception, however, is hardly one that can commend itself to critical thought. Its sharp separation of faith from experience must be set aside as an illicit abstraction, and the essentially authoritarian view of revelation which it implies must be rejected as both "irrational" and arbitrary. There is no way of completely escaping subjectivity. The very acceptance of revelation is a subjective act and so also is the determination of its content. Faith, furthermore, can become concrete and real only by being embodied in experience. In the abstract we may distinguish the two, and from this point of view we may think of mystical experience as supplementing and confirming faith. But from the concrete point of view we must think of it as the expression of a certainty inherent in faith itself.

This, however, does not mean that mystical experience has no objective ground and is illusory. It, rather, means that both faith and mystical experience have such a ground and are trustworthy. Both have a divine source. But that faith should be so produced or occasioned by the Divine Spirit as to reveal an objective order is commonly overlooked; and hence if faith does not receive a kind of independent perceptual verification in mystical experience, the skeptical conclusion is sometimes drawn that both it and the mystical experience are devoid of cognitive significance. In order to meet this objection, consequently, it has been claimed that mystical experiences are at bottom independent of faith or, at least, may be such. They have come to men who were professed unbelievers. Such a case was that of Richard Jefferies (1848–1887), "the great nature mystic of the nineteenth century."[29] He accepted the

[29] See *The Philosophy of Mysticism*, pp. 371-88, by Edward I. Watkin.

current naturalistic philosophy of his time and proclaimed himself an "agnostic" and even an "atheist." Yet he had mystical experiences that revealed to him "the existence of an inexpressible entity infinitely higher than Deity,"[30] and that led him to express himself in terms strikingly similar to those of Dionysius, Saint John of the Cross, and other great mystics. Indeed, toward the close of his life he was led by his mystical intuitions to accept the Christian faith. Now, that such an unbeliever as he had these visions and ecstatic experiences is, we are told, a "convincing vindication of the fundamental principles of Catholic theology and mysticism." It proves that the intuition of the mystic is not "the reflex of a creed previously accepted," but an independent revelation of an objective reality.

To this it may be replied that Jefferies must have actually had a profounder faith than the agnostic or atheistic creed which he verbally professed and that it was this profounder faith that gave rise to his mystical experiences. In any case these experiences were expressions of faith rather than disinterested visions of an "unutterable existence infinitely higher than Deity." What he says about them makes that evident. Still, it is significant that in his case they prepared the way for the Christian faith. His experience in that respect illustrates the true relation of nature and grace to each other. Grace, as Thomas Aquinas used to say, does not destroy nature, but

---

[30] *Story of My Heart*, p. 57. Compare the somewhat similar experience of J. Middleton Murry recorded in his recent book entitled *God, Being an Introduction to the Science of Metabiology.*

presupposes and perfects it. No doubt the natural mysticism of the soul is seriously defective and calls for drastic criticism, as does also the natural reason. But neither is antithetical to "revealed" religion. Rather is the Christian faith the crown of both.

### The Absoluteness of Christianity

Thus far we have argued that Christianity stands in an organic relation to the common reason and the common religious experience, and that it is the function of theology not only to expound the Christian faith, but also to justify it in the light of our common intellectual and religious life. The older dualistic and supernaturalistic view is then mistaken. Christianity does not stand apart from the rest of human life as alone divine. It is not an island separated from the great human mainland. It is, rather, a mountain peak rising up out of the broad plane of human need and human aspiration. It is the climax of the natural, not its antithesis. There is, we are told, a light that lighteth every man that cometh into the world. And it is this light that we have in Christianity, a light that came to its sharpest and brightest focus in the person of Christ. Between the light that we have in him and the light that we have in the reason and religious experience of the "natural" man there is no absolute contrast. The difference is one of degree. But the difference of degree is so great as to be practically a difference of kind. Whatever acknowledgments of truth and worth in other religions have come from representative Christian thinkers, they have always ascribed to Jesus an altogether unique significance. They have seen in him the one perfect revealer of God. Whether there be any other revelations of God or not, he has revealed the Father in so exclusive a sense or so pre-eminent a degree as to be entitled to be called "the Word of God." In him we have final or absolute truth. Such has been the claim of the Christian Church from the beginning. On this claim the church was founded, and from it the distinctive content of its theology has been largely derived.

The Christian claim to absoluteness was at first spontaneous, a product of the unreflective consciousness. One might call it "naïve" in the sense that it was not a reasoned conclusion. It was, rather, an instinctive conviction. This was true of Jesus' own estimate of himself and his mission as well as of that current among his immediate disciples. He and they did not institute a scientific comparison between the new faith and other religions, and then conclude that the new faith was superior to all other religions and hence absolute. Its absoluteness or finality was given immediately in Jesus' own self-consciousness and in the faith of his disciples. His Messianic claim implied it, and so, of course, also did the acceptance of the claim by others. Some scholars, it is true, have denied that Jesus made any such claim. But so deeply is it embedded in the Gospels that to eliminate it would go far toward destroying their historical credibility. If the gospel portrait of Jesus is at all to be trusted, we must ascribe to him "the consciousness of being the Fulfiller, of sitting regnant upon the throne of history."[31] And that this conception of him was accepted by his followers needs no proof. For them he was from the very beginning the climax of revelation, the inaugurator of the kingdom of God upon earth.

One might, and as a rule one does, distinguish between the message and the messenger, but in the case of Jesus the two were bound up with each other. The perfection of the messenger guaranteed the perfection of the message, and the perfection of the message pointed to the perfection of the messenger. Both put upon the Christian movement the stamp of uniqueness and finality. Jesus was more than a prophet; he was the Son, who alone knows the Father and reveals him to men (Matt. 11. 27). And his message was the fulfillment of the Law and the Prophets. Indeed, it was in a sense more than that. It introduced, according to Paul, a new kingdom of grace, distinct from and in a way opposed to the older reign of the law. Christianity did not then simply supplement Judaism, it did not simply differ from it quantitatively; it differed from it qualitatively, it abrogated it. And still more so did it stand apart from and overshadow the other religions. No believer questioned its complete supremacy. Its absoluteness was taken for granted. But for that very reason it was not at first made the subject of special study, nor was it theoretically grounded in a thoroughgoing way.

Two tendencies early manifested themselves. One was to base the absoluteness of Christianity upon its

---

[31] See *Is Christianity the Final Religion?* p. 111, by A. C. Bouquet.

isolation, the other upon what might be called its climactic relation to other religions. These tendencies, as we have seen, lay back of the long discussion concerning faith and reason and also that relative to faith and mysticism. In reviewing these controversies we decided in favor of the second view, the synthesis of the Christian faith with reason and mysticism rather than its *diastasis.* But the two views have received such definite and distinct formulations in connection with the problem of the absoluteness of Christianity that they call for further consideration.

Both views have had representatives throughout virtually the whole of Christian history. But it was the first, the belief in the isolation of Christianity, that eventually gained the ascendancy in western theology. Here the Christian religion was separated from all other religions by its supposed miraculous origin. It, and it alone, was declared to be based upon divine revelation. Other religions were referred to human or demonic sources and condemned as false. The belief was that man in his natural state as a result of the fall was entirely incapable of attaining to a saving knowledge of God. True religion must, therefore, be divinely communicated to men. And such a communication we have in the Bible. It was miraculously inspired, and this inspiration guarantees its truth. If it were not inspired, it might be true, but it would not be divine truth. What makes it divine is its miraculous inspiration. Miracle is thus the presupposition of revelation, and it is also its only adequate authentication. That a message is divinely true is confirmed by the miracle or miracles that attend it. Only in this way, it was held, could we be assured of the truth of Christianity. But such authentication is to be found in abundance in connection with its origin, and to be found there alone. Hence it is the one inspired, revealed, divinely true, absolute and eternal religion.

This exclusive supernaturalistic method of grounding the finality of the Christian religion stands close to popular religious thought. It was developed during the medieval period, and in its most pronounced form was widely held by Protestant theologians down to a century or two ago. It crumbled, however, before the advance of biblical criticism, of natural science, and of the modern philosophy of the divine immanence, and to-day represents an "overcome standpoint." Important modifications or modernizations of it have appeared, it is true, during the past century. The famous "Erlanger School," for instance, represented by such men as Hofmann and Frank, made the miracle of the new birth the fundamental datum of theology, seeking to deduce from it the historicity of the biblical miracles. Ritschl and Herrmann attributed to the inner life of Jesus an essentially miraculous character, and made it normative and in that sense authoritative in theology. Karl Barth and Emil Brunner are at present emphasizing the miracle of revelation as the basal thing in theology, but the content of revelation they determine in a quite subjective way, rejecting altogether the doctrine of biblical infallibility. These different schools have all sought to establish the absoluteness of Christianity by some sort of more or less miraculous isolation, but the older supernaturalistic authoritarianism they all repudiate. They recognize no purely miraculous authentication of truth before which the human reason must bow. Revelation for them is self-evidencing; it justifies itself. In that respect they are modernistic.

With the fall of the older exclusive and rationalistic supernaturalism a new method of establishing the absoluteness of Christianity was introduced by Hegel and Schleiermacher, especially the former. This method marked a return to that tendency in the early church which recognized a kinship between the gospel and the higher thought and life of heathendom, which saw in the superiority of the gospel to all other religions a difference of degree rather than of kind, and which held that the Logos, incarnate in Jesus, illumined also the minds of men in general. There is, however, this difference between the ancient teaching and that of Hegel, that the latter stressed the idea of development, holding that Christianity is not an isolated or unrelated fact, but the climax of an evolutionary process, the highest and completest embodiment of the idea of religion. The Hegelian teaching is, consequently, called "evolutionistic apologetics" by way of distinction from earlier types of Christian thought. It also differed from the older apologetics, especially that of the particularistic type, in that it laid stress on the content and essence of Christianity rather than upon its miraculous authentication. Indeed, the latter it excluded. It saw everywhere in the religious history of mankind one and the same process. No miracle or miracles differentiate one religion from the others. All religions it regarded as divine. But they represent different stages of development, and the culminating stage, the logical crown of the whole process, it found in the Christian faith. Christianity is, therefore, the absolute religion. In it we have the full self-realization of God in human consciousness.

This apologetic is the modern substitute for the older dogmatic supernaturalism. Its underlying idea is impressive, and there is no doubt an important truth in it. But in the logical-dialectical form in which it was developed by Hegel, it was an imaginative construction out of touch to a large extent with historical reality. History is not a field dominated by general ideas that operate with logical necessity toward the achievement of some end. It is a realm of freedom, of purpose, and of personality, and as such defies reduction to any predetermined scheme of development. It is, furthermore, a realm of the concrete and the individual, and is so infinitely varied in its ever-changing life that no concepts or system of concepts could express its full meaning and worth. Every being no doubt stands related to other beings, but over and above these relations it has its own individuality, which is, to some extent, unique and inexplicable. This was true of Jesus in a pre-eminent degree; indeed, true of him in a superlative degree if we hold to the absoluteness of his mission. Hegel recognized this and sought to provide for it by making him the perfect embodiment of the Idea. But the ascription of such supreme importance to a single individual seemed hardly consistent with the logic of the system as a whole. So there arose among Hegelian theologians a tendency to subordinate the person of Christ to the principle or idea embodied in him and to find the essence and absoluteness of Christianity in the latter. The idea, for instance, represented by Jesus, was that of the union of the human and the divine. This is the highest conceivable idea, and since it constitutes the essence of the Christian faith it stamps Christianity as the absolute religion. But in what sense and to what extent this idea was embodied in the person of Christ is a question on which there has been wide difference of opinion. Hegel himself saw in Jesus the actual God-Man, the manifestation of the Absolute in the realm of the finite. But his disciple Strauss declared that "the Idea loves not to pour all its fullness into one example in jealousy toward all the rest," and in his *Life of Jesus* sought to show that the actual historical Jesus was a very different person from the God-Man of the Christian faith.

Schleiermacher laid more stress on the particular and the distinctively religious than did Hegel. Instead of beginning with the general *idea* of religion and seeking to show that it received its completest embodiment in the person of Christ or in Christianity, he began with concrete Christian experience, as perfectly expressed in the person of Jesus, the archetypal man, and sought to show that it represents the highest conceivable type of religion and as such is the universal and absolute religion. Hegel deduced the absoluteness of Christianity from the fact that it embodies the universal and perfect idea of religion;

Schleiermacher, on the other hand, deduced the absoluteness and universality of Christianity from its own moral and spiritual perfection. In other words, according to Hegel, the absolute perfection of Christianity was derived from and authenticated by the universal idea of perfection, while, according to Schleiermacher, the absolute perfection of Christianity was inherent in itself and hence, to a large extent at least, self-verifying. But neither the self-verification nor the authentication by a universal standard furnished a logical basis for the absoluteness of Christianity in the sense of its "unsurpassability." Both involved subjective factors in the way of evaluation that excluded the possibility of their being objectively convincing. There is no way by which it can be demonstrated that Christianity will never be superseded by another and higher religion. Origen, Nicholas of Cusa, and more recently Troeltsch have held that it would be thus superseded or at least might be, and various Christian sects such as the Montanists in the early church and the Joachimites in the medieval church proclaimed a new Age of the Spirit transcending that of the Son. The theoretical possibility of such an advance beyond the Christian gospel cannot be gainsaid. Neither the evolutionism of Hegel and Schleiermacher nor the exclusive supernaturalism of dogmatic theology provides an effectual barrier against it.

The question of the "unsurpassability" of Christianity, however, is only one phase of the problem of its absoluteness, and that a phase of subordinate importance from the practical point of view. No immediate or vital interest of the church is involved in it. In the past it has been commonly assumed that the revelation of God in Christ would never be transcended, and this is, no doubt, still the general belief. But if it should be concluded with Origen and Nicholas of Cusa that an "everlasting gospel," an "eternal religion of immediate vision," will eventually displace historical Christianity, no serious evil would result. The only unfavorable effect, if any, would be to dim slightly the halo of absolute sanctity that now surrounds the Christian faith. Its present superiority and authority would not be challenged.

A more important phase of the problem has to do with the question as to whether absoluteness can be affirmed of any historical phenomenon. It has been vigorously urged by Troeltsch[32] and by G. B. Foster[33] that history is by its very nature relative and that no historical person or institution can consequently be absolute. And as against the older dualistic supernaturalism this consideration has weight. Jesus and the Bible were not miraculously isolated from the rest of the world. They stood related to other religions and other religious leaders and were to a considerable extent determined in their nature by this relationship. Jesus was in a real sense a man of his own time. But if so, how can absoluteness be ascribed to him? It is customary to distinguish between the permanent and the transient elements in his teaching

---

[32] *Die Absolutheit des Christentums.* For an exposition of Troeltsch's views in English see H. S. Sleigh, *The Sufficiency of Christianity,* and A. C. Bouquet, *Is Christianity the Final Religion?* pp. 189-240.

[33] *The Finality of the Christian Religion.*

and that of Scripture, and it is difficult to see how this distinction can be avoided. But is it really valid in a thoroughgoing sense? Are there elements in the teaching and experience of Jesus that are permanent in the sense of being eternally and absolutely true? Troeltsch seems to think not. He apparently holds that the distinction between the transient and the permanent or the shell and the kernel is merely an apologetic device and fails altogether to solve the problem under consideration. "Actual absoluteness of the kernel," he says, "absolutizes also the shell, and actual relativity of the shell relativises also the kernel."[34] It would, then, seem that we must choose between an absolute supernaturalism, on the one hand, and an all-engulfing relativism, on the other.

But this sharp antithesis between the absolute and the relative seems to me abstract and misleading. It suggests that by the absolute we must mean something static and unchangeable, and that if Christianity is to be really absolute, it must have a rigid core of being that remains the same from age to age. Then, since the existence of such a rigid core would be inconsistent with the unceasing change and consequent relativity of history, it is concluded that history and absoluteness exclude each other. But such a static interpretation of absoluteness is unwarranted. In the field of religion God is the absolute, and he is far from being a static Being. He is the dynamic source of the world; and it is through man's communion with him that religion takes on an absolute character. This is true of reli-

[34] *Die Absolutheit des Christentums*, p. 35.

gion in general, and it is pre-eminently true of Christianity. In Christ Jesus we believe we have an instance of perfect union and communion between God and man, and in this perfect union we have something absolute and final. The exact nature of the union and the precise content of the revelation mediated through it cannot be reduced to fixed and unchangeable formulæ. Nor can they be appropriated in their fullness by men. The human appropriation of the gospel will always be relative and subject to growth. But to the gospel itself, as embodied in the life and teaching of Jesus, there is no reason why we should not ascribe finality. If in Christ we come face to face with God as nowhere else, that very fact imparts to him and to his mission a character that may properly be described as "absolute."[35]

Absoluteness, as applied to Christianity, has thus for us a double meaning. It means that in Christ we have an actual revelation of the Absolute, of God, and it also means that this revelation is the highest known to men.[36] In the former sense absoluteness is a matter of Christian experience; we have what seems to us an immediate knowledge of God through Christ. In the latter sense it involves a comparative study of the world's religions. Such a study might at first seem to lead to endless complexity. But on surveying the religious field as a whole it turns out that there are very few religions that need to be taken into account

---

[35] See *The Originality of the Christian Message*, pp. 161-91, by H. R. Mackintosh.

[36] See Walter Scheller, *Die Absolutheit des Christentums* (1929), where it is argued that Christianity is *an* absolute religion but not *the* absolute religion.

in dealing with the question of the supremacy of Christianity. "It is amazing," says Troeltsch, "on how few ideas mankind has in truth lived";[37] and this is especially true in the religious realm. Among the great ethical and spiritual religions—which alone need to be considered in this connection—we have, on the one hand, Judaism, Christianity, and Mohammedanism, which have a common root and represent a common type. On the other hand, we have the great Oriental religions, Brahmanism and especially Buddhism, representing another type. Along with these there have been various forms of speculative or rational religion both in the East and the West, but these have had no independent or self-sustaining power. They have been offshoots from the historical religions and have derived their vitality from them. Only in the latter "does the productive power of religion pulsate."

The religions of the world may then be said to reduce themselves essentially to two: the prophetic-Christian and the Buddhistic-Oriental. As between these two it may not be possible to establish the superiority of Christianity in such an objective way as to convince the Buddhist. When it comes to one's ultimate world-view, subjective factors are involved that defy logical control. Nevertheless, there are norms in the religious life that enable us to determine with a fair degree of objectivity the relative rank of the different religions, and on the basis of these norms we are justified in maintaining that Christianity is superior to Buddhism and to every

---

[37] *Die Absolutheit des Christentums*, p. 61.

other religion, superior in its theological content, superior in its ethical teaching, superior in its power to meet the deepest needs of the soul. This conclusion is warranted by the comparative study of religions; but the ultimate decision of the question cannot, of course, be effected by mere study. It can be reached only in history itself, which has been described as the battlefield of standards of value. There the struggle is going on. The personal and ethical optimism of Christianity is pitted against the impersonal and quietistic pessimism of the East, and the probability is that as Western science is sweeping over the East so it will eventually be with the Christian faith. Its own intrinsic superiority would seem to guarantee its ultimate triumph, and in this sense we may hold to its absoluteness.

The Christian faith, however, to which absoluteness is ascribed, cannot be identified with any of the historic creeds, nor can it be identified with the teaching of Scripture as a whole. It is only the essence of Christianity that can be said to be absolute. But what is this essence? How is it to be defined? It was a little over a century ago that this problem in its technical sense was first raised. Previous to that time the dogmatic temper was in the ascendancy. It took various forms, that of ecclesiasticism, of biblicism and of rationalism. The first of these ascribed absoluteness or infallibility to the church, the second to the Bible, and the third to certain abstract truths of reason. None of them had any proper appreciation of the principle of historical development. They all identified Christianity with a certain definite body of truth, and hence made no effort to determine its true nature by an empirical study of its history. For them the essence of the Christian faith was already given in the objective standard of truth which was accepted, and, consequently, there was no need of defining it more precisely. This dogmatic attitude was dominant in the church down to the close of the eighteenth century; and not until it was overcome and a true historical spirit had been introduced could there be a genuine scientific inquiry into the essential nature of the Christian religion.

It was Schleiermacher who gave us the first important definition of Christianity, based on a study of its history and its relation to other religions. The older rationalism, moralism, and dogmatism he emphatically rejected. For him religion was not a mere knowing or doing. It was something deeper, a feeling, a vital experience. It was also concrete and individual, a spontaneous, historical growth. With the so-called "natural religion" of his day, the religion of reason, he had little patience. He saw in it but a faded image of real religion. The latter he found only in the positive or historical religions. These religions were related to each other, but each one had also its own distinctive nature, and any complete definition of it would involve both factors, its uniqueness and its relation to other religions. These two factors appear in Schleiermacher's definition of Christianity. "Christianity," he says, "is a monotheistic faith of the teleological type, and is essentially distinguished from other such faiths by the fact that everything in it is related to the redemption accomplished by Jesus of Nazareth."[38] In this definition the central place accorded to Jesus of Nazareth should be noted. It should also be noted that this central place is accorded him because of his relation to redemption. It is the redemptive experience made possible through him that differentiates the Christian religion from all others. It should, furthermore, be noted that Christianity is put in the same class with certain other religions insofar as it is a monotheistic and teleological faith.

Ritschl defined the Christian religion in somewhat the same way that Schleiermacher did. "Christianity," he said, "is the monotheistic, completely spiritual and ethical religion, which, based on the life of its Author as Redeemer and as Founder of the kingdom of God, consists in the freedom of the children of God, involves the impulse to conduct from the motive of love, aims at the moral organization of mankind, and grounds blessedness on the relation of sonship to God, as well as the kingdom of God."[39] The new element in this definition is the emphasis placed on the ethical side of the Christian life as represented by the idea of the kingdom of God. Jesus stands related not only to the work of redemption, but also to the moral organization of mankind. Both of these lines of activity are essential to the Christian faith. Ritschl used to say that Christian truth is not a circle with a center, but an ellipse with two foci; the foci are redemption and the kingdom of God. But apart from his special emphasis on the latter idea his defi-

[38] *The Christian Faith*, Par. 11.

[39] *Justification and Reconciliation*, p. 13.

nition of Christianity did not differ much from that of Schleiermacher.

Troeltsch objected to these and other similar definitions on the ground that they assumed that the essence of Christianity had been the same from the beginning. It was his contention that its essence changed from age to age, and that there is no self-identical concept or impulse that has persisted throughout its history and been the source of its expansive power. This view is the natural corollary of Troeltsch's historical relativism, and has no better basis than his relativistic theory in general. As a living historical movement it is no doubt true that Christianity defies encasement in any conceptual strait-jacket and also reduction to any single impulse or pair of impulses. It is too broad and too rich a movement to be exhaustively expressed in any formula; but this does not mean that there is no continuity of the Christian faith. Christianity has its own *élan vital,* and there is no reason for holding that this has not remained essentially the same through the ages. Indeed, Troeltsch himself, when he comes to defining the essence of Christianity, adopts substantially the same view as that of Schleiermacher and Ritschl. "The Christian faith," he says, "is faith in the divine regeneration of man, who, as belonging to the world, is alienated from God—a regeneration effected through the knowledge of God in Christ and resulting in union with God and social fellowship in the kingdom of God."[40]

---

[40] *Gesammelte Schriften,* II, p. 512; R. S. Sleigh, *The Sufficiency of Christianity,* p. 134; *American Journal of Theology,* 1913, p. 13.

We speak of these modern definitions of Christianity as "scientific," but they are such only in a general sense by way of contrast with the dogmatic views of an earlier day. They are not in the strictly empirical sense of the term "scientific." They are not arrived at by mere generalization. We cannot determine the essence of Christianity by purely inductive means. We must call in an objective standard which will enable us to distinguish the essential from what is accidental or perverse or peculiar to an individual or group. And this standard has necessarily a subjective origin. If a person is unfriendly to the Christian religion, he is likely to find its essence in some obsolete dogma or conception. On the other hand, if he is a Christian believer he will naturally find its essence in some ideal that appeals to the thinking man of to-day and that has about it the ring of permanence. In any case, we cannot escape a certain personal equation in our definition of Christianity. Pure objectivity is impossible. But this need not lead us to do violence to history. It should simply put us on our guard against a premature dogmatism.

The "essence" of Christianity is the modern substitute for the infallible book or infallible church of the past. Even when strict biblical or ecclesiastical infallibility was generally accepted, theologians were always implicitly guided by a more or less clearly defined conception of the essential nature of the Christian faith. They never actually ascribed equal authority to all parts of the Bible and to all the dogmatic decrees of the church. They always distinguished between what appealed to their conscience and intelligence and what did not, and in doing so they followed consciously or unconsciously the lead of what they believed to be the essence of Christian teaching. But since the infallibility of the Bible or church was abandoned, this "essence" has become the recognized source and norm of theology.

It is not so clearly defined as the older standards, but it is derived from them and retains what was really authoritative in them. We learn from Scripture and the history of the church what the Christian faith in its essence is; and the task of Christian theology is to expound its intellectual content and justify it so far as possible from the standpoint of the common reason and the common religious experience. Its ultimate justification it must find in itself.

# CHAPTER III

## SCIENCE AND THEOLOGY

THE common reason has in modern times expressed itself most effectively and most authoritatively in the form of empirical science. The commanding position now occupied by science was formerly held by philosophy. It was Greek philosophy that in the early centuries of the church's history was accepted as the secular standard and test of truth. Before its bar Christianity was forced to justify itself. It did so by reinterpreting its own sacred books, by appropriating the congenial elements in the philosophy of the day and by casting its own teaching in the molds of Greek thought. In this way it became the religion of the Græco-Roman world.

To-day it is empirical science that is in the saddle. It holds the whip-cord over the intellectual pursuits of men. Only those lines of study are admitted into good and regular standing which conform to the results and methods of the empirical sciences. Theology, consequently, if it is to maintain itself in the modern world, must somehow or other square itself with current science. This is its first apologetic task. For it to repudiate science would be to ostracize itself from intellectual circles and brand itself as false or mistaken.

The term "science" is sometimes used in the sense of systematized knowledge, and in that sense theology and philosophy are themselves sciences. But present-day usage tends to limit the term to the empirical sciences, and it is in this sense that it will here be used.

From such works as the *History of the Conflict between Religion and Science,* by John W. Draper, and *A History of the Warfare of Science With Theology,* by Andrew D. White, it might be concluded that there is a necessary antagonism between theology and science, and that when the struggle is over, very little place will be left for theology.[1] It is recorded in these volumes how time and again theology resisted the advance of science, but was eventually forced to give way and beat an ignominious retreat. The globular shape of the earth, the idea of antipodes, the Copernican astronomy, the age of the earth, the antiquity of man, the origin of species, the descent of man, evolution, the uniformity of nature, miracles, demoniacal possession, the historicity of the Flood—all of these have been the subject of strenuous debate between science and theology, and in virtually every case the scientific theory has triumphed over the traditional view endorsed by theology. The resistance of theology to science would thus seem to be entirely futile.

Nevertheless, in spite of these numerous reverses, theology still persists and religious belief is about as

[1] For a more recent work covering the same field and considerably more sympathetic with the theological side of the conflict, see *Landmarks in the Struggle Between Science and Religion,* by James Y. Simpson.

vigorous as ever. Indeed, most of the leading scientists have themselves been Christian believers. They have not been aware of any antithesis between their religion and their science; and if this has been so in their case, there would seem to be no reason why it should not be so with others. Evidently, then, the long conflict between science and theology must have been due to some serious misunderstanding. Theology must in the past have trespassed upon the territory of science, and science at times upon the territory of theology. Thus a kind of intellectual Alsace-Lorraine was created which led to repeated strife. All this, it would seem, might have been avoided if only the province of theology and that of science had been properly defined. Between the two there is no necessary antagonism. Each has its own independent field, and there is no valid reason why one should encroach upon the province of the other. They ought, rather, to supplement each other and to co-operate one with the other. Such is the growing feeling of our day, and in principle it is entirely sound.

The situation, however, is more complex than this statement would indicate. Scholars are by no means agreed as to the exact limits either of science or theology, nor are they agreed as to the relation of scientific and theological method to each other. Some argue that in its method theology ought to become an empirical science. If it should, great and extraordinary triumphs, we are told, would await it.[2] But before such a program could be carried out we would need to know just what is meant by an empirical

---

[2] See *Theology as an Empirical Science*, by D. C. Macintosh.

science; and on this point agreement has by no means been reached.

We distinguish between the "natural" or "descriptive" sciences, on the one hand, and the "historical," "cultural," or "normative" sciences, on the other; and both groups are commonly classed as "empirical," so that an empirical science might be either a natural or a cultural science. There are also two quite different conceptions of the limits of empirical science, one positivistic, the other metaphysical. Of these the first restricts science to the phenomenal realm, to the observation of facts and the determination of their relations to each other. Everything beyond this, all inquiry into causes and substances, it relegates to philosophy or banishes completely from the range of human investigation. The second interprets science in a realistic or materialistic sense. It regards the facts of our physical experience as metaphysically objective, as involving a direct knowledge of matter and force. And in a similar way it has been argued that our religious experience involves a direct knowledge of God. Furthermore, in addition to these different views of empirical science, there is a question as to whether theology can take an entirely neutral attitude toward the various sciences. Some hold that it may take such an attitude toward the science of nature, but deny that it can be indifferent to the conclusions reached by the science of history.

The relation of theology and science to each other is, therefore, not so simple a problem as some seem to think. Much confusion of thought still exists on the subject; and if a permanent *modus vivendi* is to be established between them, there must be a larger degree of agreement as to the nature and limits of each.

First, we need to decide between the positivistic and the metaphysical interpretations of science.[3] Modern science began in a naïve realistic mood. It assumed that we know matter at first hand and know that it is a real and an extra-mental cause. The fact that science was empirical did not, therefore, limit it to the phenomenal realm. Experience itself was supposed to embrace the metaphysically real. This was implied in the distinction between primary and secondary qualities. The latter were subjective, but the former were regarded as objective. They were truly real; and it was with them that science was fundamentally concerned. It had to do with "reality" as well as "appearance." Its function was "explanation" as well as "description." In other words, it was itself a philosophy; indeed, it was called "natural philosophy."

But with the keener and more thorough analysis of sense experience due to such men as Berkeley, Hume, and Kant it became evident that primary as well as secondary qualities are subjective and that we have no such immediate apprehension of metaphysical reality as was supposed. We know only phenomena. The cause or substance lying back of them completely eludes sense-perception. Science, therefore, insofar as it is empirical, has nothing to

---

[3] An excellent discussion of these two interpretations will be found in *A Philosophy of Ideals*, pp. 43-61, by Edgar S. Brightman.

do with the causal ground of things. It is purely descriptive. Its task is simply to relate and correlate the facts of experience. This positivistic conception of science has for some time past been making steady headway, and is the view now commonly held in scientific circles.[4] It is the only view that is consistent with Humian and Kantian criticism, and the only view that makes possible a clear distinction between science and philosophy. Metaphysically interpreted, science becomes a realistic or materialistic philosophy, and as such subject to the devastating criticism to which these types of philosophy are exposed. Positivistically interpreted, it has to do only with the factual order, but there it reigns supreme. It leaves to philosophy the question as to the nature of the cause and purpose that lie back of the world of phenomena.[5] This division of labor between science and philosophy is the most satisfactory one yet devised. So we accept the positivistic interpretation of science, while rejecting philosophical positivism.

## Theology as an Empirical Science

Having adopted the positivistic conception of sci-

[4] It was about the beginning of the last quarter of the nineteenth century that scientists began to adopt this view as "a definitely stated conception, corrective of misunderstandings." Kirchhoff and Mach had not a little to do in giving it currency. See J. Arthur Thomson, *The System of Animate Nature*, p. 8. Note also the following statement by Karl Pearson in the preface to the third edition of *The Grammar of Assent* (1911): "Nobody believes now that science explains anything; we all look upon it as a shorthand description, as an economy of thought."

[5] In John Wesley we find substantially this distinction between science and philosophy, but it is evident that he did not realize its full import, since he manifestly held to the realistic view of science. See Frank W. Collier, *John Wesley Among the Scientists*, pp. 65ff., 148f., 248f.

ence, our next question has to do with the attempt that is being made in some quarters to transform systematic theology into an empirical science. Such a transformation, we are told, is not only possible; it could be effected in the very near future, and with most advantageous results.[6] The plan, it seems, is to have the theologian enter upon his work with the same naïve realism that the average physicist or chemist does. As the latter assumes the reality of matter as given in sense-experience, so the theologian should assume the reality of God as given in religious experience. Then by a method of observation and experiment akin to that of the natural sciences he should study the facts of the religious life, reduce them to laws, generalize his conclusions, and in the light of his new discoveries revise or define more precisely his conception of God, just as the physicist does his conception of matter. In this way he would remove the rock of offense that scientists heretofore have found in theology and would make of theology itself a "genuinely scientific" discipline.

This theological program has its attractive features, but there are decisive reasons why it cannot be accepted. For one thing, it presupposes a substantialistic interpretation of science—an interpretation which, as we have seen, is steadily being outgrown. Substance and cause are categories with

[6] D. C. Macintosh, *Theology as an Empirical Science*, pp. 3, 25. A somewhat similar theological program is advocated by H. N. Wieman in his *Religious Experience and Scientific Method*, Chap. I, but apparently with much less confidence in the possibility of its speedy realization.

which science is dispensing. It is itself philosophically neutral, consistent alike with idealism and with realism. Matter as a metaphysical entity is not given in sense-experience, and empirical science has nothing to do with it.[7] To interpret science realistically or metaphysically is to take a step backward, and yet it is this interpretation of it that is implied in the effort to make of theology an empirical science.

Another objection to this program is that it does not make adequate allowance for the marked difference that exists between sense-experience and religious experience. Whatever be our conception of experience, idealistic or realistic, it is still true that the objective content of sense-experience is quite different from that of religious experience and that the former is amenable to scientific treatment in a way that the latter is not. It is no accident that the strictly "scientific" method has flourished in the field of "natural philosophy," while it has had comparatively limited application in the field of systematic theology. The difference of method in the two fields is inherent in the difference of subject matter. The object or objects of religious perception, if there be such, do not have the same independent and detached character that the objects of sense perception have. They do not force themselves upon our attention in the same way, they are more subjectively conditioned, they arise to a larger extent out of personal interest

[7] The methods of physical science, says A. S. Eddington, lead "not to a concrete reality, but to a shadow world of symbols, beneath which those methods are unadapted for penetrating" (*Science and the Unseen World*, p. 73). See also his larger book, *The Nature of the Physical World*, chs. XIII-XV.

and anticipation. We do not know God in the same impersonal way that we know the things of sense, and the knowledge of him is not communicable and verifiable in the same objective way that scientific knowledge is supposed to be. Knowledge, that may properly be called scientific in the empirical as distinguished from the merely systematic sense of the term, must be based on observation and experiment, and it must also be capable of being verified and communicated to others.[8] But that we have a really empirical or perceptual knowledge of God is by no means certain. We believe in him; but whether we actually have a "consciousness" of him is at least open to question. The mystics claim to have such a consciousness, but in their case it is admittedly special in character; it is not capable of experimental verification and communication to others. The belief in God, implied in the more general religious experience of the average man, is no doubt at times vivified into what may be called a "consciousness" or awareness of the Divine. But the Divine, thus laid hold of, is too dimly apprehended to be made the foundation of a science; and if scientific terminology is applied to such a vague perception, it can only be in an accommodated sense. Strictly, theology cannot be an empirical science, even on the realistic basis. Its experiential data lack the necessary concrete objectivity.

The fact is that in the proposed "scientific" the-

---

[8] For an analysis and definition of science see J. Arthur Thomson in *The Outline of Science*, IV, pp. 1165ff., and in *Science and Religion*, pp. 4ff.

ology God is forced to function in a double capacity. He serves as the analogue both of the sense-objects and of their supposed material ground or cause. Natural science, it is held, involves both. But our knowledge of one is quite different from our knowledge of the other. We have an "empirical" knowledge of the sense-objects, but we have no such knowledge of "matter." Of the latter we have either a speculative conception or a confused notion due to spontaneous thought or to an inherited prejudice. Yet God in the new "scientific" theology is supposed to take the place both of it and of the sense-objects. It is assumed that we know him in the same clear and direct way that we know the things of sense and also in the same vague and indirect way that we know their causal ground. This illustrates the confusion into which thought falls when it tries to reduce theology to an empirical science.

The correct view to take of science is the one we have called the positivistic, and from this standpoint theology could not in the nature of the case become an empirical science without surrendering its objectivity and becoming synonymous with the psychology of religion. If there were among the objects of religious experience an intermediate realm of reality akin to that of sense-objects, we might perhaps claim that theology as an empirical science would differ from the psychology of religion just as physics and chemistry do from the psychology of sense-experience, but no such middle realm exists for religious thought. Religious experience, if it has any objectivity at all, has God as its object; and this means that the purely "empirical" or positivistic plane has been transcended, for God is ultimate reality, a metaphysical Being, if he is anything. Empirical science, interpreted positivistically, excludes the idea of God and of metaphysical reality of any kind. We might from this point of view study the factual side of religious experience, but we could never advance beyond that and make any positive affirmation about the objective reality of its intellectual content; in a word, we could never be theologians. Theology, transformed into a positivistic empirical science, would be simply psychology of religion.

There is, then, no way by which theology can retain its integrity and yet become an empirical science. Nor can it ward off the attacks of scientists by claiming that it is itself a pure science. There are in it extra- or superscientific factors which cannot be discarded. Theology has its own unique character, and necessarily stands apart to some extent from the scientific movement; it cannot be merged in it without losing its identity. Not by being metamorphosed into an empirical science will it be able to maintain itself in this modern age, but by so adjusting itself to the scientific movement that the truth of both its own standpoint and that of science will be recognized.

## Views of Ritschl and Bowne

Two significant attempts at such adjustment have been made. One, which we owe to Ritschl, consists in distinguishing between existential judgments (*Seinsurtheile*) and judgments of value (*Werthurtheile*). Science, we are told, has to do with the former, and religion or theology with the latter. This does not mean that science and theology are concerned with different realms; it, rather, means that they approach the world from different points of view. Science registers its existence, the mode of it, while theology evaluates it. In this distinction there is considerable truth. It fits in with the distinction that has in recent years been drawn between the natural sciences and the cultural or historical or normative sciences.[9] The former are "nomothetic," they lay down laws, generalize, and are "*wertfrei*," have nothing to do with values. The cultural sciences, on the other hand, are "idiographic," they are primarily concerned with the concrete, with individuals. They lay stress on values, are guided by the idea of an end, and frame laws that are purposive rather than causal. In these respects theology bears a certain resemblance to the cultural sciences such as sociology, ethics, and law. It studies religion from the normative point of view and thus transcends a pure psychology of religion. But it is not itself merely a normative science. It transcends all such sciences by affirming the metaphysical reality of its ideal.

Here, however, a certain ineptness in the phraseology manifests itself. "Judgments of value," when contrasted with "judgments of being," would seem to be subjective. For if not, why should the contrasted judgments be called "judgments of being"? The latter judgments by their very name would seem

---

[9] Heinrich Rickert, *Kulturwissenschaft und Naturwissenschaft*, and *Die Grenzen der Naturwissenschaftlichen Begriffsbildung*; and G. B. Foster, *The Finality of the Christian Religion*, pp. 309ff.

to include all judgments that have to do with reality. Other judgments such as those of value would, then, have to do with the ideal or the unreal. And some have insisted that this is the natural implication of the term. But a careful analysis of value-judgments makes it evident that they imply an objective reference. Apart from it they would be meaningless. "Were there no existence," says W. R. Sorley, "there would be no value."[10] Judgments of value are not, then, purely subjective. Indeed, in the Ritschlian theory of value-judgments the very reverse is implied. Here it is assumed that the key to ultimate reality is to be found in the value-judgments of religion rather than in the existential judgments of science. There is, therefore, no antithesis or even separation between reality and worth. Rather do the two belong together. But it is still true that the term "being" in the expression "judgments of being" is commonly interpreted as synonymous with "reality," and hence the impression is left that there is, after all, a sharp divorce between reality and worth. To avoid this impression it ought to be explained that the term "being" applies only to phenomenal reality; but this is usually not done, and the result is confusion and misunderstanding.[11]

A much better way of defining and adjusting the

---

[10] *Moral Values and the Idea of God*, p. 109.

[11] In this connection it may also be noted that science as well as religion has a practical basis and that scientific facts are, as Professor R. T. Flewelling says, "meaningful and real largely from the standpoint of value." One might even find, as he suggests, a ground of reconciliation between science and religion in the fact that "both must pass through the same little door of social and moral justification" (*Creative Personality*, pp. 220f.).

relation of science and theology to each other is to distinguish with Borden P. Bowne between phenomenal and metaphysical reality and then assign the former realm to science and the latter to theology. This preserves the positivistic character of science and gives to it free rein in the space-time world. No limitations are imposed upon it so long as it confines itself to the phenomenal order. On this plane it may frame any theory it wishes, and theology will not be disturbed by it. For theology has to do with the power-world, the world of cause and purpose, in which the facts of experience find their ultimate explanation, but whose nature is not determined by any particular theory concerning the factual order itself. One might hold either the biblical or the scientific cosmogony, the Ptolemaic or the Copernican astronomy, the theory of creation or of evolution, and yet hold essentially the same view of the underlying power upon which the world is dependent. In deciding upon the nature of this power one may properly be influenced to a large extent by ethical considerations, and in that case one may retain the Ritschlian distinction between the predominantly factual character of science and the predominantly valuational character of theology. But the distinction between science and theology is better expressed by the terms "phenomenal" and "metaphysical" than by the terms "existential" and "valuational."[12] For the

[12] Canon Streeter, in his book *Reality*, uses the terms "quantitative" and "qualitative" to distinguish between scientific and religious knowledge, and since both are valid approaches to reality, he calls his theory "bi-representationism." This theory is substantially the same as that held by Bowne, though the word "qualitative" suggests a leaning toward the Ritschlian viewpoint.

nature of ultimate reality is by no means determined solely by the idea of value, and the term "existential" is, as we have seen, unfortunate in that it obscures rather than emphasizes the distinction between the phenomenal and the real. The "phenomenality" of the material world brings out its secondary and subordinate character, and thus makes it possible to avoid the dualism implicit in or at least suggested by the antithesis between the existential and the valuational. If the material world is phenomenal, there is nothing about it that is inconsistent with a fundamental monism; rather does its phenomenality point to the unity of ultimate reality.

## Sources of Conflict Between Science and Theology

In principle there is, therefore, no conflict between science, which has to do with the phenomenal, and theology, which has to do with the metaphysical. But while this is true of the scientific and theological world-views in general, there are two points at which a strained relation still exists and perhaps permanently will. One has to do with history and the other with the apparently naturalistic implications of modern science.

Christian theology is concerned not simply with a spiritual interpretation of the universe, but with the historicity of certain events, and it has had greater difficulty in maintaining the latter than the former. The distinction between phenomenal and metaphysical reality makes possible the maintenance of a spiritual view of the universe in the face of any conceivable scientific discoveries. But when it comes to specific historical events the situation is not so clear. Here Christianity invades the field of historical science, and it is a question whether the two can be completely adjusted to each other. That in the past Christianity made many historical affirmations that were unwarranted and nonessential to the Christian faith is now generally conceded. The science of biblical criticism has relegated much of what was supposed to be history to the realm of legend and untrustworthy tradition. This applies not only to the Old Testament, but to the New as well.

In this connection the question of miracle has figured prominently. It used to be argued, on one side, that miracle is impossible; and, on the other, it was maintained that miracle is essential to the Christian faith both as "authenticating" evidence of its truth and as proof of the Divine freedom. All of these contentions are now obsolete. No one knows enough about the nature of ultimate reality to be warranted in affirming the impossibility of miracle. This is at present generally conceded. And on the theistic basis the possibility of miracle is, of course, implied. On the other hand, it is equally evident that miracle cannot establish the truth of any proposition that does not commend itself to reason. As an Arabian writer once put it, "If a conjurer should say to me, 'Three are more than ten, and in proof of it I will change this stick into a serpent,' I might be surprised at his legerdemain, but I certainly should not admit his assertion."[13] It is also clear that belief in the divine

[13] J. W. Draper, *Conflict Between Religion and Science*, p. 66.

freedom does not hinge upon the fact of miracle. If it did, it would have a very insecure basis. The doctrine of the divine immanence has, to a large extent, deprived the appeal to miracle of its religious importance.

Yet the question of miracle does have a significant bearing upon the historical credibility of Scripture and upon our conception of the person of Christ. A man may admit the theoretical possibility of miracle and yet deny its actuality. This is the position which probably most scientific historians would at present take. They would regard the nature miracles of the Bible as mythical or as misunderstood natural events. Such miracles, if recorded in other sacred literatures, would be rejected by us all; and if so, why should we accept them because they are narrated in our Scriptures? We no longer hold to biblical infallibility. The middle wall of partition between the Bible and other sacred literatures is broken down. All history, we now see, is of one weave, and hence no special consideration can be accorded the biblical miracles. This position, if generally accepted, would not, it is true, destroy the historical trustworthiness of Scripture as a whole, but it would undermine it at points that have hitherto been regarded as of vital significance. There is, consequently, here still a tension between faith and historical science.

But more significant is the bearing of psychological and historical science upon the inner life of Jesus. Christianity might perhaps dispense with the physical miracles recorded in the New Testament, but when it comes to the person of Jesus, his consciousness, the situation is quite different. Here we have to do with the very citadel of the Christian faith. If we were to follow the lead of psychology and sociology in their efforts to reduce Jesus to the level of our normal or abnormal humanity and were to regard him as completely and unreservedly the child of his own time, it is evident that we would come into conflict with one of the profoundest and most tenacious convictions of the Christian Church. Psychology would, of course, be willing to allow that Jesus was a religious genius and perhaps the most exalted of all religious geniuses. But Christianity has never been contented with such a classification or differentiation of him. It has always set him apart in another and different sense, and so in modern times there has arisen the distinction between "the Christ of faith" and "the Jesus of history." The tendency of historical and psychological science has been to suppress the former in the interest of the latter; but to prevent this, it would seem, is a matter of life and death with historical Christianity. Here, then, we have an acute tension between science and theology.

The second point of discord, above referred to, had to do with the naturalistic implications of the scientific world-view. These implications are due in part to the factual and nonideal character of science. For it things are what they seem, they have no deeper meaning or purpose; and hence all ideal values seem to be illusory. This seeming grows out of the self-limitation of science. But it is also due to the fact that the modern scientific world-view does not fit in so well with the Christian scheme of things as did the older world-view. Take, for instance, the Copernican astronomy and the Darwinian theory of man's descent. Against them as a background read John 3. 16, and it becomes evident at once that the two viewpoints are not completely geared into each other. The anthropocentric standpoint of Christianity seems more or less out of place in the world of modern astronomy and modern biology. That the God of a geocentric universe should fix his attention chiefly upon man and sacrifice himself for his redemption, is not altogether strange. Even in the presence of such a God the devout mind, it is true, as it contemplated the heavens, exclaimed, "What is man that thou art mindful of him?" Yet there was a certain congruity between the anthropocentric and geocentric points of view. Peter Lombard, for instance, said in his "Sentences": "Just as man is made for the sake of God—that is, that he may serve him—so the universe is made for the sake of man—that is, that it may serve him; therefore is man placed at the middle point of the universe, that he may both serve and be served."

From the geocentric and creationist standpoint there was no particular difficulty in conceiving of man as the goal and climax of the universe. But with the introduction of the Copernican and Darwinian theories the situation was completely changed. Man now seems to be an accidental product of a blind evolutionary process, and so utterly insignificant a being that it would be preposterous to regard the universe as in any sense made for him. He seems so overwhelmed by the immensity of space and so closely linked to the lower forms of life that it would be absurd to attribute to him a high and unique destiny. He seems, rather, as someone has termed him, "cosmic scum." And when this seeming is mistaken for reality and treated as an implication of science, as it easily is, there results necessarily a sharp conflict between science and religion. But even when the provisional and more or less illusory character of science is recognized, it is still true that the scientific picture of the world is not so transparent and effective a symbol or medium of Christian truth as was the older view. The scientific world-view is capable of a religious interpretation, but it has inherent in it a naturalistic prejudice, which it is not easy to overcome. Then, too, when purged of this prejudice, it does not lend itself so readily to a Christian interpretation as did the older geocentric and creationist view. We have here, consequently, a persistent source of difficulty between religion and science.

This difficulty, however, is psychological rather than logical. In principle there is no conflict between pure science and pure religion. One has to do with phenomenal reality and the other with ontological reality; one is concerned with facts, the other with their ultimate interpretation. Science permits a theistic interpretation of the world; and that is all that theology has a right to ask of it. When it comes to certain historical events, it may not always be easy to fix the limits of science, on the one hand, and the limits of theology, on the other. At this point there will probably continue to be more or less of conflict, and so there will also be more or less tension between the spirit of science and that of religion, often within the very same person. But in general and from the logical point of view there is no reason why theology and science should not live peaceably together. Each has in the main its own independent field, and each may well learn from the other.

## CHAPTER IV

## PHILOSOPHY AND THEOLOGY

PHILOSOPHY does not enjoy the prestige it once did. It has in modern times surrendered one field of inquiry after another to the empirical sciences, so that some predict its fate will be like that of King Lear, who divided his goods among his children and then was himself cast out as a beggar upon the street. The actual outlook for it, to be sure, is not so discouraging as this. But it is true that its right to a place in the university curriculum alongside of the special sciences has been called in question, and it is also true that among philosophers themselves there are wide differences of opinion as to its true nature and function. There is in philosophy no generally accepted body of knowledge such as there is in science. Indeed, there is a question as to whether the conclusions reached in philosophy can be called knowledge in the proper sense of the term.

Still, in spite of these uncertainties, philosophy cannot be dispensed with. We each have a philosophy, whether we will or no. The rejection of metaphysics is itself a metaphysics. No thinking person can escape having a world-view of some sort, and the most significant thing about him is perhaps the world-view which he consciously or unconsciously holds. Men struggle for their world-view. They do so on the field of battle, they do so in their cultural life. Indeed, culture is largely the result of the struggle for different world-views. People support their own particular world-view with arguments of one kind and another, and in this way philosophy in the more specialized sense of the term arises. One type of philosophy, such, for instance, as the Aristotelian, may for a time become so dominant as to be synonymous with philosophy itself, and in that case a reaction may set in against all philosophy,[1] but the reaction turns out to be itself only another type of philosophy. On the other hand, the fact that there is often so much disagreement among philosophers may give rise to a prejudice against philosophy in general, but the prejudice when thought through proves to be itself a philosophy. It is only philosophy that can displace philosophy. Even though philosophy may then have lost some of its former prestige, it by no means follows that its power is broken. It remains consciously or unconsciously about as potent a force as ever in the intellectual life of the world, and it is, therefore, important to determine the relation of theology to it as well as to science.

### Positivistic Philosophy

In the preceding chapter we distinguished philosophy along with theology from science by saying that it has to do with metaphysical reality while science is concerned with the phenomenal realm. And as applied to much of the philosophy of the past this

---

[1] This is illustrated by early Protestantism. Compare Georg Wobbermin, *Theologie und Metaphysik*, p. 5.

way of stating the distinction would perhaps be quite generally accepted as substantially correct. But it does not hold for much of current philosophy. As there are both a positivistic and a metaphysical interpretation of science, so there are both a positivistic and a metaphysical conception of philosophy. The positivistic type has wide vogue at present; it is the popular philosophy of the day. It decries metaphysics. It seeks to be empirical and scientific in method, and professes to differ from the special sciences only in its scope. What it aims to be is a systematization of the sciences.[2] But it also differs from them in another important respect. It is dogmatic. It affirms that knowledge is limited to the empirical sciences, and in so doing ceases itself to be scientific. Pure science has nothing to say about the limits of human knowledge. Such affirmations are philosophical in the older sense of the term.

Philosophy in its traditional form is commonly divided into epistemology, or the theory of knowledge, and metaphysics, or the theory of reality. Both of these are nominally rejected by the philosophical "modernist." But as a matter of fact epistemology is a presupposition of the positivistic quite as much as the metaphysical type of philosophy. No philosophy is complete without a theory of knowledge. Epistemology is the necessary foundation alike of

[2] According to John Dewey, philosophy is "a liaison officer between the conclusions of science and the modes of social and personal action through which attainable possibilities are projected and striven for." Its true function is not the "knowledge of reality." When it assumes this rôle, it becomes a "rival instead of a complement to the sciences" (*The Quest for Certainty*, pp. 309, 311).

metaphysics and of anti-metaphysics. No one is warranted either in affirming or denying the possibility of a knowledge that transcends experience until he has inquired into the nature, conditions, and limits of human thought. At this point the positivistic and metaphysical philosophies are agreed. They are antithetical in their conclusions; but they both, insofar as they are logical and critical, necessarily begin with a study of the problem of knowledge and in that respect transcend the sphere of the empirical sciences.

The positivistic type of philosophy differs, then, from pure science in its greater range, in its taking account of the epistemological problem, and in its anti-metaphysical dogmatism. The last feature is the one that is most characteristic. While it constitutes a point of difference with science, it is also a point of kinship with it, so that positivism in its various forms has come to be known as the "scientific philosophy" of the day. It limits knowledge to the realm covered by the empirical sciences, and by means of its epistemology erects this limitation into a dogma. It thus breaks down the traditional distinction between the method of philosophy and that of science. The same method, we are told, is to be followed in both.[3] Philosophy, like science, has ultimately to do merely with the relation and correlation of facts, with description. For it, as Paul Natorp

---

[3] "Philosophy," says Bertrand Russell, "is distinguished from science only by being more critical and more general" (*Philosophy*, p. 297). It is or should be as ethically disinterested as pure science. It can do nothing to ground men's higher hopes (*Our Knowledge of the External World*, p. 37).

said, "The way is everything, the goal is nothing." It recognizes no purpose and no power back of the world of experience. It sees in the phenomenal order simply a "flapping drapery hanging upon no solid form, but folded round the empty outline of a ghost."[4]

Such a philosophy can manifestly lend no positive support to Christian theology. In a negative and indirect way, however, its aid has occasionally been invoked by theologians. It has, for instance, been pointed out that positivism implies the overthrow of materialism; and since materialism has in the past been the great foe of religion, its overthrow, we are told, is a distinct service to faith. But to invoke the aid of positivism in overthrowing materialism is very much like casting out devils by means of Beelzebub. One set of demons is thus disposed of, but another demon takes their place. For positivism with its negative attitude toward the superworld is quite as hostile to religion as is materialism. Indeed, Karl Pearson goes so far as to say: "Strange as it may seem, it is nevertheless true, that in materialism lies the next lease of life for theology."[5] By this he apparently means that materialism affirms the reality of a metaphysical something called matter. What this "something" is we do not know, and since it is unknowable, the theologian can safely take refuge in it. He can claim for it the support of philosophic materialism, and then with the aid of revelation transform it into an object of worship.[6] But whether such an alliance

[4] James Martineau, *Types of Ethical Theory*, Vol. I, p. 6.

[5] *The Ethic of Free Thought*, p. 40.

[6] See *Die Gottesbeweise in der neueren deutschen philosophischen Literatur*, by Dr. Franz Schulte, p. 20.

between theology and materialistic agnosticism is possible or not, positivism as over against materialism offers no real aid or comfort to religion.

Another way in which some theologians have tried to turn positivism to their account has been to treat its agnosticism as proof of the metaphysical bankruptcy of the human mind and hence as evidence of man's need of a divine and authoritative revelation. If men were able through their own reason to arrive at a knowledge of God, a divine revelation would hardly seem to be necessary; at the most, it would serve as a supplement, more or less valuable, to man's native insight. But if men are entirely incapable through their reason of arriving at a knowledge of God, as they are according to the positivistic philosophy, it is evident that a supernatural revelation is absolutely necessary if he is to be known at all. Those who are interested in maintaining the necessity of an objective authority in religion, consequently, find in philosophical skepticism a natural foil to their authoritarianism. It has often been so in the history of Christian thought. The tendency in that direction was strong at the time of the Reformation. Luther denounced in unmeasured terms the dominant Aristotelian philosophy, seeing in the helplessness of reason a ground for affirming the necessity and sole authority of Revelation. This tendency has reappeared in modern theology, especially in Germany, where it has been closely associated with Neo-Kantian positivism. Such a use of philosophical positivism, however, has never been thoroughgoing, and has always involved a transformation of positivism itself. As the handmaid of theology positivism wears a very different mien from what it does in its native heath. Pure and unadulterated positivism is naturalistic, dogmatically and arrogantly so. It leaves no place for a divine revelation, and for it to be yoked with the latter puts it in a position that is foreign to its native purpose and spirit. Between the two there is and can be no inner bond of union. Only as the positivistic philosophy lays aside its arrogance and its anti-theistic cast, only as it assumes the rôle of intellectual humility, can it become the ally of biblical authoritarianism, and by that time it has lost much of its distinctive character as a philosophy.

The theology with which positivism in this modified form has been allied has been both conservative and liberal. In the one case the positivistic principle has been used to support the idea of an objective authority, either biblical or ecclesiastical; in the other it has been employed in the interest of the independence and primacy of the emotional or practical nature. The latter is illustrated by the Ritschlian theology. Here the idea of an external and coercive authority is renounced, and revelation is interpreted in a vital and practical instead of an intellectualistic sense. A certain normative and authoritative character is ascribed to revelation, but both the authority and content of revelation are grounded in the spiritual capacity and receptivity of man rather than in anything objectively miraculous. Faith, in other words, takes the place of miracle as the foundation of Christian truth. It gives man the insight which on the positivistic basis cannot be attained through the intellect. It is itself not miraculous in character, and hence the contrast between the view of the world which it implies and that of naturalistic positivism may not seem quite so sharp as in the case of the older supernaturalism. But the content and spirit of the two world-views are totally different, and the attempt to hold them both by making one independent of the other results in an intolerable dualism. No satisfactory working agreement between positivistic agnosticism and the Christian faith in either its authoritarian or liberal form can be established.

### Metaphysical Philosophy Morally Grounded

We turn then to the metaphysical type of philosophy. And here we distinguish between an intellectually grounded metaphysics and a morally or spiritually grounded metaphysics. It is Kant to whom we chiefly owe this distinction. He rejected metaphysics in its older intellectualistic form and sought to re-establish it on a moral basis. He found in conscience an adequate ground for affirming God, freedom, and immortality. These affirmations do not rise to the plane of knowledge in the strict sense of the term. They, rather, express a faith; but it is a rationally grounded faith, a faith inherent in the practical reason.

This morally grounded or "faith" metaphysics has been developed in various ways since the time of Kant. In recent years it has come to be known as the philosophy of value, and has been most conspicuously represented by the pragmatism of William

James and the transcendental idealism of Windelband and Rickert. Neither of these philosophic movements contains a clean-cut and coherent metaphysic. But both stress the idea that the needs and aspirations of men warrant our making affirmations concerning reality. These affirmations may not be objectively valid, but they are at least in principle justified; and if they can be shown to represent permanent needs of the human spirit they may be accepted as verified. In this way the door is opened to a metaphysical philosophy.

The philosophy thus arrived at stands midway between modern positivism and the Platonic-Aristotelian intellectualism. To the former because of its anti-metaphysical dogmatism it denies the character of true philosophy, and the latter it charges with ascribing to the pure reason powers which it does not possess. Positivism, so far as it is true, is science, not philosophy; and the traditional intellectualistic theism is negated by the Kantian criticism. Kant taught us that knowledge in the strict sense of the term is limited to experience. What lies beyond that can only be an object of faith. This, we are told, is his great contribution to philosophy. He transformed it into a *faith*-philosophy. His doctrine of the creative activity of thought, which is often singled out as his greatest achievement, is intellectualistic in character and really belongs to the philosophy of the past. The new and most significant thing in his teaching was his doctrine of the primacy of the practical reason. It was this that inaugurated a new era in the history of philosophy. Henceforth, it is claimed, all true philosophy must be a philosophy of value or of faith, a philosophy for which "the goal is everything, the way nothing."[7] But the faith expressed in philosophy is one that is being constantly translated into logical forms and into reasoned convictions, and so philosophy takes on both a scientific and a religious character. It "distinguishes itself from religion," says Kaftan, "in that it is science, and from science in that it is religion."[8]

Such a practical view of philosophy is naturally congenial to the Christian religion, especially in its Protestant form. Indeed, it has been maintained that this particular type of philosophy is "the philosophy of Protestantism"; and because of his supposed advocacy of it Kant has been called "the philosopher of Protestantism." The point on which stress has been laid in this connection has been the practical character of the Protestant conception of faith. In Roman Catholicism faith meant intellectual assent. This was the view that naturally fitted in with its dogmatic and authoritarian system. As distinguished from it the reformers emphasized the volitional and emotional nature of faith. With them faith meant decision, trust, something far deeper than the mere assent of the mind. And in this conception, since faith is the organ of religious knowledge, it was implied that the profoundest insights come to us through the will and feeling, rather than through the perceptual and logical faculty. Kant laid hold of this truth, and in his doctrine of the primacy of the

---

[7] J. Kaftan, *Die Philosophie des Protestantismus*, p. 388.
[8] *Ibid.*, p. 241.

practical reason made it basal in his system. A new approach to philosophy was thus introduced, and a new conception of its nature. At present, says Windelband, "We do not so much expect from philosophy what it was formerly supposed to give, a theoretic scheme of the world, a synthesis of the results of the separate sciences, or, transcending them on lines of its own, a scheme harmoniously complete in itself; what we expect from philosophy to-day is reflection on those permanent values which have their foundation in a higher spiritual reality above the changing interests of the times."[9] A philosophy of this type, whether it eventuates in a clearly defined metaphysics or not, is manifestly favorable to religious belief. It holds to the objectivity of values, and so takes at least an important step in the direction of personalistic theism.

At this point a difference of opinion emerges as to the way in which the knowledge of the higher realm of values is arrived at. The Kantian tradition favors what might be called the postulatory method. According to it, we have no direct experience of the supersensible world. The existence of such a realm is implied in our moral and spiritual nature, but it is not given to us in experience. It is a postulate, an object of faith, not an intuition. The idea that we have an immediate experience of the Divine Kant regarded as fanatical. But in spite of Kant this "mystical" view has had wide currency in Protestant circles and is to-day contesting the field with the pos-

[9] *Die Philosophie im deutschen Geistesleben des XIX Jahrhunderts*, p. 119.

tulatory or "faith" theory. At first it might seem as though these two theories were necessarily opposed to each other, and this they would be if the mystical experience were wholly unmediated. But such it is not. All articulate experience is subjectively conditioned, and so it is with mystical experience. It is conditioned by faith. Without faith there would be no mystic-state, and without the immediacy of mysticism the faith-state would never become a vital conviction. It is, then, possible to combine the mystical theory of religious knowledge with the "faith" theory, implied in the Kantian doctrine of the primacy of the practical reason.

This ethical or ethico-mystical philosophy has had a pronounced influence on modern theology. The Ritschlian theology is, to a large extent, based upon it. Indeed, Ritschlianism might be said to be the philosophy of value applied to the field of Christian theology. Its distinction between judgments of being and judgments of worth presupposes an ethically grounded metaphysics. By means of this distinction new light has been thrown upon the nature of religious faith, and a new bond of connection established between it and the higher faiths of men in general. All these faiths are idealizing processes, and all rest upon the fundamental conviction that the gleaming ideal is the everlasting real. It was this conviction that Lotze had in mind when he said, "The true beginning of Metaphysic lies in ethics. . . . I seek in that which *should* be the ground of that which *is*."[10] A philosophy thus founded has manifestly a religious

[10] *Metaphysic*, p. 536.

motive and is at bottom akin to religion. It justifies in principle religious belief, and leaves room for an independent Christian theology, a theology which stands in its own right and which requires no other support than that furnished by the Christian religion itself.

But however comforting such a philosophy may be from the religious point of view, there are serious objections to it, when taken as complete in itself. For one thing, it assumes too sharp a contrast between the theoretical and the practical reason. The theoretical reason is supposed to stand by itself, to be free from subjective interest, and to be guided solely by its own categories and by the pressure of objective events. It recognizes simply the factual order and the reign of law in it. It is, therefore, mechanistic and deterministic. The practical reason, on the other hand, takes its cue from the will and the ideals of life. It stresses freedom and an objective moral order. It thus runs directly counter to the naturalism of the theoretical reason. But such a conception of the theoretical reason is quite mistaken. The theoretical reason is not sufficient unto itself. It cannot take the first step toward knowledge without faith—faith in the intelligibility of the world and faith in our ability to understand it—and such faith is practical in nature. It is an assumption whose truth cannot be demonstrated. Furthermore, the theoretical reason is not deterministic. Determinism, if logically carried out, would mean the overthrow of all knowledge. Only through freedom can the possibility of knowledge be harmonized with the fact of error. It is, then, a serious mistake to assume that there is a sharp antithesis between the theoretical and the practical reason, and that the former is entirely disinterested and necessarily mechanistic in its view of the world. The very unity of the human spirit renders such a dualistic view inherently improbable.

Another objection to a philosophy or metaphysics that is exclusively grounded in the moral or spiritual nature is that it unduly limits the range and function of the intellect. It assumes or maintains that the theoretical reason is incapable of transcending the phenomenal order. With merely its aid we can never know the thing-in-itself. Speculation gives us no insight into ultimate reality. But such a dogmatic limitation of knowledge is, as we have seen, unwarranted. We cannot very well escape the idea that there is a power or energy back of the world of appearance, nor can we very well avoid thinking about it. And if we are warranted in thinking about it, there would seem to be nothing violent in the supposition that there are a more correct and a less correct way of conceiving it. No matter how baffling the universe may be, we instinctively and inevitably believe that it is intelligible. All science presupposes that it is such; and on that supposition we must hold that it conforms to the laws of reason. We must believe that reality is rational. And if so, not only are we justified in seeking to form a self-consistent view of it, but it is our duty as philosophers to do so. To draw a line at the gateway to ultimate reality and to say to the human intellect, "Thus far mayest thou come but no farther," is an act of caprice, not of reason.

It has still further been objected to an exclusive philosophy of value that it leads to illusionism. This objection is valid only to a limited extent. It is true that our first and firmest persuasion of reality comes from sense-perceptions and logical deductions from them, and that natural science, consequently, has come to be with many the signature of truth. In contrast with it the realm of the ideal and every philosophy based upon it seem unreal. In science reality is forced upon us and we are compelled to accept it, whether we will or no; in the philosophy of value or of faith, on the other hand, we have to do with hopes and wishes, and these may be far removed from the real. To base a philosophy or theology exclusively on value-judgments seems, therefore, to desert the solid ground of objective reality and to launch forth upon a sea of dreams. But while this seeming has some justification and while the philosophy of value is weakened by its complete detachment from the theoretical reason, it is a mistake to suppose that it logically leads to illusionism. The element of faith or of value in knowledge by no means discredits it. For all knowledge of reality implies faith. And the faith of science is logically no more valid than the faith of religion. Each is ultimate and stands in its own right. We may, then, with a good conscience base our philosophy of reality upon the moral and spiritual nature of man; but if we rest it there exclusively, we lose to some extent the note of objectivity characteristic of the theoretical reason, and expose ourselves needlessly to the charge of subjectivism.

## Metaphysical Philosophy Intellectually Grounded

From the purely ethical metaphysics we turn now to the third type of philosophy, which we have described as an intellectually grounded metaphysics. The latter has taken three main forms—that of materialism, pantheism, and theism. Materialism denies both the reality and worth of spirit and thus negates religion. Faith can form no alliance with it. We need, therefore, take no account of it. Pantheism also in its more radical and distinctive form is destructive of faith, for it denies freedom and reduces spirit to the level of things. It virtually makes spirit one with matter and in so doing starts on the road to materialism; for when spirit and matter are put on the same plane, the latter always proves itself the stronger.[11] We need not consequently here concern ourselves with it. Theism with its teleological and idealistic implications is the only form of metaphysics with which the Christian faith can ally itself. Every other metaphysic leads eventually to skepticism and despair.

In speaking of theism as an intellectually grounded metaphysic we are not, however, to suppose that it rests on a purely theoretical basis. No philosophy does, not even materialism or pantheism. Every philosophy is based to some extent on practical considerations. Either negatively or positively it is to

[11] See E. Troeltsch, *Glaubenslehre*, p. 68.

some degree a philosophy of value, whether it is aware of it or not. Every philosopher, in spite of himself, has his bias. But a distinction may nevertheless be drawn between a pure philosophy of value and a philosophy that bases itself on the theoretical as well as the practical reason. It is in the latter sense that we speak of theism as an intellectually grounded metaphysic. It does not exclude practical considerations; it gives large place to moral values; but it also appeals to the theoretical reason and finds support in it.

Against theism in this traditional sense of the term the charge of "intellectualism" is frequently made. And by intellectualism is meant the view that the truth of religion can be established by arguments of a purely theoretical character. That such a view of the theistic "proofs" was not infrequently taken in the past, is no doubt true. It was believed that the existence of God could be "demonstrated." But since the time of Kant this view has been quite generally relinquished by theistic writers. It is now seen that strict demonstration is impossible when it comes to objective reality. All knowledge rests on faith. This is true of God as of objective reality in general. And in the case of God it is chiefly moral faith on which knowledge rests. But moral faith may and needs to be supplemented by theoretical considerations; and in this supplementary way the inductive and speculative arguments in support of religious belief have a permanent value. Such is the position taken by current philosophic theism. Nevertheless, against it the old charge of intellectualism and scholasticism is still made. The assumption seems to be that in the field of religious belief the theoretical reason in any form is an intruder and that it must be forthwith banished if the gospel of the purely practical nature of religion is not to be contaminated.

Various objections have been raised against any attempt at an intellectual grounding of religion. For one thing, such a grounding is said to be necessarily inadequate. And this is no doubt true in the sense that no theoretical proof can yield the full religious idea of God. But no theist to-day, so far as I know, puts forth such a claim. Again, it is objected that philosophic theism places undue stress upon the doctrinal element in religion such as the belief in God and personal immortality. Religion, we are told, is something other and older than these beliefs. And this too may be true. But religion in its present and highest form has so completely expressed itself in these beliefs that without them there would be very little of value left in religion. The Christian faith stands or falls with them; and if so, traditional theism cannot have been far astray in centering attention upon them.

Another objection to the theoretical justification of religion is that it does not square with the actual grounds of religious belief. People, as a matter of fact, do not believe in God because of the proofs that have been offered of his existence. Faith with them is instinctive. It springs up spontaneously in their lives. Various causes contribute to its genesis, but its justification it finds within itself. It is self-evidencing. It is based on direct spiritual insight. At least such is the form that it takes in vital piety; and if in this respect it is mistaken, it can lay no claim to truth. If it is not in itself trustworthy, no argument can make it such. We must, then, assume the validity of faith or fall into skepticism. And if so, our task as theologians should be, not to prove the truth of religion, but to show how faith is actually produced, to exhibit its inner nature and grounds. When once produced, it justifies itself.

The trouble with this position is that it fails to distinguish between the psychological causes of faith and its logical grounds. The psychological causes are numerous and from the practical point of view are worthy of careful study. In the actual religious life of men they are far more important than the logical grounds of faith. But this does not mean that they are self-sufficient or that they justify faith. Nor does it mean that faith has no logical grounds, or no need of them. These grounds may not have the significance that was once attributed to them; and they certainly are not essential to faith; nor do they impeach its self-verifying power. But they do serve as supplements to it; and the fact that the direction of attention to them has historically followed rather than preceded faith, does not impair their worth.

Yet the further objection is raised against an intellectually grounded theism that it is superfluous, both logically and practically superfluous.[12] The argument from the moral consciousness, we are told, represents the *actual* source of religious faith. It alone,

[12] Compare John Baillie, *The Interpretation of Religion*, pp. 92f., where this view is emphatically indorsed.

therefore, has any real practical value. Then, too, if valid at all, it establishes the existence of God as well as his goodness, and hence there is no need of a purely theoretical argument to prove his existence and his intelligence. These are both involved in his moral character. The one argument from moral experience, consequently, is sufficient. We need no other.

But this line of reasoning implies a very one-sided view of human nature and of religious experience. The human mind has other interests than the ethical, and so has religion. There is no single factor in human life so isolated as to be completely self-sufficient. The moral consciousness may be the chief source of religious faith, but even if it were the sole source—which it is not—it would not make religious faith so independent as to need no support from the theoretical reason. The very fact that Christian philosophy throughout almost the whole history of the church has been theoretically as well as ethically grounded, is itself the most convincing evidence that the theoretical grounding of faith has not been devoid of practical value. Some have, no doubt, responded more readily to it than others, and many may have been cold to it; but to rule it out as worthless and superfluous is an arbitrary and doctrinaire procedure, entirely unwarranted by actual experience and by the constitution of human nature. Men are unitary beings and what they do along the religious line must find its echo in the parallel activity of thought. A house divided against itself cannot stand.

Such has been the conviction of the church during the greater part of its history, despite the influence of authoritarian obscurantism and epistemological sophistry; and hence a working alliance has been quite steadily maintained between theology and the theoretical reason. The philosophy with which the main stream of Christian thought has allied itself has been naturally of the theistic type. But theism has taken various forms. In the course of its development it has gone through four main stages: the Platonic or Neoplatonic, the Aristotelian, the Cartesian, and the modern idealistic. It would be interesting and instructive to trace in detail the relation of each of these theistic philosophies to the Christian faith, but that would here take us too far afield.

It will suffice for our present purpose if we point out two or three common aspects of the theistic systems which have tended to confirm the Christian faith.[13] One has to do with the problem of knowledge. Christianity manifestly implies that the human mind is not limited to the sense plane, that it is able to transcend the empirical, to lay hold of the metaphysical. It does not define how this may be done. It talks about "revelation" and "faith," but these are religious terms which cast no light upon the mental process by which the transcendental is apprehended. They do, however, imply that in some way or other the human mind does have power to grasp the supersensible. This power is sometimes conceived in an anti-intellectualistic sense, and a sharp distinction is, consequently, drawn between faith and knowledge. But this sharp distinction is, as we have seen, unwarranted. For there is no knowledge without faith,

[13] Cf. Georg Wobbermin, *Theologie und Metaphysik*, p. 1901.

and no faith without more or less knowledge. The two imply each other. And if it be insisted that religious faith is entirely different from intellectual faith, it may be replied that logically one is as good as the other, and that the natural tendency will be for the two to stand or fall together. If faith in the metaphysical capacity of the intellect is denied, there is no good reason why faith in the metaphysical capacity of the religious nature should not also be rejected.

Any philosophy, therefore, which attributes transcendental powers to the human intellect, to that extent lends support to religious faith. And *that* theism in its four main forms has always done. It has given good grounds, though these differ to some extent in each of its main forms, for believing that the human reason is endowed with the capacity to think correctly concerning ultimate reality, and insofar as it has done this it has created a presumption in favor of the validity of religious faith. If our intellectual nature is worthy of being trusted, it is inherently probable that our religious nature also is.

A second philosophical problem in which Christian theology is deeply interested, is that of the "I." Christianity affirms the reality of the self, of personality. This is one of its most characteristic doctrines, both as applied to man and to God. It holds to the survival of human personality after death, and it places the utmost emphasis upon the personality of God. It has also devoted an extraordinary amount of attention to the question as to how the personality of Christ should be conceived. With it the reality of personality is thus a subject of major concern. Its primary interests here as elsewhere are, of course, practical. But the practical needs the support of the theoretical, and this is especially so in connection with such a problem as that of personality. For to all appearances the human self is a mere bubble on the great sea of cosmic energy; it has no abiding reality. This conclusion has been proclaimed again and again in the materialistic and positivistic philosophies. To their negations it is, therefore, a matter of prime importance that an adequate response be made, if faith is to be at all rational. And this response is to be found in the theistic philosophies. They have realized that if there is no spirit in the microcosm, there can be no spirit in the macrocosm, and hence with united effort they have sought to establish the reality of the human spirit.

Two great contributions have been made toward this end. The first was the Platonic contention that spirit or personality is immaterial. It is, therefore, in its inner being independent of the body and need not necessarily cease to exist when the latter is dissolved. The second contribution is the modern insight into the fact that personality alone fills out the notion of being or reality. The real must provide for change, for this is a changing world; but if it is truly real, it must also in some sense abide and remain identical with itself. In a word, it must combine in itself identity and change, unity and plurality; and this, as a matter of fact, is done only in personality. We change and do many different things, yet through memory we remain or constitute ourselves one and the same. In this unique fact of self-consciousness we have, therefore, the key to reality. This insight and the allied insight into the immateriality of spirit give the lie to our sense prejudices, and thus prepare the way for and confirm the affirmations of faith.[14] Indeed, without these insights faith would find its personalistic assumptions unrelated to if not directly contradicted by reason; and this state of affairs could not but eventually prove detrimental to faith.

A third philosophical problem, which stands closely related to Christian theology, is that of causality. The idea of a real cause is implied in the Christian conception of God as Creator and in the Christian belief in Providence. To dissolve the principle of causality away by reducing it in positivistic fashion to a mere order of succession or coexistence, would then be to undermine these fundamental Christian doctrines. Faith, if it is to maintain its rationality, must ally itself with a philosophy which makes a place for real causality and for causality in its volitional form. Such a philosophy we have in a thoroughgoing theism. Here it is not only made clear that the idea of a real cause is essential to meet the mental demand for ground and connection, but it is also shown that only in its personal form can causality be thought through without self-contradiction. For causality implies change and it also implies permanence. There must be some abiding being that produces the change; otherwise the change would not be accounted for. And this union of permanence and

[14] See my *Philosophy of Personalism*, pp. 237-46.

change inherent in causality is found, as we have seen, only in personality. A personalistic philosophy thus solves the problem of metaphysical causality and at the same time furnishes a foundation for the Christian belief in the divine creatorship and providence.[15]

From the foregoing discussion it is evident that there can be no theology without metaphysics, and it is also evident that there can be no adequate theology without a metaphysics that is theoretically as well as ethically grounded. But while theology thus stands closely related to metaphysical philosophy, it is not to be identified with it. It has its own distinctive character and its own method. This will be made clear in the next chapter.

---

[15] Cf. my *Philosophy of Personalism*, pp. 210-25.

## CHAPTER V

## SOURCES AND METHOD

THUS far we have dealt chiefly with the general field of theology, and our positive argument has been comparatively simple. We have defined theology as the systematic exposition and rational justification of the intellectual content of religion, and in support of this definition have argued, first, that religion has a valid intellectual content and, second, that this content in its Christian form admits, to a certain extent, of rational justification. The first position we have maintained as over against illusionism and the second as over against both an authoritarian and a romantic irrationalism. Religion, it is true, like every other fundamental interest of the human spirit, must, in the last analysis, justify itself. But self-justification does not exclude rational justification. Rather should the two go together. If religion is self-evidencing, it ought also to find support in the common reason. And this is the view that has been represented by the main stream of Christian thought.

Some have tried to find a rational support for religion in science by transforming theology into an empirical science and thus giving to it the same recognized intellectual standing as any special science. But this attempt, as we have seen, has led to confusion and self-contradiction. Science in its traditional common-sense interpretation is a confused compound of philosophy and empirical science, and in its positivistic sense it excludes theology altogether. For there can be no theology without metaphysics. Religious belief by its very nature implies the metaphysical. It is only in metaphysics, consequently, that religion can find its ultimate rational basis. Such a religious metaphysics may be either ethically or theoretically grounded or both. Only the double grounding meets the needs of both the religious mind and heart.

Theology, then, stands in a close relation to metaphysical philosophy. It differs from it in that it concentrates attention upon the subject of religion. In this respect it resembles the philosophy of religion. It differs, however, from the latter in that it is conditioned by its relation to the church. Theology has grown up in connection with the church; it was its child, and to a large extent remains such. It is the servant of the church; and this relationship it cannot well disown, at least not under existing conditions. It may be conceived of as related only to a particular religious communion, as Schleiermacher did; he defined theology as "the science which systematizes the doctrine prevalent in a Christian church at a given time."[1] Or its relation may be extended to all Protestantism or to the entire Christian Church. But in any case it remains linked up with the church. It has a place within the church, and has a function to perform there. This fact differentiates it from the general philosophy of religion.

---

[1] *The Christian Faith*, p. 88.

So far as the validation of religious belief is concerned, the two are on the same plane. In the past theology appealed to an external authority for the authentication of at least a large part of its teaching. It distinguished between natural theology and revealed theology. The former was made up of "mixed articles" (*articuli mixti*), that is, articles based both on revelation and reason; the latter had to do with "pure articles" (*articuli puri*), that is, articles based on revelation alone. But this distinction between natural and revealed theology has now largely fallen into disuse. The present tendency is to draw no sharp line of distinction between revelation and the natural reason, but to look upon the highest insights of reason as themselves divine revelations. In any case there is no fixed body of revealed truth, accepted on authority, that stands opposed to the truths of reason. All truth to-day rests on its power of appeal to the human mind. There is no external standard of truth. The only standard is within the human mind itself. At this point there is, therefore, no difference between theology and the philosophy of religion. Both have the same basis. But while this is true, theology, in view of its ecclesiastical associations, has its own special province. It concentrates attention upon the teaching of the Bible and the church, seeking to interpret and commend it to the modern mind, in a way that the philosophy of religion does not. It thus has its own peculiar approach to the religious problem. It comes to it from within the Christian Church. This fact gives to it a content and a character that are more or less distinctively its own, and raises certain questions with reference to sources and method that require consideration. It is with these questions that the present chapter is concerned.

### Sources

The question as to the sources of theology was in the past closely bound up with the idea of an infallible revelation made through a divinely inspired book or church or both. This idea we no longer hold. We do not believe in either biblical or ecclesiastical infallibility. But the question of sources still has its interest and significance for us. Indeed, the problem is, theoretically at least, as vital and important as ever. If we are to determine what Christianity is and expound its doctrines, we must be agreed as to what the normative source or sources of information concerning it are; and we must also be agreed as to the method by which they are to be interpreted.

That the Bible is or should be the chief source and norm of Christian theology would probably be generally admitted. But that it should be the only source and norm is open to question. Some Protestant theologians insist that it should be, but in so doing they seem to me to reflect the influence of an earlier ecclesiastical and supernaturalistic exclusivism. One may attribute to Scripture an altogether unique degree of inspiration without denying that Christianity has learned important truths from other sources also; and one may believe that the Protestant Reformers were justified in opposing the authority of the Bible to that of the church without denying that original and significant contributions to the deposit of Christian truth were made by the Church Fathers. That the great creative ideas of the Christian faith came from Scripture is no doubt true, but that they have been supplemented and developed by the creeds and confessions of the churches and by the reason and experience of believers would seem equally true. To know what Christianity is, then, we must take into account not only the teaching of Scripture, but the whole history of the Christian Church. Indeed, it is not sufficient to study the Christian Church alone. We need to extend our inquiries so as to take in the religious life and beliefs of men in general. Only against the background of other religions and in relation to them can Christianity be fully understood. To our study of biblical exegesis and church history we need, therefore, to add the study of the psychology and history of religion. All of these subjects, to which the philosophy of religion might be added, may be regarded as contributory to Christian theology.

Still, it is the Bible that in a special and pre-eminent sense is the source and norm of Christian belief. In it we have the earliest and most trustworthy record of that unique revelation of God which was mediated to the world through Jewish and early Christian history and which constitutes the foundation of the Christian faith. To this record we must go for the original documents of our religion, for its classic expression. Much might be said in favor of the unique inspiration of these documents, but entirely apart from this question they occupy historically a position of primacy from which they can never be dislodged. They are at once the earliest literary embodiment of our faith and the one original and authentic record of God's special revelation of himself. In the latter respect they are properly spoken of as the Word of God and in the former respect they contain the only adequate data for scientifically determining the nature of primitive Christianity. In both respects they are unique, and this constitutes adequate ground for ascribing to the Bible a position of transcendent significance. To it, therefore, as to no other source Christian theology will necessarily go back for its material and for its validation. Of this the whole history of the church furnishes ample confirmation. The only question has to do with the exclusiveness of its authority and the limits of its normative content. On both of these points there have been historic contests.

With reference to the limits of the biblical canon there is a difference between Protestants and Roman Catholics. The latter include the Apocrypha, while the former do not. But this difference has no important doctrinal significance. So far as doctrine is concerned, there has been only one important debate with respect to the limits of the canon, and this had to do with the Old Testament. A serious effort was made in the early church by the Gnostics, and especially by Marcion, to eliminate the Old Testament from the Christian canon. It was their contention that the God of the Old Testament differed in character from that of the New. He was just and righteous, not merciful and loving like the God of Jesus, a Judge, not a Father. But what they particularly objected to in him was that he was the creator of the present evil world, from which Christ came to redeem us. Such a being, they held, must in the nature of the case be imperfect, if not evil, a demiurge, not the true God. So they distinguished between the Creator-God of the Old Testament and the Redeemer-God of the New Testament. To the former they allowed no place in the Christian faith.

This attempt to limit the canon to the New Testament failed, and for manifest reasons. It ran counter to the teaching of Jesus and Paul and to Christian tradition in general. It overlooked the large Christian element in the Old Testament, especially in the Psalms and prophetic books. And it directly contradicted a fundamental Christian conviction with reference to the present world and its relation to God. However imperfect the world may be, it is still, according to Christian teaching, his handiwork and the field of his providential and redemptive activity. Redemption does not negate creation; it completes it. Furthermore, only he who is Creator can be Redeemer. The two offices do not exclude each other; they belong together. Such was the profound conviction of the early church, and under its influence the Gnostic teaching was rejected as heritical. Since then a hostile or unappreciative attitude toward the Old Testament has occasionally been expressed by distinguished Christian thinkers, but no attempt to dispense with it has been made comparable in vigor and range to that of the Gnostics.[2] The church as a whole has throughout its history been

[2] See *An Outline of Christianity*, Vol. IV, pp. 339ff., 365ff., where I have discussed the subject more fully.

persuaded that there is an organic connection between the two Testaments, that the New is implicit in the Old and the Old explicit in the New, and that the Christian faith requires both if it is to be fully understood.

But while the Old Testament has a well-established place in the Christian canon, it is not to be placed on a level with the New Testament. At this point the old theory of biblical infallibility erred. It formally at least attributed an equal degree of inspiration and of authority to all parts of the Bible. This view runs counter to the idea of a progressive revelation, is inconsistent with the claims of the New Testament, and is completely negated by modern criticism. As the historical presupposition of the New Testament and as the independent source of imperishable religious truth, the Hebrew Scriptures have a permanent value and are properly incorporated in the Christian canon. But there is much in them that is sub-Christian or extra-Christian, and this needs to be distinguished from the Christian element. What is truly Christian can be determined only by appealing to the New Testament. It is the revelation made in and through Christ that is the source and norm of Christian truth.[3] Only in a supplementary, preparatory, and corroborative way does the Old Testament have authority for us, but in these respects it serves an important purpose. It was against the background of the Old Testament that Jesus did his work, and much of this background passed into his own teach-

---

[3] Cf. *The Use of the Scriptures in Theology*, by William Newton Clarke.

ing so as to form a permanent part of it. It would, then, do violence to the New Testament to detach it from the Old. The two belong together in fact as well as by the authority of the Master. Such may be said to be the considered judgment of the Christian Church.

Aside from the attempt of the Gnostics to divorce the Old Testament from the New, no serious effort has been made to reduce materially the Christian canon. Nor does any great doctrinal significance attach to the modern relegation of the Old Testament to a subordinate position within the canon. But there is at present a tendency to limit the authority of the New Testament and of the Bible as a whole to the Synoptic Jesus, or what is supposed to be "the Jesus of history," in a way that implies a very significant doctrinal change. It is argued that the Jesus of Paul and John and the later Christian Church is the "Christ of faith," and that as such he is the product of the Christian imagination. He never existed. It is the Jesus of history, and he only, who has authoritative significance for us. Our task, therefore, to-day is to "reconstruct our Christianity, not in the light of Paul or John, or later accepted and official beliefs, but in the light of the religious experience of Jesus himself."[4] The most authentic picture of the historical Jesus is to be found in the Synoptic Gospels. A unique significance, therefore, attaches to them. They are the Holy of Holies of the Christian

---

[4] This program is elaborated with marked ability, learning, and enthusiasm by Professor Walter E. Bundy, of DePauw University, in two interesting volumes entitled *The Religion of Jesus* and *Our Recovery of Jesus.*

canon. The rest of the New Testament and the Old Testament as a whole belong to the outer courts.

This view is often set forth as though it were self-evident, a necessary implication of the historical method. But it is, rather, an instance of what the Germans call "historicism." It puts the human process above the divine content. Indeed, it is inclined to exclude the latter altogether. It assumes that our one interest is or ought to be "the religion of Jesus." "The religion about Jesus," by which is meant the belief in his divinity, is treated as though it were a degenerate offshoot from the pure gospel. The fact, however, is that it was this faith that created the Christian Church and that has since maintained it. Christianity owed its origin to the impression made by the personality of Jesus upon his disciples. This impression was double. The disciples saw in Jesus and his work not simply a human quest after God, but a divine quest after man. They beheld in him not merely the perfect sanctity of a man, but the gracious advent of Deity. They heard in the message of his life and death not only the voice of man, but the voice of God. That this double impression was made upon them is not open to question. The whole New Testament is witness to it. And here it is that we have the characteristically Christian point of view. We cannot resolve it into anything simpler without dissolving it. The double impression was original and ultimate.

To construct a picture of Jesus with the divine factor eliminated and represent such a Jesus as the source of Christianity, pure and undefiled, is to fly in the face of history. It was not the so-called "historical Jesus" on whom the church was founded, but the real Jesus, a man who had the power to awaken in others faith in himself as the mediator of the divine grace. It was this "Christ of faith" who actually existed and from whom the Christian religion took its start. The "Jesus of history," whose significance was exhausted in his teaching and in his exemplary religious experience, is a figment of the modern imagination, a product of the naturalistic mode of thought. The truly historical Jesus was a generator of faith in himself both as the perfect man and as in some sense the incarnation of the Divine. To suppose that in the latter respect an erroneous impression was produced on Paul and John and to suppose that on so fundamental a point the Christian Church has for nineteen centuries been mistaken, would go far to discredit not only the entire Christian consciousness, but the whole religious nature of man. In any case there can be no doubt that the belief in Jesus as something more than a great teacher or a perfect moral and religious example is an essential part of historical Christianity and that to exclude this belief from the articles of our faith would involve a reconstruction of the Christian system almost as radical as that involved in the Gnostic rejection of the Creator-God of the Old Testament. As the latter movement failed because it broke with the Christian tradition and the Christian consciousness, so we may be confident it will be with the modern movement, if such it may be called, which would discard the Pauline and Johannine conception of a divine Christ, and restrict the authority of Scripture to a nebulous "Jesus of history." It is the whole New Testament, not any selected portions of the Synoptic Gospels, that is and that will remain the chief source and norm of Christian theology.

But is the Bible, either in whole or in part, the exclusive source and norm of theology? This question, to which we have already referred, has figured prominently in the disputes of the past. The controversy has taken three main forms. Some have maintained that the church, others that reason, and still others that Christian experience is a supplementary or a coequal, or even a superior source of religious truth.

The question as to the relation of the authority of the church to that of Scripture has been one of the main grounds of contention between Protestants and Roman Catholics. The latter hold that the revelational activity of the Divine Spirit is continued in and through the church, and to this there is in principle no valid objection. The inspiration of the Bible does not necessarily exclude the inspiration of the great creedal and other utterances of the church. Nor does the fact that we have in Christ the supreme revelation of God exclude other and supplementary revelations to the church. But Roman Catholics go further than this. They maintain that the church is the sole authoritative interpreter of Scripture, and that the ultimate basis for accepting the authority of Scripture must be found in the authority of the church. Here we have a sharp clash between the Catholic and Protestant points of view. The characteristic thing in Protestantism is not its belief in the inspiration of the Bible, but its belief in the inspiration of the individual. As over against the tyrannical authority of the church it vindicates for the individual the right and the duty to interpret the Scriptures for himself. It also finds the ultimate ground for accepting the biblical revelation in its power of appeal to the individual soul or, to use the language of the older Protestantism, in the *testimonium spiritus*. It thus rejects the authority of the church insofar as it comes into conflict with the conscience and the intelligence of the individual believer.

But it is, of course, impossible for the individual to detach himself completely from the influence of the church. It is through the church that he comes to know the Bible, and he could not, if he would, escape the influence of the past in its interpretation. Indeed, no sane exegete would wish to do so. The church has through its scholars made important contributions to the correct interpretation of Scripture which no honest student could or would disregard, so that in spite of ourselves we see the Bible through the eyes of the church. These contributions it has made not only by philological studies, but by the new perspective it has given to biblical teaching. It has emphasized the Christian elements and allowed the others to sink into the background. The process has varied from generation to generation, reflecting the changing thought of the church. Progress has not been steady. There have been reactionary movements which could be met only by a fresh return to Scripture. But it is a radically mistaken view which sees in the main stream of the church's doctrinal development a defection from the faith. It is in and through its history that Christianity unfolds and expresses itself, and it is only by taking into account its total history that we can determine its true nature. Its history thus supplements Scripture and regulates our interpretation of it. Hence the church with its creeds and confessions may properly be regarded as a secondary source of theology.

The basis on which reason is singled out as another source of Christian theology is somewhat different. We have here to do with the contributions made by theistic philosophy to the Christian faith. These contributions, derived chiefly from the Greeks, have, as we have seen, been rated very differently by Christian thinkers. Some have appraised them highly, while others have branded them as foreign importations that have done more harm than good. Naturally the latter have not been disposed to see in reason a true source of Christian theology. But the former are manifestly quite justified in doing so. For them the natural reason appears as both a supplement to and support of the biblical teaching; and that this represents the main stream of Christian thought has been made clear in previous chapters.

Reason, however, has not always been willing to serve as merely a supplementary source of Christian theology. It has at times claimed to be the sole ultimate source. In the deistic movement, for instance, it was maintained that all true religion is based on the natural reason and that Christianity is true only insofar as it is not "mysterious," only insofar as it is as old as creation or a republication of the religion of nature.[5] Hegel also represented about the same standpoint, though he expressed himself differently. He looked upon the fundamental doctrines of the Christian Church not as echoes of an earlier natural religion, but as symbols of the absolute truths of reason. Christianity, he held, is true insofar, and only insofar, as it foreshadows and symbolizes the higher abstract principles of the idealistic philosophy. These two historic forms of rationalism thus virtually set aside the Bible as an independent source of religious truth and put reason in its stead. In so doing they broke with the Christian point of view. Christianity is willing to recognize "reason" as a supplementary and regulative or formal source of theology, but it cannot without renouncing its own distinctive character recognize it as the chief and much less as the sole ultimate source.

With respect to religious experience as a source of theology the situation is somewhat different from what it is with the church and the natural reason. The latter have both made distinct contributions or additions to the content of Christian theology. But this can hardly be said to be the case with religious experience viewed as something direct and unmediated. The mystics have claimed for themselves an immediate apprehension of the Divine, but they have admitted that while this experience has given them a greater assurance of the reality of God, it has not increased their insight into what he is. Insofar as

[5] See John Toland, *Christianity Not Mysterious*, 1696; Matthew Tindal, *Christianity as Old as the Creation, or the Gospel a Republication of the Religion of Nature*, 1730.

the mystic experience has had a definite content, it has derived it from earlier training. This is also manifestly true of "the Christian consciousness" which Schleiermacher set up as the main source of theology. No doubt it is true that there was a Christian consciousness before the New Testament and that the New Testament was to a large extent an expression of it. It is also true that as a reaction against a dogmatic biblicism, on the one hand, and a barren rationalism on the other, Schleiermacher's emphasis on Christian experience marked an important step forward in the history of theology, the founding of theological empiricism. But if this emphasis be construed into meaning that the Christian consciousness of to-day is independent of Scripture, it is evident that we have here a serious error. The Christian consciousness is, to a large extent, the product of biblical teaching and the society that biblical teaching has created. Apart from them it could not, without a miracle, come into being. Its content is, therefore, derived, not original. What the Christian consciousness does is to reflect the teaching of the church. But it not only reflects it, it exercises a selective function as over against it. It picks out those truths that seem to it to be of the greatest value, and neglects others. In this way it modifies to some extent traditional Christian teaching and gives it a new direction. But it cannot be said to have added anything to its content by virtue of any transcendental experience of its own. Its function is regulative, not creative, and only in this sense can it be viewed as a source of Christian theology.

We have, then, as definitive of the unique or special field of theology, one main source, the Bible, and particularly the New Testament, and three additional sources which may be described as supplementary or regulative; namely, the church, the natural reason as expressed in the theistic philosophies, and Christian experience.

## Method

The question of theological method has been much discussed during the past century. This has been due to the breakdown of the older dogmatic and rationalistic method and the failure to agree upon a method to take its place. We hear about the "theocentric" and "anthropocentric," the "speculative" and "empirical," the "religio-historical" and the "religio-psychological" methods, and in the past few years the "dialectic" method has been attracting wide attention. This diversity of method is at first rather confusing, and has led some to the conclusion that the question of method is at present of fundamental theological significance, that everything, indeed, depends upon it. The one great need of the day in theology, we are told, is the attainment of a "unified and unambiguous method."[6] In one sense this is perhaps true. The establishment of a clearly defined and commonly accepted theological method would be highly desirable. It would bring unity into what is at present a somewhat distracted

---

[6] So Georg Wobbermin, *Die Religionspsychologische Methode in Religionswissenschaft und Theologie*, pp. viif.

field. But the ideal is hardly one that is likely to be realized in the near future. The reason is that method is, after all, secondary, a reflection of one's philosophical or theological standpoint. It is not method that determines one's theological conclusions, but, rather, the reverse. The various methods above mentioned are all the outcome of certain theological or philosophical convictions. The "empirical" and "religio-psychological" methods owe their origin to a more or less empiricistic theory of knowledge. The "theocentric" and "speculative" methods are due to the persistence or revival of the older dogmatic and rationalistic standpoints and the term "anthropocentric" is applied to any method that stresses the human conditions of religious knowledge. The "religio-historical" method grows out of the modern philosophy of history, and the "dialectic" method of Barth and Brunner is the natural accompaniment of their Neo-Kantian epistemology. Complete agreement in theological method is, therefore, practically impossible without agreement in philosophical and theological presuppositions, and this is not likely to be attained for an indefinite time to come. Nevertheless, the question of method is one which the theological student should understand and about which he should be clear.

The fundamental cleavage in theological method is that between the "dogmatic" and what may be called the "critical" method. It was Schleiermacher who first clearly established the contrast between these two methods. The dogmatic implies an authoritative standard which is regarded as objective and more or less self-operative. The standard may be the Bible or the church, or even reason itself, if the latter be conceived of as involving certain definite and necessary religious beliefs. With such an objective standard the method in constructing a theology will be to systematize and, so far as possible, justify what is taught in the accepted standard without taking adequately into account the subjective factors that condition its acceptance and the actual influences that determine religious belief. These subjective and empirical factors were first developed in a thoroughgoing way by Kant in the field of philosophy and by Schleiermacher in the field of theology. Kant emphasized the moral and Schleiermacher the emotional basis of religious belief, but both stressed the practical element in religion as over against the theoretical. The doctrinal and intellectual element as represented by biblical theology, the creeds of the church and speculative theism they made secondary, an effect of religion rather than its cause. In this way they undermined the earlier dogmatic and rationalistic method and introduced in its place the "critical."

By the critical method is thus meant the method that begins with an inquiry into the subjective conditions of knowledge or belief and that makes this inquiry basal. In its more characteristic form this method is variously called "anthropocentric," "empirical," "scientific," "religio-historical" and "religio-psychological." What all of these terms emphasize is the inductive character of theology and the human approach to it. Theology from this point of view finds its starting-point in faith rather than the object or objects of faith. It is a *Glaubenslehre,* a science or doctrine of faith, rather than a *doctrina de deo et rebus divinis.* The latter was the conception of theology current up to the time of Schleiermacher. He rejected it in favor of the critical method. It was this fact that Neander had in mind when, in announcing his death in 1834, he said, "We have now lost a man from whom will be dated henceforth a new era in the history of theology."

The critical method, however, is not to be identified with that introduced by Schleiermacher, nor with any one specific period. The term might, it is true, be applied in the Kantian sense to a nonmetaphysical theology. But there is no established usage to that effect. Here the term is used in a comprehensive sense to denote any method that excludes an external and definitive authority and that takes serious account of the subjective conditions of knowledge and belief. Virtually all current theological methods do this except the purely traditional, and hence they may in a general way be described as "critical." They renounce the idea of biblical infallibility, and are also agreed in recognizing the necessity of finding a basis for their own particular position in some sort of religious epistemology. But within this general agreement there are several important differences, two of which call for brief consideration. Reference has already been made to them. One is the difference between the anthropocentric and the theocentric methods. It has been argued by Erich Schaeder,[7]

[7] *Theozentrische Theologie.*

and still more radically by Emil Brunner,[8] that Protestant theology was diverted into a false channel by Schleiermacher, that the human was wrongly substituted for the divine standpoint, and that the hope of the future lies in a return to the theocentric emphasis of earlier times. Theology, we are told, must again become objective. The subjectivism of modern thought must be overcome, and revelation must be reinstated in its central and supreme place. Instead of fixing attention on religion or faith as a human experience we must fix attention on God. Interest must be centered in the object of faith rather than in faith itself.

For this reaction against the anthropocentric and subjectivistic tendency in modern theology there is some justification. There is danger that religion may lose its grip on the eternal and transcendent and become purely humanistic. To meet this peril there is need of the theocentric emphasis. But taken by itself, as determinative of a whole system of theology, the theocentric method would mean a revival, in modified form, of the older dogmatism. For while it rules out biblical infallibility, it clings to the idea of revelation as an objective and authoritative body of truth. It recognizes that subjective factors are involved in the determination of the exact content of this body of truth, but when determined absoluteness is ascribed to it. And this means that theology becomes again a *doctrina de deo et rebus divinis.* It loses to a large degree its critical character and becomes dogmatic. It fails to see that in our day

[8] *Die Mystik und das Wort.*

theology must be anthropocentric in its starting point. Otherwise it would have no point of contact with modern thought. It must, to be sure, transcend this anthropocentric point of view. In its outcome it must be theocentric, if true to itself. Both methods must be combined in any complete and adequate theology.

The second difference in modern theological method calling for attention in this connection is that between the speculative and the empirical. In its more extreme form the speculative method subordinates the concrete facts of Christian history and experience to the general ideas or truths symbolized by them. For instance, the person of Christ is said to have significance only insofar as it is the embodiment of the principle of Christianity;[9] the latter alone is absolute; and so with biblical and Christian history as a whole. Not in its concrete events or personages, but in the ideas operative in them is that ultimate truth to be found with which theology is concerned. To develop and ground these ideas is, therefore, the main task of the theologian, and hence his method must be fundamentally speculative.

The chief objection to this method is that it implies an intellectualistic conception of religion and marks a return in principle to the discredited rationalism of a century or so ago. Opposed to it stands the empirical or scientific method, which is the popular theological method of our day. Here the stress is placed on the individual instead of the universal, on the concrete instead of the abstract, on experience in-

[9] Cf. A. E. Biedermann, *Christliche Dogmatik*.

stead of reason. But experience is a vague term and is used in a variety of different senses. In seeking to determine its meaning more precisely it should first be noted that there is no such thing as "pure experience." All articulate experience is interpreted experience; that is, it implies the activity of thought or reason. Still there is a difference between knowledge of the concrete perceptual type and abstract or conceptual knowledge; and to the former the term experience may be applied. But experience is not purely cognitive, it is also appreciative. It has not only a registering, but also an evaluating function. Then, too, there is a past as well as a present experience, and the past is irrevocable. In the case of the individual past experience may be remembered, but in the case of the race it is only figuratively that we can speak of a memory of the past. All remembrance is individual; but even when remembered the past is not experienced. It was once experienced and as such belongs to experience, but as past it is irrevocable and separated from us by a gulf which no magic can bridge. A record of it may be transmitted to us and it may within limits be recalled in memory, but as a past experience it is unrepeatable. It belongs to history. The experience that underlies or constitutes history is, therefore, different, so far as we are concerned, from present experience. We have, then, three different senses in which the term "experience" is used: the purely perceptual, the evaluational, and the historical.

Each of these different aspects of experience has been made the basis of a special group of empirical sciences. The natural sciences are based on the purely perceptual side of experience, the normative sciences on its evaluational side, and the historical sciences on the recorded experiences of the past. And each of these forms of empirical science has been carried over into theology. We have a type of empirical theology that lays stress on history, another type that emphasizes value-judgments, and a third that puts the stress on the perceptual character of religious experience. These three types do not exclude each other. They are often fused together with very little recognition of distinction between them. They all claim to be empirical, and in that sense anti-speculative and anti-metaphysical. But a fundamental confusion usually inheres in their conception of experience. We have seen that popular thought oscillates between a positivistic and a metaphysical interpretation of experience; and this uncertainty and confusion vitiates a large part of current empirical theology. If religious experience be interpreted in a positivistic sense, theological empiricism degenerates into psychologism and historicism. It surrenders all transcendent reality and with it the very essence of religious faith. If, on the other hand, religious experience be interpreted in a metaphysical sense, we have in empirical theology a confused compound of science and philosophy; and under the guise of this hybrid empiricism the older metaphysical types of thought are revived in a diluted or modified form. In the historical positivism of Ritschlianism we have an attenuated form of the older authoritarianism; in the Ritschlian theory of value-judgments we have an abbreviated form of the older rationalism; and in the perceptual theory of religious experience we have a modernized version of the older mysticism and pietism. If biblical history had in it no note of authority, if value judgments were devoid of all objective and existential reference, and if there be no such thing as a mystical apprehension of a Divine Being, the whole appeal to religious experience, past or present, valuational or perceptual, would be utterly futile. It is only a metaphysically interpreted experience that can serve the purposes of theology.

The current empirical method in theology is, then, complex and confused. But so also is present-day thought in general with reference to "experience," "science," and "metaphysics." And it is to this confused state of thought that theological empiricism to a large extent owes its present vogue. It seeks to win for theology the prestige of being a recognized science without inquiring fully into what is involved in such an attempt and without analyzing, clarifying, and defining its own fundamental concepts.

The fact is that the current theological quest after a "unified" method, and particularly the quest after a thoroughly "scientific" method, is to a large degree a mistaken one. Theology is composite in character. It is partly a science and partly a philosophy; and to this composite character its methodology should correspond. To seek to reduce theology as a whole to an empirical science is as mistaken as is the effort to reduce it to a metaphysical philosophy. The latter is the error of the speculative method, and the former the error of the scientific or empirical method. Both methods are essential to a complete and adequate theology. Then, too, theology has a practical aim, that of meeting the actual needs of the church, and this should also be taken account of in its methodology, so that a sound theological method should be partly scientific, partly philosophical, and partly practical.

The first task of theology is to determine and expound the essential nature and content of the Christian faith. In fulfilling this task its method must be that of a normative science. It will gather together the relevant data from the various recognized sources, but after doing so it will not simply generalize on the basis of these data, as is done in the natural sciences. It will erect within the data a norm or standard by which they will be evaluated and arranged in a graded scale according to their importance. Some will be rejected as foreign to the true nature of Christianity and others as incidental elements in its history. This method will be followed in the use of Scripture as well as in that of Christian history as a whole. The accepted norm for determining what is truly Christian and what is not will be found in Jesus Christ. But what in him is actually normative? Is it his teaching? Is it the principle of Christianity embodied in him? Is it his inner life? Or is it the transcendent fact that he is the incarnate Son of God? All of these are value-judgments. To some extent their correctness can be determined by a study of biblical and Christian history. But the question to which they are answers cannot be decided by purely objective considerations. A subjective factor is involved in every answer to it. And so it is with the determination of practical standards everywhere. It holds in every normative science. That it obtains in Christian theology, therefore, casts no reflection upon its scientific character. Insofar as theology has the function of determining the nature and intellectual content of Christianity, and insofar as it does so by an impartial study of the relevant facts, it is a normative science in the strict sense of the term, even though it cannot altogether divest itself of subjective criteria.

But theology has also the task of establishing the validity of the Christian faith, and this it cannot do without invading the field of philosophy. It may, indeed, be said that the Christian faith is self-verifying and requires no defense, but this very affirmation is in need of justification and can find justification only in a theory of knowledge which makes it clear that the fundamental moral, religious, æsthetic and intellectual interests of the human spirit are to a certain extent independent of each other and stand in their own right so that one cannot be overthrown by the others. But theology has also the duty of elaborating the intellectual content of Christianity and exhibiting its deep inner unity, and insofar as it does this it renders an important apologetic service. For it is not only as a vague subjective conviction, but as "a profound and homogeneous system" that Christianity is, as William Shedd said, "its own best defense."[10] Thus to present Christian belief, how-

[10] *A History of Christian Doctrine*, I, p. v.

ever, requires a high degree of speculative ability. Then, too, the Christian system needs to be brought into harmonious relation with the general field of philosophy, and this also calls for the use of the speculative method. The latter, therefore, is as inescapable in theology as is the scientific method.

A practical purpose lies back of the work of scientists and philosophers in general, but it stands especially close to the work of the theologian. For he stands within a definite organization and has the duty of ministering to its needs. This should not in the least divert him from his fundamental quest after the truth, but it should give direction to his inquiries and determine to some extent his method of exposition. He cannot cut loose from the terminology of the past nor break with the historic continuity of the faith without in a measure defeating the very purpose of his work. A sound practical method must, therefore, in theology supplement the purely scientific and speculative.

The question as to the order in which the different Christian doctrines should be treated has received considerable attention. To me it does not seem to be a question of any special consequence. One may, if he wishes, follow the psychological order in which the Christian system seems naturally to unfold itself, or one may adopt the logical order in which the different doctrines stand to each other. The latter, since it is clearer and less disputable, seems to me preferable from the pedagogical point of view. Adopting it, we take up in the present volume the doctrine of God. Then in a later volume, referred to in the Preface, we shall treat of the world and sin, and of Christ and redemption. These three in any case are the main topics to be considered in any and every Christian theology; and under these general heads a natural and proper place can be found for anything that needs to be said concerning the intellectual content of the Christian faith.

# PART II

# THE DOCTRINE OF GOD

## CHAPTER VI

## THE EXISTENCE OF GOD

THE existence of God is a fundamental presupposition not only of the Christian religion, but of all religion in its more highly developed forms. There probably was a kind of religion anterior to the rise of the belief in a Divine Being or beings, but of it we know very little. Original Buddhism was atheistic, but whether it was a religion or not is a question. Certainly, it represented a very one-sided and inadequate expression of the religious nature, and it was not until it was transformed into a polytheism that it became a truly popular and vital religion. In modern times various efforts have been made to start a religion without God, but the results have not been encouraging. No such effort could be successful without a radical change in the religious nature of men. So long as religion implies a trustful feeling of absolute dependence and a deep longing for redemption, it will inevitably tend not only toward a belief in a superworld, but toward a belief in a transcendent personal Being.

The theism of Christianity does not, therefore, set it apart from the other religions of the world; it is, rather, a bond of union with them. For, however vague, impersonal, and agnostic the latter may be, they contain an implicit theism. There is in them a native urge toward something clearer and more adequate. Their impersonalism and agnosticism are not finalities; they are, rather, way stations on the road to a more definite and more satisfactory world-view. And this more adequate world-view Christianity offers them in its own clear-cut theism. It says to them what Paul said to the Athenians on Mars' hill: "Whom ye ignorantly worship, him declare I unto you." It does not, then, negate their claims; it, rather, affirms and fulfills them. And this it is able to do because all religion by its very nature is implicitly theistic. It is in the thought or assumption of a transcendent and divine reality that all religion roots. What Christianity does is simply to make more explicit and carry to its logical consequences what is involved in the nature of religion in general. As it is said of the Old and New Testaments that the New is latent in the Old and the Old patent in the New, so it may be said of Christianity in its relation to other religions that it is latent in them and they are patent in it. A common theistic interest binds them all together.

In beginning, then, our exposition of the Christian faith with its doctrine of God we are adopting a method suggested not by the uniqueness of Christian teaching, but by the logical structure of religious belief in general. All vital religion rests ultimately on faith in God. But God is differently conceived by different religions and by different philosophies. The fundamental problem of theology is, therefore, to determine, if possible, what is the true conception of God. Some there are who resent all such attempts and condemn them in advance. They do so not simply because they regard them as futile, as incapable of being carried to a successful issue, but because they look upon them as more or less out of harmony with the true nature of religion. To them it is the vagueness, the indefiniteness, the indefinability of Deity that is most appealing. If his being carries with it the vague notion of some supernal value, they are content. They care for nothing more definite. They have no interest in defining his nature more precisely. Indeed, they look with disfavor upon any such attempt, branding it as "rationalistic," "scholastic," or something still more reprehensible. But intelligible as all this is by way of reaction against an overdone intellectualism, it cannot satisfy the permanent religious needs of men. If God is real and if he means anything to us, it must be possible to form some more or less definite conception of his being. If it were not, religion would degenerate into an amorphous feeling, and for the mass of men would lose both its credibility and its worth. That God may be known is implied in the idea of revelation upon which the historical religions are based; and on this assumption men have built up their various conceptions of God. These conceptions have no doubt at times been analyzed and defined by their adherents with too great minuteness and precision; but it is nevertheless true that it is in the distinctness of its conception of God that the genius and strength of a religion are most clearly revealed. This has manifestly been the case with Christianity.

In the history of Christian theology there are three

main problems with reference to God that have been discussed. The first has to do with his being or existence; it is for the most part an apologetic problem. The second has to do with his attributes, and the third with the doctrine of the Trinity. The last is a distinctively Christian doctrine; in it the unique element in the Christian view of God comes to its clearest and fullest expression. The being and attributes of God are problems that Christianity shares with other religions and with philosophic theism.

In the discussion of the divine attributes there has been considerable difference of opinion among theologians. They have not agreed as to what an attribute is. Some of the older theologians seemed to regard the attributes as standing in an external relation to the divine being or nature, as something like pins stuck in a cushion. This is obviously a mistake. The attributes have no existence apart from the being of God, and the being of God has no reality apart from its attributes. The two belong together. Taken separately they are abstractions. The attributes are simply expressions of the nature of God. On the other hand, some of the profoundest theologians have denied that the attributes express any real differences within the divine nature. Augustine, for instance, said: "God is truly called in manifold ways great, good, wise, blessed, true, and whatsoever other thing seems to be said of him not unworthily; but his greatness is the same as his wisdom; for he is not great by bulk, but by power; and his goodness is the same as his wisdom and greatness, and his truth the same as all those things; and in him it is not one thing to be blessed, and another to be great, or wise, or true, or good, or, in a word, to be himself."[1] Somewhat more explicitly still Schleiermacher said: "All attributes which we ascribe to God are to be taken as denoting not something special in God, but only something special in the manner in which the feeling of absolute dependence is to be related to him. . . . The divine thinking is the same as the divine will, and omnipotence and omniscience are one and the same."[2] These statements by Schleiermacher and Augustine, if taken strictly, would lead to virtual agnosticism. For if the divine attributes are subjective with us and represent no distinctions within God himself, it is evident that we have no valid knowledge of him, since it is only through his attributes that he can be known. We must, then, regard the divine attributes as truly expressive of the divine nature; and from this point of view we may, with O. A. Curtis, define an attribute as "any characteristic which we must ascribe to God to express what he really is,"[3] or we may, with H. B. Smith, define it as "any conception which is necessary to the explicit idea of God, any distinctive conception which cannot be resolved into any other."[4]

If these definitions of an attribute be accepted, the question still arises as to what specific aspects of the Divine Being should be singled out as attributes and how they should be classified. Here too there is no

---

[1] *De Trinitate*, VII, 7; English translation by A. W. Haddan, pp. 173f.

[2] *Der Christliche Glaube*, Pars. 50 and 55; English translation, pp. 194, 221.

[3] *The Christian Faith*, p. 474.

[4] *System of Christian Theology*, p. 12.

general agreement, but the differences are not of any particular moment. Yet in seeking to determine how we ought to think about God it is a matter of some importance that we should single out those characteristics which are most significant in themselves and in their relation to current thought. In the past it was not uncommon to string together the various attributes without any attempt to relate them logically to each other. Richard Watson, for instance, discussed the following attributes in the order given: Unity, spirituality, eternity, omnipotence, ubiquity, omniscience, immutability, wisdom, goodness, holiness.[5] More recently it has been customary to distinguish between the metaphysical and the ethical attributes; and this distinction is valid and important.[6] But beyond it no scheme of the divine attributes has been agreed upon. Rather has the tendency been against any such schematization, and also against a multiplication of attributes. Interest now centers in a few fundamental characteristics or attributes of Deity, such as absoluteness, personality, and goodness. Is God to be thought of as absolute, as personal, as good, and, if so, in what sense? These are the questions now attracting attention, and it is with them that we shall deal. They do not exclude the older and more exhaustive inquiry into the divine attributes. But they approach the problem from a

---

[5] *Theological Institutes*, Pt. II, Chaps. II-VII.

[6] Biedermann substitutes "psychological" for "ethical." Others have distinguished between "positive and negative," "proper and metaphorical," "communicable and incommunicable," "internal and external," "immanent and transeunt," "quiescent and operative," "absolute and relative" attributes. But none of these distinctions has any particular value.

broader point of view, seeking to simplify it and to relate it more closely to the living thought of the day.

It is sometimes urged that the discussion of the question as to the existence of God should follow the exposition of the Christian conception of his nature, on the ground that it is only after we know what this conception is that we are prepared to justify it.[7] But in reply it may be pointed out that in seeking to justify the belief in God we are concerned with only the more general aspects of his being, and that the argument does not require a knowledge of the full Christian doctrine. Such a general knowledge as any well-educated Christian may be supposed to have will suffice. We begin, then, our study of the doctrine of God with an inquiry into the question of his existence, following it with three chapters on the absoluteness, the personality, and the goodness of God respectively, and concluding the study with an exposition and criticism of the Trinitarian teaching of the church.

In taking up the problem of the divine existence we are confronted at the outset with the question as to what existence or reality means. The common man answers the question by pointing to things. But it was long ago discovered that things are not what they seem, and so a distinction came to be made between appearance and reality. "Only in opinion," said Democritus, "consists sweetness, bitterness, warmth, cold, color; in truth, there is nothing but atoms and empty space." This limitation of reality to atoms or material things Plato rejected. He found a higher realm of reality in immaterial Ideas or souls.

---

[7] So W. N. Clarke, *The Christian Doctrine of God*, pp. 357ff.

And at the beginning of the modern era Descartes reduced all finite reality to two radically different modes of being—extended and thinking substances, or material things and minds. But Berkeley denied the substantial reality of matter, and a little later Hume denied the substantiality of the soul. Thus the older metaphysical conception of reality, both material and immaterial, both physical and mental, both static and dynamic, was called in question; and in its place or alongside of it there arose a positivistic view, which rejects the ideas of substance and cause and in principle reduces all reality to the phenomenal plane. This type of thought has never been carried through with complete consistency, but as a tendency it is perhaps the most characteristic feature of contemporary philosophy; and by its alliance with current empiricism and certain impersonal forms of idealism it has so modified or blurred the conception of reality that the subjective elements in human experience and thought are often declared to be as real as the objects of sense-experience. The latter, we are told, have no substantial or causal reality in them or back of them, and hence are real only insofar as they enter into experience or into some unsubstantial web of relations.

Under the influence of this positivistic view of reality efforts have been made to redefine God in such a way as to eliminate the older metaphysical implications of the term and yet to retain the idea of his real existence. He is, for instance, said to be real in the same sense as Alma Mater, Uncle Sam, and Humanity, though in a "greater" degree. He is "reality idealized," he is "experienced reality taken in a socialized way," he is "the Spirit of the world of living beings, taken in their associated and ideal experience."[8] Or from a slightly different point of view he is identified with a part or aspect of nature. He is said to be that "most subtle and intimate complexity of environmental nature which yields the greatest good when right adjustment is made."[9]

In this redefinition of God it is evident that he is not regarded as real in the same sense as is that larger Nature of which he forms a part. It is, indeed, stated that "his reality is as demonstrable as the world itself," but the world or nature is manifestly thought of as the more inclusive and original reality. It is real in the metaphysical sense of the term, while God is real only in a secondary sense as a part or product of nature. No individuality or independent activity is ascribed to him. He may be spoken of as "the Power which makes for righteousness," but this is only in an accommodated sense. He is, rather, a law or process, and is real only in the sense in which a law or social group is real. If a deeper reality is attributed to him, it is in a pantheistic sense. The system under consideration, however—if it may be called a system—is far from being a consistent pantheism. It is a compound of positivism, naturalism, pantheism, and sociology, together with a dash of Platonic idealism and a persistent profession of empiricism. In such a fusion—if not confusion—of different points of view it is not always easy to determine

[8] E. S. Ames, *Religion*, pp. 133f., 154.
[9] Henry N. Wieman, *The Wrestle of Religion With Truth*, p. vi.

exactly what is meant by the various statements concerning God. But it is clear that he is not to be regarded as the ultimate ground of the universe. He is a part or aspect or expression of it.

Insofar as he is identified with a social process, or a social group, or a social ideal, or some observable phase of nature, it may perhaps be justly claimed that he is as demonstrably real as the world about us, but he is not real in the only sense in which religion is interested in his reality. What religion is alone concerned about is a righteous and loving will upon which the world is dependent. No social process, no phase of the natural order, no vague universal can fill out the religious idea of Deity. For religion God must be an individual, absolute and personal Being. At least such is the Christian view. And the fundamental question of religion is whether such a Being exists. Existence as applied to him means, therefore, metaphysical existence, an independent, dynamic and spiritual mode of being.

That such a God exists is the basal affirmation of the Christian faith. But on what does this affirmation rest? It comes to us through tradition. We accept it as a part of our religious inheritance, or we reject it. The question consequently arises as to how we are to determine whether it is valid or not.

An early method of dealing with the problem, and one that is not yet obsolete, was that of inquiring into the origin of the belief. If the belief had a worthy origin, it was to be accepted; if not, it was to be rejected. Under this assumption the friends of religion traced the belief to a divine source, to revelation, while the foes of religion insisted that it not only had a purely human origin, but that it originated in some unworthy element or aspect of human nature or life, such as fear, selfish desire, perverted sexuality, priest and statecraft, social injustice, dreams, trances, or the belief in ghosts. The theories upholding the latter view were considered at some length in Chapter I. Here I need do no more than remind the reader that a belief or institution is not necessarily discredited because of its historical antecedents. Astronomy, chemistry, and manual labor do not lose their validity or dignity because they grew up out of astrology, alchemy, and slavery respectively. And so it is with the belief in God. It may have been preceded by various superstitions and its development may have been influenced by unworthy motives or pathological states of one kind or another, but the question of its validity cannot be decided by considerations such as these. Its truth or falsity can be determined only by its intrinsic rationality and worth or by its lack of these qualities.

Much has been made by critics of the human origin of the belief in God and of the anthropomorphic character of our conception of Deity. It has been said that "God is the noblest work of man"; and to Heine we owe the taunting remark that "if God made man in his own image, man made haste to return the compliment." Back in the early days of Greek philosophy Xenophanes satirized the anthropomorphisms of his day by saying that "the Ethiopians make their gods black-haired and flat-nosed, and the Thracians make theirs red-haired and blue-eyed." "Yes," he added, "and if the beasts had hands and could paint and carve, the horses would make their gods like horses, and the oxen make theirs like oxen." The assumption underlying such utterances as these, which have been repeated through the centuries, is that the idea of a personal God is man's creation, the giant reflection of his own personality, and that on this account it cannot have objective validity. But in response it may first be pointed out that nothing can exist for us except as we think it. Our idea of the world is our creation quite as much as is our idea of God, and the only significant question in either case is as to whether the idea is correct or not. That it has a human source does not compromise its validity any more in one instance than in the other. And as for the anthropomorphic element in the conception of God it should be noted that "man is organic to nature" and that there is consequently as good ground for attributing cosmic significance to personality as to any other form of existence. Indeed, weighty reasons, as we shall see later, may be offered for the view that it is only in and through personality that a rational understanding of ultimate reality is possible. There is, then, nothing in the charge of anthropomorphism nor in the charge that the idea of God had a human origin that invalidates the theistic belief.[10]

On the other hand, one cannot justify the belief

---

[10] Canon Streeter has pointed out that if theism is anthropomorphic, materialism is "mechanomorphic." It fashions the Infinite in the image of a machine, and this conception is "essentially myth." The mechanistic view, as he shows, is "doubly anthropomorphic," for it is derived from human constructions made for human purposes (*Reality*, pp. 9ff.).

in God by attributing its origin to divine revelation, for revelation implies the existence of God. Without God there could be no revelation. To base the belief in God on revelation would, therefore, be to argue in a circle; for revelation itself is in turn based on the belief in God. The fact is that the belief in revelation is simply an expression of the belief in God. If we really know God he must have revealed himself. Revelation is a corollary of religious faith. It does not ground faith, it presupposes it. No argument in support of a supernatural revelation would have the slightest cogency apart from the belief in God. The whole rationale of revelation is grounded in the theistic faith.

It is also important to note that revelation does not stand opposed to what may be called the "human" or "natural" mode of acquiring knowledge; it does not necessarily involve the miraculous. History and psychology might conceivably describe the exact process by which the belief in God arose, but this would not exclude a divine agency. The revelational activity of the Divine Spirit is entirely consonant with a synchronous activity of the human spirit. Indeed, the two involve each other; they are different aspects of one and the same process. From one point of view the quest after God is a human search, a human striving, but from another point of view it is a divine revelation.

This, however, does not mean that everything is equally divine and that there are no degrees in the divine nearness to men. God has revealed himself more fully to some peoples and to some individuals than to others.[11] This is the basis on which the Christian claim to a special divine revelation rests, and much with reference to the uniqueness and high character of the prophetic-Christian view of God may be said in support of it.[12] Nowhere else do we find so pure and lofty a conception of the divine righteousness and love, and nowhere else do we find the monotheistic idea developing and maintaining itself under such untoward circumstances. It is a significant fact that it was not in a world-empire such as Assyria or Egypt, but in the two puny Hebrew kingdoms, and that at the very time they were going down to political ruin, that the idea of one God, and he a God of righteousness, emerged into distinct human consciousness. So contrary is this to all natural human calculation that the religious mind can hardly resist the conviction that the history of Israel was touched in a unique way by the finger of God. Israel was also the only nation whose religion survived the national downfall. When other ancient nations fell they threw their gods, as Isaiah said, to the moles and the bats, and this in all probability Israel also would have done if it had not been for the work of her prophets. Then, too, her religion was the only religion in southwestern Asia that succeeded in resisting the encroachments of Hellenic naturalism. These remarkable facts put the stamp of uniqueness upon Israel's religion and upon the Christian religion based upon it, and justify us in seeing in both a special revelation of God. But

[11] Cf. *The Diviner Immanence*, by Francis J. McConnell.

[12] Cf. *The Evidential Value of Prophecy*, by E. A. Edghill; *The Belief in God*, Chap. IV, by Bishop Charles Gore.

this, after all, is a religious judgment. There is nothing in either Israelitic or Christian history that to the nonreligious mind necessarily excludes a naturalistic interpretation. No logical ground for either accepting or rejecting the theistic belief can, therefore, be found in the various theories of its historical origin. These theories are secondary, not primary, the effects of faith or unfaith, not their causes. One might, like the sage of whom Von Hügel tells us, trace the origin of religion back to "the scratching by a cow of an itch on her back,"[13] and yet not undermine the religious belief of to-day; or, on the other hand, one might find the ultimate source of religion in a primitive revelation and yet leave it with as little rational justification as ever.

We come back, then, to the Christian religious tradition with which we started and which is the immediate source of our belief in God. That this belief is traditional is, to some extent at least, in its favor. That it has been tried and tested through the centuries, that it has been the settled conviction of generation after generation of men, that it has passed through the fires of criticism, seven times overheated in modern times—all this is manifestly to its credit. No doubt there have been errors hoary with age, no doubt falsehoods have at times been tenacious of life. But this has been due to sense prejudice, to selfishness of one kind or another, or to mental inertia. In the Christian belief in God, on the other hand, we have a conception that rises above the sense plane, that transcends all selfishness, both individual and

[13] *Essays and Addresses on the Philosophy of Religion*, p. 141.

corporate, and that has been subjected to the keenest and profoundest critical investigation. That it has persisted through the ages and still persists as the professed faith of the leading peoples of the world is, therefore, a weighty consideration in favor of its truth. But there is dissent from it, increasing dissent; and the modern man is in principle opposed to resting his faith on the mere authority of tradition. He recognizes in religion no external authority, either human or divine. Tradition, he insists, must present to him its credentials. It must justify itself, and this it can do only by awakening within him an inner persuasion of its truth. Mere assent to it will not suffice. There must be something deeper, genuine personal conviction; and the fundamental question in religion is as to how this conviction can be generated. What valid basis or bases, if any, are there for the Christian belief in God?

Current religious thought begins its defense of theism with what may be called the religious argument. It then passes to the moral argument and from that to the theoretical or "rational" argument. This analysis and order of treatment will be adopted in the following discussion.

### The Religious Argument

The religious argument is based on the uniqueness of man's religious nature. It is maintained, not that there is a separate religious faculty in the human mind, but that man has a capacity for religion as original and distinct as is his capacity for art, for morality, and for science, and that this capacity when fully and consistently developed leads to the belief in God. The latter part of this claim has already been discussed at sufficient length; the former was first clearly and definitely formulated by Schleiermacher. Before his time the uniqueness of religion was to some extent implied in the current supernatural and authoritarian conception of revelation and faith, but it was not scientifically developed and grounded. Schleiermacher was the first clearly and explicitly to distinguish religion psychologically from other forms of the mental life. Religion, he insisted, is not knowing or doing, but is a unique feeling, the feeling of absolute dependence. As such it is ultimate and justifies itself. But the method of self-justification has been differently conceived.

Some argue that religion is akin to an instinct or some other natural human endowment by means of which adjustment is made to one's environment. The existence of such an instinct or endowment presupposes the existence of the object toward which it is directed. The autumnal flight of the birds of passage implies the existence of the warmer southland,[14] the eye implies light, the ear sound, hunger food, reason a rational world; and so also, it is argued, religion implies the reality of the Divine Object after which it reaches out. If there were no such correspondence between the inner and organic world and the outer world, life would be impossible. The very fact of human life requires, therefore, that to every deep-seated human power or need there be an objective

[14] See Jer. 8. 7, where religion is likened to the instinct of the birds of passage.

counterpart. And not only is this conclusion involved in an analysis of the conditions of human life, it is genetically grounded. For our human powers, our senses, instincts and other capacities owe their origin to their environment. They have grown up as responses to the realities by which they were surrounded. Causally as well as analytically they consequently point to real existences corresponding to them. This is as true of the religious as of other capacities. Our yearning after God implies that he exists both as the cause and the object of our yearning.[15]

This argument, if it may be called such, is not "religious" in the strict sense of the term. It is not rooted in the religious consciousness, nor is it a direct expression of it. It is, rather, a theoretical argument, based on the genesis and structure of the religious nature. Its main contention is that religion, like the other natural human capacities, is a response to an objective reality and that for it this reality is God. Without God religion would be inexplicable as a normal factor in human life.

In this line of thought it is assumed that there must be a correspondence between the inner and outer world; and some such correspondence, it is clear, must be assumed if knowledge is to be possible. But error and illusion are patent facts of human life; and it is a question whether religion might not serve an important biological function, even though its ideational content be misleading. Perception, as applied

---

[15] For an elaboration of this argument see W. N. Clarke, *The Christian Doctrine of God*, pp. 402-28.

to the physical world, is, we know, largely deception. Things are not what they seem. And so it may be in the spiritual realm. There may be no God, even though religious faith seems to require it; and yet faith in the ideal may be of the greatest practical value, just as our normal perception is. Whether faith in the ideal is permanently detachable from the belief in God is doubtful. But in the past popular faith in the superworld has varied so much and has often been so vague and confused that not a little can be said in favor of the view that the utility of religion is not dependent upon a clear-cut theism. The bare principle of adjustment to environment, such as we see illustrated in the organic realm, does not guarantee the truth of religious belief. The adjustment, it is true, would be more complete and our world-view more harmonious if our highest religious beliefs squared with reality; but there is nothing in the biological analogy that necessarily requires such a parallelism. As a mere instinct or mode of behavior, as a mere adjustment to environment, religion might conceivably be geared into a naturalistic system. How long it would in such a system retain its dynamic, is a question. But so long as it did, it would fulfill a social function. And when its dynamic failed, it would, like other obsolete institutions, become a kind of social vermiform appendix which had better be excised.

Against such a possibility as this stands a deep-seated feeling that religion has played so important a rôle in human history and has been of such supreme value in human life that we cannot regard it as a mere transitory phase of human development. It must, we feel, be permanent. But this conviction is much more deeply grounded than the principle of social adjustment or anything logically contained in it. If it were not, it could hardly be regarded as self-evidencing.

A profounder way of presenting the religious argument for theism is that represented by Schleiermacher, Troeltsch, and Otto. They turn for the self-verification of religion not to a more or less dubious biological analogy, but to the structure of the human mind itself. Schleiermacher, for instance, says that the "feeling of absolute dependence, in which our self-consciousness in general represents the finitude of our being, is not an accidental element, or a thing which varies from person to person, but is a universal element of life; and the recognition of this fact entirely takes the place, for the system of doctrine, of all the so-called proofs of the existence of God."[16] In thus affirming the universality of the feeling of absolute dependence Schleiermacher may go beyond what the facts warrant; but insofar as he means to assert that religious experience is structural in human nature, that it "takes its place alongside of science and practice, as a necessary, an indispensable third, as their natural counterpart, not less in worth and splendor than either,"[17] so that it stands in its own right as fully as they, he is on solid ground. No moral or rational "proof" is necessary to give validity to reli-

---

[16] *Der Christliche Glaube,* Par. 33; English translation, pp. 133f.

[17] *On Religion; Speeches to Its Cultured Despisers,* translated by J. Oman, pp. 37f.

gious belief. Religion is as independent, as ultimate and as irreducible as any other factor or element of our mental nature, and hence it may be regarded as verifying itself.

Troeltsch gave somewhat greater precision to this line of thought by linking it up with the Kantian doctrine of the categories and maintaining that there is a religious *a priori,* just as there are a moral, an æsthetic, and an intellectual *a priori.*[18] The term "*a priori*" suggests the logical or rational; and Troeltsch does speak of a "rational *a priori* of religion" and a "rational kernel of religion." He looks upon religion as belonging to "reason." But he uses the word "reason" in a broad sense as about equivalent to the human spirit in its normal and normative activity. "Rational" with him does not then mean "intellectual"; it does not denote the theoretical reason. Indeed, the religious *a priori,* though rational, is said to be "anti-intellectualistic." It has its own unique and distinctive nature. But beyond that it cannot be defined. It is "formal" in character, as are the other categories, and manifests itself only in and through experience. Religious experience presupposes a religious *a priori,* and without it would be impossible. But this *a priori* or immanent principle has no detachable existence of its own. It is the condition of the religious consciousness, but not a separate factor in it. It denotes a rational capacity, "an autonomous validity"; and it is here that its significance lies. Grounded in a rational *a priori,* religion,

---

[18] *Psychologie und Erkenntnistheorie in der Religionswissenschaft; Gesammelte Schriften,* pp. 754-68, 805-36.

like science, morality, and art, carries within itself the law of its own being and needs no validation from any other source.

Rudolf Otto accepts the idea of a religious *a priori,* but his conception of it is somewhat different from Troeltsch's, and he has analyzed it more fully.[19] He, for instance, distinguishes between a rational and an irrational *a priori.* The former manifests itself in the conceptions that we form of the Deity, such as his absoluteness, his personality, and goodness; the latter manifests itself in what Otto calls the "numinous" feeling, an awareness of the divine. Both of these have their roots in the hidden depths of the spirit and are in that sense *a priori.* But not only are they *a priori,* there is a connection between them, and it, too, has an *a priori* character. The numinous feeling and the conception of the divine goodness are bound together in an inward and necessary union, so that when the moral character of God is affirmed the religious spirit instinctively ratifies it. A striking illustration of this is found toward the close of the second book of Plato's *Republic,* where Socrates says, "God, then, is simple and true in deed and word, and neither changes himself nor deceives others," to which Adeimantos replies, "Now that thou sayst it, it is also quite clear to me." What he had not thought of before, the high moral character of Deity, commended itself to him as self-evident the moment it was stated by Socrates. And so it was with the Hebrews to whom Amos addressed himself. Their religious consciousness almost in spite of themselves

[19] *The Idea of the Holy,* pp. 116-20, 140-46.

acknowledged the validity of his conception of Jehovah as a God of absolute righteousness, although it was a novel doctrine. There are, then, three religious *a prioris*—one rational, another irrational, and the third the bond of union between the other two. But interesting and suggestive as this analysis is, it cannot be said to advance in any material way the apologetic problem. Whether the religious *a priori* be single or triple, clearly defined or not, the main truth underlying it is that of the autonomous validity of our religious nature. Religion is as structural in reason or in our total personality as are science, art, and morality, and may, therefore, be regarded as equally permanent and equally trustworthy. As these other interests justify themselves, so also do religion and the belief in God.

Yet another form of the religious argument may be briefly considered. This one is more empiricistic and consists in maintaining that the existence of God is given immediately in religious experience. It is not an explication of a hidden *a priori,* nor a mere postulate of our moral nature, nor an inference from experience. It has the same kind of objectivity that the material world has. It is an intuited and verifiable reality. We may be said, then, to know God through our religious experience in the same direct way that we know the physical world through our sense-experience.

To this putting of the case there are two main objections. The first is based on the Berkeleyan and Humean criticism of sense-experience, and the second on the Kantian criticism of metaphysical and religious knowledge in general. Berkeley and Hume showed once for all that matter as a substantial and causal reality is not an empirical datum. We may ascribe our sense-experience to such a hypothetical matter, but it is important to bear in mind that matter in this metaphysical sense is hypothetical and not an immediately experienced or intuited reality. The analogy of sense-experience fails, therefore, to establish the reality of the metaphysical object in religious experience. In the latter the belief in God is a plus added to the original empirical data in the same way that matter is in sense-experience. And we have in each case the same problem to decide as to whether the addition is valid or not.

Then, too, Kant made it unmistakably clear that we cannot know God or any metaphysical object in the same way that we know the sense world.[20] Our knowledge of ultimate reality is subjectively conditioned. Volitional and moral factors enter into it so that it would more properly be called faith than knowledge. Faith, it is true, may become so vivid as to take on a perceptual form; but this holds true only of the more extreme type of mysticism. As a rule, it moves on a different plane, and confusion may result from assimilating it too closely to sense-perception and scientific knowledge. Certainly, our perception or knowledge of God is quite different from our perception or knowledge of the phenomenal order. The former is volitionally and morally conditioned in a way that the latter is not. That faith has an object is emphatically true, and from this point of view we

[20] Cf. Georg Wobbermin, *Das Wesen der Religion*, pp. 374-95.

may speak of it as religious perception or religious experience or religious knowledge. But we need to be on our guard against being led astray by these terms. They by no means guarantee the validity of our faith. By whatever name or terms faith may be known or described, it is still faith, and as such differentiates itself from mere perception. It does not become more objective, nor more certain, nor more immediate because of the partial analogy that exists between it and sense-experience.

The truth and strength of the religious argument do not lie in the magic of a new religious nomenclature or in the mystical immediacy of religious cognition, but in the fundamental independence of religious faith, in its *a priori* character. All the ideal interests of mankind—science, art, morality, and religion—rest ultimately on faith;[21] and faith in one form is logically as good as faith in any other form. Religious faith has in this respect nothing to fear. It occupies as impregnable a position as does the faith that underlies science, morality, and art. It cannot be dislodged by merely theoretical considerations. It stands in its own right. This is the invincible truth of the religious argument for the divine existence.[22] Wherever faith in God is spontaneous, vigorous and

---

[21] It is a matter of interest that even naturalistic writers are now beginning to admit that science roots in faith and that it is itself a faith. See, for instance, Chap. III of *Religion and the Modern World*, by J. H. Randall and J. H. Randall, Jr. The profounder implications of this admission, however, these writers do not seem to realize.

[22] I know no more effective putting of this argument than that found in the Introduction to Borden P. Bowne's *Theism*, pp. 1-43.

sincere, as it is, for instance, in Scripture, it justifies itself.

### The Moral Argument

The moral argument stands closely related to the religious argument. I have elsewhere[23] treated the two as parts or aspects of one and the same argument, to which I gave the name "valuational." The term "pneumatological" has also been applied to it on the ground that it has to do with the logic of the spirit rather than that of the pure reason.[24] Such a fusion of the religious and moral arguments is natural in view of their close relation to each other. But there is still a sufficient difference between them to warrant our treating them separately.

The main line of cleavage between them lies in the fact that the religious argument emphasizes the *immediacy* with which faith or religious experience lays hold of its object. God is given to us in an act of faith or mystical intuition which resembles perception both in its objectivity and its certitude. We know him directly or have a conviction or awareness of his reality akin to that with which we apprehend the presence of another person. The moral argument, on the other hand, stresses the spiritual necessity of the belief in God. We have from this point of view no immediate experience of him. But without him conscience would fall into contradiction with itself. If we are, therefore, to avoid ethical inconsistency, we must affirm his existence. Our moral

---

[23] *The Philosophy of Personalism*, pp. 306-14.

[24] Adolf Fricke, *Darstellung und Kritik der Beweise für Gottes persönliches Dasein.*

nature requires it. God is an implication, a postulate of our practical reason.

This moral argument has taken on several different forms. We may distinguish three. The first and simplest starts with the fact of the moral law and argues from it to a lawgiver. The essence of morality, we are told, consists in the recognition of an objective and binding law, and this law implies a moral ruler. Without a ruler there could be no law. But this line of reasoning manifestly rests upon a naïve, heteronomous and monarchic conception of the moral life. In our actual experience duty does not come as an external command. It is autonomous, it arises within us, is self-imposed. That it furnishes some basis for the belief in a supreme judge may be true. But the existence of such a Being is not given directly in the moral consciousness itself, nor is it a necessary logical inference from the fact of duty or of moral law. Law in the moral realm does not necessarily imply an external lawgiver. Neither psychology nor ethics lends any support to such a claim.

The most famous form of the moral argument is that given it by Kant. The great Königsberger, after destroying, as he believed, the traditional theistic "proofs," sought to re-establish theism upon a purely ethical basis. The moral nature, he held, implies two things: first, an *a priori* moral law to which unconditional obedience is due, and, secondly, "the distribution of happiness in exact proportion to morality." But such a proportionate distribution is not to be found in the world as we know it. Hence, he argued, we must assume or postulate a Supreme Being who will bring it about; and, furthermore, since complete virtue cannot be attained in any finite period of time, we must assume for man an endless life. To this argument it has been objected that it presupposes a eudemonistic view of morality. But this is a mistake. Kant strenuously maintained the contrary view. Virtue does not consist in seeking well-being. It is, rather, independent and self-sufficient. It is itself the supreme good. But while the *supreme* good, it is not the sole good nor the *summum bonum*. The latter includes happiness; and this means that our moral aspiration is directed toward outward fortune as well as toward inner worth. The good will is all-important, but it is not all that is important. In order to be good, it must will the good; and this means that there is an objective good which it can will. In other words it means that the universe is not indifferent to the distinction between good and evil. It means that there must be, as Kant says, "a harmony between nature and morality." If there were not, the moral nature would be thrown back upon itself. It would have no object, no end, and would thus contradict itself. It would be an alien in the world, a rebel against all that is; and the ultimate consequence would be its elimination from human life as essentially false.

This, however, Kant regarded as virtually a *reductio ad absurdum*. The moral law is structural in human reason, it is a rational *a priori*, and as such must be as permanent as reason itself. With it we may, therefore, start as a universal and necessary fact, and from it deduce whatever is logically involved in it. It, for instance, requires that the virtuous man be the recipient of moral approval and that he be treated accordingly. But such approval and such treatment in the present world-order are uncertain and limited in extent, and never will be fully realized unless there be a Supreme Ruler who will bring nature and morality or happiness and virtue into harmony with each other. We are, therefore, morally and rationally justified in affirming the existence of such a Ruler. For conscience cannot be content with a purposeless obedience to a formal law. Beyond the law there must be an end to be attained and in this end man must find "something which he can love." Our moral nature requires this, and hence we may say with Kant that "morality inevitably leads to religion."

This line of argument could be considerably strengthened by pointing out the disastrous ethical consequences of a refusal to draw the religious or theistic conclusion.[25] Atheism reduces men to automata, and automata could hardly have duties as duties are ordinarily understood. They might perhaps recognize the formal moral principles, but these are conditioned in their application by our general world-view and by our conception of human personality, its nature and destiny. If we held an atheistic or naturalistic view of the world and of human life, our formal moral judgments might readily be applied in such a way as to undermine our existing ethical code; and certainly in such a world-view there would

[25] For a vigorous and convincing statement of these consequences see B. P. Bowne's *Theism*, pp. 291-314.

be no basis for ethical idealism. The moral life would lose its inspiration and would sink to a low level of individual or social expediency. It is only in a theistic world-view that a rational basis for a high and noble morality can be found. Without such a world-view life would have no meaning, its ideals would collapse, and its springs of action be broken.[26] At least this would be the logical result. To one, consequently, who believes in the sanctity of the moral life and who would regard its overthrow as an act of unreason, the theistic conclusion must seem inevitable.

Kant regarded the foregoing line of thought as the sole valid basis for the belief in God, and many of his disciples have taken the same view. Some, however, have felt that he interpreted morality in too narrow and formal a way. To define religion as "the recognition of all duties as divine commands" does not do justice to the uniqueness and breadth of religion. If the moral consciousness is to be made the one source and justification of religious belief, it must be broadened so as to take in life as a whole. It must be understood as including "the awareness of all ultimate ends of desire of whatever sort."[27] But this puts a new construction upon the word "moral" and virtually transforms the moral argument into what I have called the "valuational" argument. If all the ideal values of life are included in "moral" aspiration, there is, of course, no objection to deduc-

[26] For a suggestive and helpful exposition of the religious implications of moral optimism see D. C. Macintosh, *The Reasonableness of Christianity*, pp. 40-133.

[27] Cf. *The Interpretation of Religion*, pp. 256ff., by John Baillie.

ing religion from morality. But in that case morality loses its distinctiveness and becomes synonymous with faith in and devotion to the ideal in general. That religion has its ultimate source and ground in such a faith is no doubt true. Beyond faith in this sense we cannot go for the validation of any ideal interest. But this, it is important to note, holds true also of knowledge. All knowledge rests on faith. The quest after truth is a quest after an ideal value quite as truly as is the quest after goodness, beauty, and God; and each of these quests finds its ultimate justification in an immanent faith. Religion stands alongside of or transcends the other quests and yet at the same time embraces them. It has the same fundamental basis as they, and whether we call this basis "moral" or "practical" or "valuational" does not matter much so long as we bear in mind what is meant. In view, however, of the fact that it is customary to use the word "moral" in its narrower sense, it would seem best to retain the distinction between the moral and religious arguments and to use another term to designate the common element in them. By the moral argument we understand, then, the Kantian form of it, as above expounded. It consists in pointing out the moral necessity of religion. The religious argument, on the other hand, dwells on the self-evidencing power of religious faith. Both see in religion the product of an evaluational process, and both imply confidence in the validity of that process.[28]

[28] For a concrete and vital exposition of the moral and religious arguments see *The Meaning of God*, by Professor H. F. Rall.

## The Theoretical Argument

Rather sharply differentiated from the preceding practical or evaluational arguments stands the theoretical argument or arguments. We have already seen that the theoretical, or pure reason, is not free from assumptions. It is guided by an ideal. It assumes that the world is intelligible and that we are able to understand it; and this understanding of the world constitutes for it an ideal end. It aims at the satisfaction of a subjective interest just as our moral, religious, and æsthetic natures do. In its fundamental ground and aim it is, therefore, practical, and hence it is permissible to speak of the *primacy* of the practical reason. It is in the latter that the theoretical reason finds both its setting and its justification. But while the theoretical reason thus has certain points of kinship with the quest after goodness, beauty, and God, it has its own unique laws, its own distinctive logic; and these laws have a quasi-mechanical character. They operate with a kind of inner necessity, and seem to be concerned more directly with objective reality than is the practical reason. We consequently set the theoretical reason apart by itself, and ask what it has to say about the belief in God.

Up to the time of Kant the chief stress was placed on the theoretical argument, and from the standpoint of pure logic this was justified. In strict logic we cannot pass from what ought to be to what is, and yet this is what we do in the moral and religious arguments. If we then wish a logical demonstration of the divine existence, we must turn to the theoretical reason; in the traditional theistic arguments such a demonstration was attempted. But since the time of Kant it has been evident that these arguments attempted the impossible. There can be no strictly logical demonstration outside of the field of mathematics and formal logic. In the objective and concrete realm the law we follow is to assume that whatever the mind demands for the satisfaction of its subjective needs and tendencies is real in default of positive disproof.[29] This law forms the basis of the moral and religious arguments, and it also underlies the theoretical arguments. The latter as well as the former furnish no demonstration of the divine existence. But the objective validity of the theoretical reason is more generally accepted than that of the practical reason, and hence in the past it was customary to begin the defense of theism with considerations drawn from it. Of late, however, the reverse has been the tendency, and not a few under the influence of Kantian teaching have gone so far as to deny all cogency and validity to the theoretical arguments.

Considerable stress has been laid on the fact that Scripture offers no "proofs" of the existence of God.[30] The Old Testament does now and then refer to the heavens and to the wonders of creation in general as evidence of the divine wisdom, power, and glory, but it does so, not to prove that there is a God, but, rather, to illustrate and make more vivid an already existent belief in him. In the New Testament there are a few passages such as Rom. 1. 19-20, Acts 17. 24-

[29] See B. P. Bowne's *Theism*, p. 18.
[30] Psa. 8. 1; 19. 1; 104. 5-11; Isa. 40. 12, 26.

28 and 14. 15-17 which imply that God has revealed himself in nature so that we may not only infer his existence, but come to know him. Indeed, the first of these passages declares that the revelation is so unmistakably clear that no one has any excuse for being without the knowledge of God. But this thought is nowhere elaborated. In Scripture the belief in God is spontaneous. Where not merely traditional it is an immediate expression of the religious and moral nature, and its validity is taken for granted without argument of any kind. But this does not mean that the theistic arguments are of no value. It simply means that in ancient Israel there was little or no need of them. People generally accepted the belief in God without question. Even the fool, who, according to Psa. 14 and 53, said in his heart there was no God, did not mean to deny the divine existence. What he meant was that he himself acted as though there were no God; he took no account of his existence. His atheism was practical, not theoretical.[31] Then, too, it should be noted that the Semitic mind was not speculative. There is in the Bible no philosophy in the theoretical sense of the term. Belief among the ancient Jews and the Christians of apostolic times was immediate and instinctive. They needed no formal arguments to support their faith. But this fact has no dogmatic significance for us. It imposes no obligation upon us to semitize the modern mind. We are Greek as well as Hebraic in our intellectual and religious inheritance, and in any case the value of the theoretical

[31] See my *Religious Teaching of the Old Testament*, pp. 51f.

arguments for the divine existence must be determined by current rational standards and not by appeal to biblical authority.

We have already seen that our moral and religious natures can find ultimate satisfaction only in the belief in God, and it would be in harmony with the unity of our personality if a similar affirmation could be made with reference to our intellectual nature. That such an affirmation is warranted has been the conviction of most of the profoundest minds in the history of Christian thought. In support of this conviction various arguments have been developed. From the historical point of view these arguments may be reduced to two groups, the conceptual and the causal,[32] the latter including the cosmological and teleological arguments and the former the ontological and other allied arguments based on Platonic realism. From the standpoint of modern thought, however, the conceptual arguments have lost, to a large extent, their cogency, and in their place has arisen the epistemological argument.

This argument takes two main forms. The first directs attention to the dualism and parallelism of thought and thing or idea and object involved in knowledge. There is no way of escaping this dualism. To identify idea and object is not only to fly in the face of our fundamental conviction of an objective otherness, but to subvert the true nature of knowledge and leave us without a tenable conception or explanation of error.[33] The dualism of thought

[32] Cf. *The Philosophy of Personalism*, pp. 258ff.

[33] *Ibid.*, pp. 104ff.

and thing we must, then, accept, but knowledge also requires that there be a parallelism between them, and this parallelism can only be accounted for by a theistic monism. If an intelligent Being cast the world in the mold of thought and then created us in his image, we can see how the thought-series might correctly grasp the thing-series, but without this assumption the parallelism of the two series must remain an insoluble riddle.

The second form of the epistemological argument dwells upon the intelligibility of the world and from it infers an intelligent Author. If the world is intelligible, there must be intelligence back of it. Language can express thought only in case it is itself produced by thought, and so it is with the world. Logically this is probably the strongest argument for the divine existence. Borden P. Bowne so regarded it, and the very last sentence he wrote was an expression of it. "The problem of knowledge," he said, "implies thought at both ends—thought at the further end to make nature the bearer of meanings and thought at the nearer end to receive and rethink the meaning."[34]

The causal argument has also taken two main forms. Traditionally these have appeared as distinct arguments—the cosmological and the teleological; but no sharp line of demarcation between them can be maintained. From the modern point of view one form of the causal argument seeks to establish the unity of the world-ground, and the other seeks to establish its intelligence. The first is a modification

---

[34] The *Methodist Review*, May, 1922, p. 369. See also the Life of *Borden Parker Bowne*, pp. 122ff., by Bishop Francis J. McConnell.

of the older cosmological argument, and the second a continuation or development of the older teleological argument.

The argument for a unitary world-ground begins with the admitted fact of systematic interaction and consists in showing that such an interacting system as the material universe is recognized to be can be rationally conceived only as the work of a co-ordinating One. There is and can be no actual transference of states or conditions from one independent thing to another, nor are there forces playing between them or influences passing from one to the other. These are simply figures of speech. The real explanation of systematic interaction can be found only in the immanent action of an underlying One. Independent things cannot in and of themselves form an interacting system. The very idea of such a system excludes a fundamental pluralism. If such a system exists, there must be a unitary Agent that mediates the interaction of the many or is the dynamic ground of their being. Only a fundamental monism can, therefore, account for such a universe as that revealed to us by science, or, more exactly, assumed by it. In other words, science supports monotheism as over against polytheism.[35]

But the underlying One might be an impersonal and blind energy. We need, therefore, some evidence of its intelligence, and this we find in the order of the material universe, the indications of design in the organic realm, and the existence of finite minds.

---

[35] See B. P. Bowne's *Theism*, pp. 44-63, and my *Philosophy of Personalism*, pp. 197ff.

Order, which is the mark of reason, points to a rational world-ground; the marvelous adaptations of means to ends in animate nature point to an underlying purpose; and intelligence in man points to intelligence in his Maker.

> "He that planted the ear, shall he not hear?
> He that formed the eye, shall he not see?"

These lines of reflection have not been invalidated by modern physical science nor by the Darwinian theory of evolution. They create in the present, as they have in the past and as they will in the future, a strong presumption in favor of the theistic world-view.

There is a third form of the causal argument that may be briefly mentioned. It consists in showing that causality can be clearly and consistently conceived only on the plane of free intelligence. On the impersonal plane the cause disappears in the production of the effect, and metaphysical predication becomes, consequently, impossible. We have either a subject without a predicate or a predicate without a subject. In other words, there is no persistent or abiding cause that produces effects of one kind or another and yet remains the same. Only on the personal plane do we have identity coupled with change and unity with plurality. Here the conscious and free agent constitutes itself one and the same and yet does a great many different things. How in the midst of its changing and plural activities it maintains its identity and unity, we do not know. But that it does, is a manifest fact of experience; and it is in this empirical fact that we have the one and only key to the nature of ultimate reality. The causal ground of the world must be self-conscious and free if it is to be rationally conceivable.

These theoretical arguments—epistemological and causal—do not demonstrate the existence of God. Such a demonstration, as we have seen, is impossible. But when thought through they do make it clear that the theistic world-view is "the line of least resistance" for the intellect as it is also for the moral and religious nature. And more than this the Christian faith does not ask. It is quite content, so long as the middle wall of partition between the theoretical and practical reason is broken down and both are seen to point toward a common spiritual interpretation of the universe.

## CHAPTER VII

## THE ABSOLUTENESS OF GOD

THE most general and distinctive characteristic of Deity in its monotheistic sense is absoluteness. It is this which differentiates the divine from the human and from all finite beings, and gives to it its uniqueness. Personality and goodness are characteristics that God shares with men, but absoluteness sets him apart from all creaturely existence.

The word "absolute" is not biblical, nor is it religious. It is a philosophical term, and one that has come into common use only in modern times. But the idea expressed by it is as old as philosophy. It is inherent in the distinction between reality and appearance, a distinction whose explicit recognition led to the rise of the philosophic movement. Philosophy began as a quest after the real, the abiding, the absolute. Since the time of Wolff and Kant it has been customary to speak of this quest as a search for "the thing-in-itself." The latter phrase, however, expressed nothing new. The idea contained in it has, according to Windelband,[1] had at least sixteen ancestors. Indeed, why he should stop with that number is not clear. Every monistic metaphysician has fathered the idea, and most metaphysicians have been of the monistic type. But for that matter the dualistic and pluralistic metaphysicians have also been in

[1] *An Introduction to Philosophy*, p. 34.

search of the thing-in-itself. Only they have been persuaded that there are two or more things-in-themselves instead of one. Some sort of ultimate reality, some sort of absolute—unitary, dual or plural—has thus been the object of every form of the metaphysical quest.

The first Greek philosophers sought for a first principle or substance that would account for the changing phenomena of the world. Thales found it in "water," Anaximenes in "air," and Anaximander in "the Infinite." The same quest led to the "elements" of Empedocles, the "Being" of Parmenides, the "atoms" of Democritus, the *nous* or reason of Anaxagoras, the "numbers" of the Pythagoreans, the "Ideas" of Plato, the "entelechies" and "Prime Mover" of Aristotle, the "One" of Plotinus, the "essence" of the scholastics, the "Substance" of Spinoza, the "monads" of Leibnitz, the "thing-in-itself" of Kant, the "Universal Ego" of Fichte, the principle of "Identity" in Schelling, the "Will" of Schopenhauer, and the "Absolute Spirit" of Hegel. All these metaphysical conceptions and the many others allied to them grew out of discontent with the world of sense-experience. It was felt that reality must be more permanent, more unified, more substantial, more rational than the things of sense seemed to be. Hence the effort was made to reconstitute the world so that it would conform more completely with the demands of reason; and the world so reconstituted was regarded as the "real" world by way of contrast with the world of experience or phenomena. The latter world is relative; relative to our sensibility, and relative also in the sense that its individual phenomena are determined by their relation to each other. The "real" world, on the other hand, is *absolute* in the sense that it is self-existent and in some way the source of the world of "appearance."

### THE MEANING OF ABSOLUTENESS

Disregarding the dualistic and pluralistic conceptions of ultimate reality as lacking in logical thoroughness and as in any case irrelevant for our present purpose, we may distinguish three different views or types of thought with reference to the Absolute. One is agnostic. It affirms the Absolute, but declares that he or it is beyond the reach of theoretical knowledge. Kant and Spencer represent this standpoint, and so also did many of the mystics of the past. An approach to it is found in the book of Ecclesiastes (7. 24), where the author says, "That which is, is far off and exceeding deep; who can find it out?"

The second view looks upon the Absolute as the highest universal, as the sum of all being, actual and potential, as all-comprehensive, taking up into itself and surmounting in its own unity all possible distinctions and differences. This standpoint is represented by Hegelianism and by pantheism in general. Its controlling idea is that of logical subordination. The third view conceives of the Absolute as world-ground or as an infinite energy producing and sustaining the world. Such a conception may be either materialistic or spiritualistic. It is dominated by the category of causality.

In harmony with these three views there are three different interpretations of the word "absolute." Some understand it to mean the "unrelated." Thus understood the Absolute cannot stand in a causal relation to the world, nor can anything be affirmed of it that implies relationship of any kind. But such a Being would have no intelligible character whatsoever. In fact, it would be not only unknowable, but also unaffirmable. For the only reason for affirming an Absolute is to account for the world of experience. To ascribe to it a nature that unfits it to perform this function is to render it useless from the standpoint of human thought; and to do so because of the supposed derivation of its name is to substitute etymologizing for philosophizing.

Others understand by the word absolute the "unlimited," and hence regard it as applicable only to a Being that embraces the entire universe, a Being that cannot be identified with personality nor any definite mode of existence. This is the pantheistic interpretation of the term.

The third meaning given it is "independent" or "self-existent." This meaning may be presupposed by the other two; but here it is made central, and the other two are excluded. The Absolute is not the "unrelated" nor is it the "unlimited" in the sense of being the All; it is the independent and self-existent cause or ground of a dependent world. The world is not a part of the Absolute, but a consequence of its activity, an effect, and as such distinguishable from its cause. It may even as effect have a measure of independence due to the self-limitation of the Absolute. This is the causal and theistic view of the relation of the world to the Absolute as distinguished from the logical and pantheistic, on the one hand, and the agnostic, on the other.

The agnostic view is, as we have seen, inconsistent and self-destructive. The other two have not been always sharply distinguished from each other. Numerous attempts have been made to combine them; and they are not entirely opposed to each other. But they are guided by different ideals. The key to the one is found in the logical subordination of the individual to the universal. The greater the universality, it is believed, the greater the reality. Hence the all-inclusive universal is the supreme reality, the Absolute. The key to the other is found in the principle of causality and particularly volitional causality. Here the real is the individual, the concrete; the universal has no independent existence. Ultimate reality is, therefore, to be thought of as the highest form of concrete individuality. The Absolute is purposive energy, will, rather than abstract reason. From the point of view of the latter the individual is included in and fused with the universal. This conception fits in with the mystical type of piety, a sense of oneness with the Divine. The other view of the Absolute lays stress on the independence of the individual and on the supreme importance of moral obedience as the condition of being in tune with the Infinite.

To the Absolute in all three senses of the term—the agnostic, the logical, and the causal—it has been customary to apply the divine name. But that there is a considerable disparity between some of the philosophical conceptions of the Absolute and the religious idea of God is evident, and consequently the question has arisen as to whether it is proper to equate the two ideas. In answering this question it is important to bear in mind the different senses in which the term "absolute" is used and also to inquire into the relation of the metaphysical and the religious craving to each other.

That a thoroughgoing agnostic view of the Absolute is out of harmony with the Christian idea of God calls for no argument. One might, it is true, combine philosophical skepticism with a positive faith in Christianity, as do Barth and Brunner; but that is another matter. It is also evident that the all-inclusive Absolute of pantheistic speculation is a different Being from the Christian God, though the two have not always been regarded as mutually exclusive. Some of the medieval mystics distinguished between the Godhead and God, looking upon the latter as a personal emanation from the former; and some moderns have taken the view that God should be included in the larger whole represented by the Absolute.[2] Whether the full Christian idea of God can be fitted into such a frame is extremely doubtful. But in any case the distinction between God and the Absolute has been made, and in view of the agnostic and pantheistic senses in which the term "absolute" is so frequently used this is not strange, nor is it strange that some theologians should have rejected the idea

---

[2] Cf. H. Rashdall, *The Theory of Good and Evil*, II, pp. 238ff.; *Philosophy and Religion*, pp. 101ff.

of absoluteness altogether and refused to apply it to God. Ritschl, for instance, took this position.[3]

But the word "absolute," as we have seen, does not mean that which is out of all relations and hence unknowable, nor does it necessarily mean that which is inclusive of all existence; it may mean the independent or self-existent ground of the world and in this sense it is practically synonymous with the idea of creatorship. There is, then, no conflict between the Christian conception of God and the idea of the Absolute. The Christian God is absolute by virtue of the fact that he is "the Father Almighty, Maker of heaven and earth." Almightiness and creatorship mean absoluteness. They mean that the entire world is dependent upon God for its existence and that there are no limits to his power except those which he himself has imposed.

In spite of this the feeling persists that there is a disparity between the idea of absoluteness and that of Deity. One, it is said, is philosophical in origin and the other religious; and philosophy and religion, it is added, are quite different things. This view, which is rather widely current and not without some justification, necessitates an inquiry into the psychological impulse that lies back of metaphysics, on the one hand, and religion, on the other.

## Origin of the Idea of the Absolute

We have already pointed out that metaphysics grew up out of discontent with the immediate world of sense-experience. Things as we perceive them do not

[3] *Theologie und Metaphysik* (zweite Auflage), pp. 17ff.

have the inner unity or rationality that reason demands, and so the mind builds up a conceptual world which it regards as more real than that of sense. It substitutes the world of physics and astronomy for that of immediate experience, and then beyond all purely scientific theories it constructs a world of ultimate or metaphysical reality. The driving force in this whole movement is dissatisfaction with the world as given to us in spontaneous thought. And this too is the source of religion. It also grows up out of discontent with the world. The things of sense fail to satisfy us, our ideals are thwarted, and so we seek a higher and better world. Religion and metaphysics thus have a common rootage, they spring up out of a common craving of the human spirit. Both are objectifications of the ideal.

There is, however, this difference, that the ideal is in one case predominantly logical and in the other predominantly practical. Consequently, the question arises as to whether these ideals both require an Absolute and a common Absolute. Insofar as they both carry with them an implicit faith in their own validity, it is evident that they imply a transcendent reality that may be called absolute by way of contrast with the imperfect and transitory things of sense. But over and above this vague faith in the ideal there are factors in both the intellectual and the religious nature of man that point to and call for a more definitely conceived Absolute. On the intellectual side there is, for instance, a fundamental demand for unity, a demand that cannot be met by the mere togetherness or systematic totality of such objects as we see about us, but one that requires us to transcend the phenomenal order and postulate a unitary Being as its ground and source. This monistic tendency of the human mind is deep and ineradicable. Closely associated with it and to some extent involved in it is the idea of the infinite, an idea that is forced upon us by the inexhaustibility of the spatial and temporal synthesis. We cannot imagine an end either to space or time, and yet the mind cannot rest in the thought of mere endlessness. So it forms the conception of an infinite, that is more and other than the sum total of spatial and temporal phenomena and that is somehow their ground. Infinitude and unity thus enter by a kind of necessity into our thought of the rational ideal. But how this ideal as an objective reality should be conceived is a matter of dispute. No inflexible logic here guides us. If we are, however, not to conceive of it as a "spectral woof of impalpable abstractions or an unearthly ballet of bloodless categories," it would seem that it must take on a spiritual or personal form. At any rate there is a deep personalistic bias in the human mind which points strongly in that direction. Either a theistic Absolute or complete philosophical skepticism would seem to be the alternatives that confront us; and as between the two a healthy reason ought to have no difficulty in making its choice. Theism cannot be demonstrated, but it fulfills the demands of the rational ideal more completely than any other world view.

Turning now to the religious nature, we find that it more immediately than the theoretical reason affirms a supramundane reality. Indeed, it is in this affirmation, or rather intuition, that religion takes its rise. How we come to have such intuitions has been much debated. The main question at issue is as to whether they have a moral origin or not. Both views are confidently asserted. Olin A. Curtis, for instance, declares that the "sense of the supernatural originates only in the experience of the moral person." It "is created by a movement of the moral life; and had man no conscience, he never would have such a sense at all." "When, in conscience, a man first feels the ultimate authority of the moral overmaster he gets his first idea of the supernatural." Then from this moral center he extends it to "all sorts of things, even nonmoral things."[4] This is a common view and is supported by the Kantian and Ritschlian tradition.

On the other hand, Rudolf Otto, like Schleiermacher, argues strongly for the nonmoral origin of the sense of the divine. This sense, he maintains, is altogether unique. Among the ancient Semites it was connected with the idea of the holy, which was originally a nonmoral term.[5] Inasmuch, however, as this term came later to have a moral connotation and still has, Otto invented, as we have previously noted, the word "numinous" to designate the pure and unmodified experience of the divine. This experience he has analyzed with extraordinary insight. In general, he characterizes it as a *mysterium tremendum et fascinosum.* It begins with a feeling of fear, and this feeling implies on the part of the object

[4] *The Christian Faith*, pp. 82f.
[5] See my *Religious Teaching of the Old Testament*, pp. 137ff.

(1) the element of awefulness or absolute unapproachability, (2) the element of majesty or "overpoweringness," and (3) the element of energy or urgency. Associated with this complex feeling, properly described as *tremendum*, is (4) the sense of mystery, the consciousness of the "wholly other," the supernatural; and to these four elements is to be added (5) the element of fascination, of rapture.[6] These various elements are nonmoral. How they take their rise in our consciousness, we cannot say. They are ultimate, as ultimate as the categories of thought. Neither conscience nor the quest after life can account for their appearance and for their unique blending in our intuition of the divine.

But while the numinous experience may thus be differentiated from the moral, it should be noted that it is itself an experience of value. The terms that describe it or its object—awe, majesty, urgency, the "wholly other," fascination—imply valuation or disvaluation, and in this respect the numinous resembles the moral. Indeed, the word "moral," as we have already seen, is sometimes used as equivalent to "valuational," and from that point of view the numinous experience might be said to involve the moral. There is in it a note of authority, a sense of oughtness. The *numen* has value for us; but it is a different value from that which is commonly designated as moral. Then, too, its existence is not derived directly from its value. We do not say that it *is* because it ought to be. Both its existence and its value are grasped in a single, unique, and immediate intuition. It seems,

[6] *The Idea of the Holy*, pp. 12-41.

therefore, best to distinguish, with Schleiermacher and Otto, between the religious and the moral consciousness.

But what we are here concerned about is not to establish the uniqueness of our elementary religious experience, but to show that it contains in itself the germ of the Absolute. Complete unapproachability, "overpoweringness," the "wholly other"—these are aspects of the primitive or purely religious-object that with the development of thought lead inevitably to the idea of an absolute power, upon which the whole world is dependent. The feeling of trust and the longing for redemption, awakened by the "fascination" and "urgency" of the religious object, lead also to the same conclusion. The history of religion teaches this fact so plainly that no serious student can fail to be deeply impressed by it. Through demonology, polytheism, and monolatry the religious spirit has moved steadily and irresistibly toward the belief in one God, Creator and Preserver of the world. Nothing short of such an absolute Being can satisfy the religious needs of men. If there is a valid basis for that feeling of trustful dependence and that quest after salvation which constitute the essence of religion, the universe must be grounded in free intelligence. Anything less than such a theism would leave religion in its highest and purest form without an adequate object. The absoluteness of God is inherent in the very structure of a spiritual faith.

Our conclusion, then, is that both the religious quest after redemption and the intellectual quest after truth lead to the affirmation of an Absolute.

Both owe their origin to discontent with the sense world, both imply faith in a transcendent reality, and neither can find complete satisfaction apart from the belief in one Supreme Being. This Being is absolute in the sense that he is self-existent, that he has no limits except those which are self-imposed, and that the world is dependent upon him. In these respects the Absolute of religion is one with the Absolute of philosophy. God would not be God if he were not metaphysically absolute in the sense just stated. Absoluteness is the fundamental and differentiating characteristic of Deity.

### The Idea of a Finite God

It is necessary to emphasize the foregoing point, not only because the word "absolute" has fallen into disfavor on account of its agnostic and pantheistic associations, but because there is at present a pronounced reaction against absolutism in general in philosophy and a consequent attempt to dispense with it in theology also. We have already referred to Ritschl's antipathy to the word "absolute," due partly to a mistaken interpretation of it and partly to a mistaken desire to divorce theology completely from speculative theism. But with that I am not here concerned. What I have in mind is the current idea of a finite or growing God. This idea is in principle, of course, not new. It is implied in polytheism and in every dualistic and pluralistic system that has a place for God. But in recent years it has come into new vogue because of the prevalence of empiricistic, pragmatistic, and other anti-monistic types of thought.

A distinction should perhaps be made between the idea of a finite and that of a growing or changing God. The former idea was broached by David Hume.[7] J. S. Mill[8] indorsed it, William James[9] advocated it, H. G. Wells,[10] the novelist, popularized it, and many others have echoed it.[11] The idea of a changing or growing God has been especially emphasized by the followers of Henri Bergson,[12] but it is not uncommon in other circles[13] and is naturally associated with the idea of a finite God. The motives lying back of these two conceptions are somewhat different, but both are reactions against what William James called "the rationalistic block universe" and "the static, timeless, perfect absolute." The idea of a changing and growing God is directed against the "static," "perfect," and "block" part of the rejected view, and the idea of his finitude is directed against the notion of the "absolute" and of a completed "universe." But at this point two questions arise on which the exponents of the new doctrine are either not agreed or not clear.

One has to do with the relation of growth to the universe viewed as the totality of being. Bergson does not make it clear whether he thinks of the whole

---

[7] *Dialogues*, Pt. XI.

[8] *Three Essays on Religion*, pp. 242ff.

[9] *A Pluralistic Universe*, pp. 310ff.

[10] *God the Invisible King.*

[11] Cf. R. B. Perry, *Present Conflict of Ideals*, pp. 316-30.

[12] For example, H. W. Carr, *The Philosophy of Change*, pp. 187f. See chapter on "The Notion of a Changing God," in *Pantheistic Dilemmas*, pp. 107ff., by H. C. Sheldon.

[13] Cf. Harold Höffding, *Philosophy of Religion*, pp. 67f.; George B. Foster, *The Function of Religion in Man's Struggle for Existence.*

universe, including the creative source of the life-movement, as growing or whether he restricts growth to the phenomenal realm. The latter view would be in accord with current theism. James, however, seems plainly to apply the idea of growth to the universe as a whole which he regards as an aggregate rather than as a system. It is, he says, an "unfinished" world, "spread out and strung-along." He speaks of it as a "mass of phenomena," but recognizes no Absolute upon which it is dependent. It is itself a growing whole. But what growth would mean when applied to the whole of reality is difficult to see. A finite individual grows by drawing upon its environment. But the universe as a whole has no environment upon which it can draw, and the application of growth or progress to it seems, therefore, quite unintelligible.[14] The world as a phenomenal order may grow and develop, but such development defies explanation and understanding except on a theistic basis. Without free intelligence there can be no *real* progress in a rational world.

The other question referred to relates to the idea of a finite God. According to James, he is to be thought of as "having an environment, being in time and working out a history just like ourselves."[15] But is he to be regarded as morally perfect from the start? Or is he a struggling and achieving being like ourselves? If the latter, he would have a religious experience similar to our own

---

[14] This line of thought has been developed at some length by Pringle-Pattison, *The Idea of God*, pp. 366ff.

[15] *A Pluralistic Universe*, p. 318.

and would need a God as much as we. Under those circumstances why he should himself be called God one is at a loss to know. Moral self-sufficiency is inherent in the idea of Deity. To attribute to God the same kind of moral struggle as that in which we are engaged, is to do violence to our profoundest religious sentiments. J. S. Mill is mistaken when he says that the belief in a finite God admits of "one elevated feeling, which is not open to those who believe in the omnipotence of the good principle in the universe, the feeling of helping God—of requiting the good he has given by a voluntary co-operation which he, not being omnipotent, really needs, and by which a somewhat nearer approach may be made to the fulfillment of his purposes."[16] It is not the limitation of the divine power and the divine need of human aid that constitutes the true religious stimulus to moral endeavor. The greatest moral dynamic of life is that which comes from the conviction that right is omnipotent and that its ultimate victory is assured. He who does not know this is a stranger to any deep religious experience. It is not sympathy with God, but faith in him that saves.

A special advantage claimed for the theory of a finite God is that it solves the problem of suffering. This problem grows out of the fact that we ascribe to God both omnipotence and goodness. To harmonize these two attributes with each other in the light of the imperfection and suffering of the present world-order is extremely difficult, if not impossible. "The notion of a providential government by an om-

---

[16] *Three Essays on Religion*, p. 256.

nipotent Being for the good of his creatures," says J. S. Mill, "must be entirely dismissed."[17] It seems to be entirely inconsistent with the facts of experience. But if we limit the power of God by denying that he is the creator and preserver of the world, it becomes possible for us to believe in his goodness, for the evil of the world may now be ascribed to other beings and forces. The rejection of the divine absoluteness thus removes the rock of offense contained in the fact of suffering. But on reflection it turns out that it also removes something more. It removes all ground for any profound faith in the divine providence. If God did not create the world and does not actually govern it, what basis have we for trusting him? God may be perfectly good, but if he is impotent, his goodness will mean little to us. It is the union of goodness with power that is the sole ground of faith. To purchase relief from a theoretical difficulty by drastically limiting the divine power is no aid to true religion; it undermines faith rather than supports it. When it comes to such a question as that of suffering, religion has no interest in creating difficulties for the intellect; but it is not willing because of these difficulties to surrender the richness and depth of its own faith. In any case it would naturally in such a position seek relief by a limitation of human knowledge, rather than by a limitation of the divine power. Human ignorance is for it a much easier assumption than the divine impotence. Indeed, the latter in the extreme form represented by the current idea of a finite God is virtu-

[17] *Three Essays on Religion*, p. 243.

ally a denial of faith. The very essence of faith is trust both in the power and goodness of God in spite of appearances to the contrary. The fact of suffering may baffle us if we hold to the divine omnipotence, but better a baffled faith than no faith at all.

From the religious point of view the doctrine of a finite and growing God is, then, unsatisfactory. It leaves us with a truncated and disintegrating faith. It is also unsatisfactory from the metaphysical standpoint. We have already seen that a growing and struggling God would himself need a God in much the same way that we do; and, in a similar way, if we were to account for his existence, we should have to refer it to the Absolute. As a finite being he would not be self-existent. In him we could, therefore, find nothing ultimate. One might, it is true, hold to a fundamental pluralism and think of the universe as a mere aggregate, but that, as Pringle-Pattison says, would be "trifling with one's intellect." A basal monism the human mind demands, and from this standpoint a finite God would at the best play only a secondary rôle. Indeed, the very idea of such a being suggests the mythological. He is not immanent in the structure of reality in the way that a living God should be and must be. He has no cosmic significance. So far as the explanation of the world is concerned he might easily be dispensed with.

The point is occasionally made that if God enters into human experience he must be finite, for our experience is finite and can apprehend only finite objects. As absolute God lies beyond the reach of experience. He becomes a truly living God only in finite form. This view rests upon a narrow and confused notion of what experience is and of the elements that enter into it. It is also usually associated with an agnostic or pantheistic conception of the Absolute. The assumption underlying it seems to be that experience is a purely receptive process, that external objects somehow enter into it, and that in the nature of the case an infinite Being could not gain access into so limited a receptacle as the human mind or human experience. To this assumption the sufficient reply is that experience is the result of a creative activity on the part of the mind, that no object enters the mind either physically or metaphysically, that the mind builds up its own objects on the condition of external stimuli and in accordance with principles immanent within itself, and that among these principles there may be a religious *a priori* by virtue of which the mind is sensitive to the supernatural or infinite and lays hold of it. In its earlier attempts to conceive and define the supernatural object the mind was naturally pluralistic and dualistic, but by a law of its own being it has moved steadily toward the monotheistic view. It may be that William James is right in saying that even monotheism in its popular religious form has never gotten beyond the conception of God as merely *primus inter pares*.[18] But if so, it is not because a thoroughgoing monotheism is a metaphysical rather than a religious doctrine, but because of the inconsistent and inconsequential character of popular religious thought. Certainly, in popular Christian monotheism there are elements

[18] *Pragmatism*, p. 298.

such as that of the divine creatorship which require, when thought through, a higher and more absolutistic view of God than that of "first among equals." Indeed, creatorship is itself the true mark of absoluteness. A being who is Creator is by virtue of that fact self-existent and the independent ground of the universe. As such he stands apart from all other beings and constitutes a class by himself. In a word, he is absolute. No other view of him will satisfy the demands of either the religious or the theoretical reason.

It is unfortunate that the word "absolute" has been used in such an abstract and purely logical or etymological sense that prejudice has arisen against it in religious circles. There is a tendency either to repudiate it altogether as inapplicable to God or to use it gingerly and along with it to assert that God is also a "limited" and "finite" Being. The result is widespread confusion of thought on the subject. The fact is that the Christian God is an absolute Being, in the sense that he is the creator of the world, its self-existent and independent ground. This is the specific sense in which the word "absolute" should be used. "Limited" and "finite," on the other hand, should be applied only to the God of a polytheistic, pluralistic, or dualistic system. More particularly they should at present be used to define such an artificial and truncated Deity as that represented by H. G. Wells and other apostles of a good but noncreative and nonprovidential Divine Being.

In view, however, of the fact that absolutists of the abstract and etymological type are accustomed to bring the charge of finitude and limitation against the God of Christian theism, there is need of such a presentation of the case as we have in Bishop Francis J. McConnell's well-known book entitled *Is God Limited?* Here it is argued at length and with richness and felicity of illustration (1) that "if we are to think of God at all, we must think of him as under some sort of limitation," and (2) that in the derogatory sense of the term the unlimited God of abstract thought is really more "limited" than the Christian God. "It is the abstract theologians," says Bishop McConnell, "who limit God." "The movement away from the concrete toward the abstract" is itself a "limitation." To empty "all the concrete out of divine experience" is to impoverish the idea of God and lock him away "behind the bars of estranging limitation." The real question, then, is not whether God has limitations, but how these limitations are to be conceived. We may distinguish two kinds of limitations—those that are imposed from without and those that are self-imposed or that inhere in the divine nature. It is only the latter that may be affirmed of God. "What the Christian consciousness demands is a God not dependent on anything else." "Self-dependence in God" is the basal truth to be observed in thinking about him. In this sense of the term Bishop McConnell not only admits, but firmly maintains that there is a "legitimate demand for an *absolute* God,"[19] but he is so keenly sensitive to other uses of the term that he thinks it important at present to emphasize the limitations of God rather than his

[19] *Is God Limited?* Pp. 17, 20, 21, 52, 53.

absoluteness. A self-limited God, however, he regards as more truly absolute than the illimitable Absolute of abstract philosophy. To deny to God the power of self-limitation would itself be to limit God, and that in an unworthy way.

A more radical method of conceiving the divine limitations has been recently proposed by Professor E. S. Brightman.[20] He suggests that there is in the divine nature "a retarding factor," a "datum akin to sensation in man," a "content," a "Given," which needs to be overcome and whose presence accounts for the irrational aspects of suffering and for "the cosmic drag which retards and distorts the expression of value in the empirical world." In other connections later I shall have occasion to consider this theory more fully. I mention it here simply to observe that, while Professor Brightman describes his conception as that of a "finite God," and while he introduces into the divine nature a larger degree of limitation than is customary, he still holds to the divine creatorship in the current theistic sense of the term and hence ascribes absoluteness to God in the sense in which this term should be understood in theistic discourse.

No matter, then, what limitations may be ascribed to God, he is absolute so long as he is regarded as the independent and self-existent source or ground of the universe. What the older theologians called *aseity,* self-caused existence, expresses the essential content

---

[20] *The Problem of God,* Chaps. V and VII. This is an interesting, informing and stimulating study, characterized by originality, breadth of view, and personal conviction.

of the divine absoluteness. But the term carries with it also the idea of perfection, and from this point of view the divine absoluteness manifests itself in three different realms: the metaphysical, the cognitive, and the ethical. The last of these will come up for consideration in Chapter IX. The second will perhaps most naturally be dealt with in Chapter VIII. Only the first needs to be treated in the present chapter. Metaphysical absoluteness, however, is itself complex. It may be analyzed into various elements. Of these there are three of outstanding significance—omnipotence, omnipresence, and eternity. In these attributes the metaphysical absoluteness of God comes to its completest expression, and to an exposition of them the remainder of the chapter will be devoted.

## OMNIPOTENCE

Of the three attributes just mentioned, omnipotence is the most fundamental. Indeed, it may be said to be virtually synonymous with metaphysical absoluteness. For omnipresence means that the divine power is not limited by space, and eternity means that it is not limited by time. Even aseity may be said to be implied in omnipotence. For an omnipotent being would in the nature of the case be able to maintain its own existence. It may also be added that omniscience and moral perfection would be empty possessions apart from a corresponding and sustaining power. It is power that gives reality to the Divine Being and to all beings.

The idea of the supernatural was implied, as we have seen, in the earliest numinous experience, in the sense of the "holy"; and it has been the presupposition of every vital religious faith. The Hebrew word for God, *El* or *Elohim,* was probably derived from a root meaning "to be strong"; and according to a popular etymology current in ancient Israel the name "Jehovah," or "Yahweh," expressed originally the idea of independent power or self-existence. "I am that I am" was supposed to be the thought lying back of it.[21] It was, of course, only gradually that the Hebrews arrived at the idea of the sole deity and absolute power of Jehovah. These ideas formed the staple of the preaching of Deutero-Isaiah in the sixth century, but they did not originate with him. How far back they may be traced is uncertain. They are assumed in the teaching of the eighth-century prophets, and cannot have been entirely unknown before their time. The idea of Jehovah's creatorship probably goes back to a considerably earlier date.[22] But whatever may have been the early history of these ideas, there is no doubt that by the sixth century B. C. they had emerged into distinct consciousness and had become the basis of an enthusiastic faith. Jehovah was now recognized by people as well as by prophets as Creator and omnipotent Lord. He measures, we are told, the waters in the hollow of his hand (Isa. 40. 12); and all the marvels of the stellar universe, we read, are but as a whisper when compared with the mighty thunder of his power (Job 26. 14).

---

[21] Exod. 3. 13-15. E.

[22] For a detailed study of this and other related questions, see my *Religious Teaching of the Old Testament,* pp. 115-136.

This conception of the divine omnipotence was carried over into the New Testament and forms the background of its teaching.[23] In both Testaments the motive of the doctrine was practical rather than theoretical. It was personal trust that inspired it, not logic. The Israelites instinctively believed that Jehovah was equal to all their needs, and hence with the expansion of their needs extended their conception of his power until it embraced heaven and earth, and time and eternity. It was so also in the New Testament. What led Jesus and his disciples to accept the belief in the divine omnipotence was the recognition of its religious value or, rather, necessity. It was faith, not reason, that led Jesus to say that "all things are possible with God"[24] and that led Paul to speak of God as one "that is able to do exceeding abundantly above all that we ask or think."[25] When, then, the church later refused to follow the lead of Marcion and reject the Creator-God of the Old Testament in favor of the Saviour-God of the New Testament, it was but carrying out the demands of faith itself. Only omnipotence can guarantee redemption. This is the implicit logic of the religious reason. Faith can become an actual triumph over the world only insofar as it includes the idea of the divine omnipotence. And, on the other hand, only he truly believes in the divine omnipotence who is led by it to a world-transcendent trust in God. The classical

[23] Matt. 11. 25; 5. 34; Rom. 1. 20; 11. 36; 1 Cor. 8. 6; 15. 28; 2 Cor. 5. 18, etc.

[24] Mark 10. 27. Cf. 14. 36.

[25] Eph. 3. 20.

expression of this faith is found in the great Christian pæan of victory in the eighth chapter of Romans.

In view of the practical origin and nature of the biblical doctrine of the divine omnipotence it is not strange that we find in Scripture itself no effort to define it or to carry out its speculative implications. But with the development of Christian theology it was inevitable that this effort should be made. What exactly is implied in the idea of omnipotence? Are there any limits to the divine power, and if so, what are they? Is truth a barrier to the divine will? Does God have a nature, and if so, does it limit his power and his will? Is his power exhausted in the actual universe, or has he reserves of power as yet untouched? Are will and ability distinguishable factors in his being as with us, or do they coincide with each other so that one involves the other? Such are some of the questions that have been asked by theologians, and a brief response may be made to them.

As in the case of the divine absoluteness, so here the etymologists have been active. They have told us that divine omnipotence means that God can do everything, and to "everything" there is no exception. If omnipotent, God must be able to create a universe in which the law of Identity, the law of Contradiction and the law of the Excluded Middle would not be valid. He must be able to create a being of such a nature that he himself could not destroy it, though the existence of such a being would contradict his own omnipotence. He must be able to "make the past not to have been," as Thomas Aquinas put it.[26] He must be able to "draw a triangle which is courageous or which has two right angles." He must be able to "make a straight stick with only one end." If he is not able to do such irrational and self-contradictory things as these, he is not omnipotent. So the etymologist has argued, and that this barren type of thought does not belong wholly to the past is indicated by the fact that a distinguished English philosopher not long ago devoted upward of twenty pages to revamping it.[27]

The sufficient response to such argumentation is that omnipotence does not mean that God can do the nondoable. There are limitations within the structure of reality that establish a distinction between the possible and the impossible. And all that any sane advocate of the divine omnipotence has ever meant is that "God can do all things that are possible" (Aquinas); the intrinsically impossible lies beyond the scope of divine power as it does beyond that of rational conception. The self-contradictory has no meaning, it is a mere juxtaposition of words, and cannot be translated into reality. Nor can any reason, practical or theoretical, be offered for ascribing to God the power to do that which is inherently irrational. The fact is that in affirming the divine omnipotence religion is interested simply in the redemptive purpose of God. So long as the realization of this purpose is guaranteed, faith is content. It has no further concern about the divine power. And philosophy in attributing omnipotence to God has

---

[26] *Summa Theologica*, Pt. I, Qu. 25, Art. 4.
[27] J. M. E. McTaggart, *Some Dogmas of Religion*, pp. 202-20.

manifestly no other interest than to maintain that there is a unitary and absolute power upon which the world depends. To say that God, if omnipotent, must be able to do everything, whether conceivable or inconceivable, is not only to go beyond the demands of faith and reason, but to contradict them both.

Reason and faith both imply that God has a nature. Without it his will would have no content or direction; its activity would be like that of the man of whom it is said that he leaped upon a horse and rode off in all directions. Only as it is linked up with the divine nature can the divine will escape being a vague and empty abstraction. It becomes real and significant only insofar as it is expressive of the divine character, and this means that it has limits, but limits only by way of contrast with mere vacuity. The word "limitation" has unfortunately two different meanings which are often not distinguished. It denotes imperfection or diminution of reality, and it also denotes definiteness and concreteness of being. Now, it is in the latter sense only that we affirm limitation of the divine will and the divine nature. Rationality and goodness, for instance, imply a certain definiteness, and in this sense limitation of the Divine Being, but they are not limitations in the sense that they imply imperfection or a lessened degree of reality. They are, rather, expressions of the divine perfection. When we, then, speak of the omnipotence of God, we do not mean that he has power to act contrary to his own nature; we mean that his power expresses itself perfectly and completely in and through his nature. In thus giving direction to the divine will the divine nature may be said to limit it. But without such a limiting nature God would not be God. He would be sheer emptiness. Limitation in the sense of definiteness of nature is of the very essence of being.

But if God has a nature and his nature conditions his will, the question arises as to what the constituents of his nature are and how far his will is conditioned by them. That truth and right are grounded in the divine nature would perhaps be generally conceded. We could not regard them as made or unmade by the divine will. They stand in their own right and are in a sense immutable. Yet they are not external authorities to which the divine will must bow. They have no objective existence. They inhere in the divine nature and are laws of the Divine Being. As such they may be said to be deeper than the divine will; still, they are not independent of it. Like other necessities of the divine nature, they are made real only through the activity of the divine will. But they are not arbitrary creations of it. They are grounded in the very being of God. On this point there probably would be general agreement.

Differences, however, arise when it comes to the question of the relation of the divine will to creation, the question of the relation of the divine will to the divine ability, and the question as to whether there may be in the divine nature an imperfect or incomplete factor which limits the divine will. With reference to the first of these questions the prevailing tendency in Christian thought has been to refer creation to the free will of God; if he had chosen so to do, he might have entirely abstained from creative activity. The other view, however, has had its advocates—that creation is eternal and that it is an outgrowth of the divine nature. God, it is said, would not be God if he were not Creator. It is not, then, a matter of choice with him whether he will create or not.[28] If we adopt this view, it is evident that we have in the creative activity of God another constituent of his nature that determines or that gives direction to his will.

The second question above referred to may be put in this form: Omnipotence, we say, means that God can do whatever he wills. But the converse, we have been told by Schleiermacher[29] and Biedermann,[30] also holds true, that God *wills* to do and *does* whatever he *can* do. There is, in other words, no difference between will and ability. The divine ability, inherent in the divine nature, carries with it the divine will and expresses itself automatically in creative action. There is no possible beyond the actual. The two are one. The actual world is, therefore, the complete expression of the divine will and ability. There are no transcendent reserves of divine power. Nature reflects all there is of God. But this pantheistic view is manifestly inconsistent with the divine omnipotence. God, if truly omnipotent, cannot have exhausted himself in the present temporal order. The very idea of omnipotence implies that of the

---

[28] Cf. A. S. Pringle-Pattison, *The Idea of God*, pp. 298-321. For a criticism, see Bishop Charles Gore, *Belief in God*, pp. 69-73.

[29] *The Christian Faith*, Par. 54, pp. 211ff.

[30] *Christliche Dogmatik*, pp. 462ff.

supernatural, as does also the idea of Deity itself in its spontaneous and vital form. So to those who identify the divine will with the divine ability and equate both with the actual energy operative in the world of nature—to such naturalistically and pantheistically inclined thinkers we may say, as Jesus said to the Sadducaic skeptics of his day: "Ye do err, not knowing . . . the *power* of God" (Matt. 22. 29).

The last of the three questions mentioned above had to do with a resisting or retarding element in the divine nature. This brings us back to Professor Brightman's theory. Here we have a situation almost the reverse of that dealt with in the preceding paragraph. There the divine will and ability, the possible and the actual, were fused into one and equated with the immanent energy of the universe. The resulting limitation was that of an exclusive immanence—a limitation that runs counter to the implicit transcendence not only of an omnipotent Deity, but of religious faith itself. Here, however, we have a conflict between the divine will and the divine nature. There is a tension between the possible and the actual. Within the divine nature or experience there is an element or content that resists the divine will. God himself is perfectly good and rational. He wills the highest values, but within his own being there is an intractable or recalcitrant factor that frustrates their realization. Whether it merely delays or permanently thwarts their realization is not altogether clear. It only delays apparently the attainment of certain specific ends. But it would seem to thwart permanently the full realization of the divine purpose,[31] for it is said to be an "eternal" aspect of the divine consciousness, and as such would seem to impose a permanent limitation upon the divine will. God, then, is absolutely good, but he is not omnipotent, and because of that fact he is involved in an endless struggle with a resisting element in his own nature. He "appears to be a spirit in difficulty."

This theory has the advantage of offering a specific reason for the divine activity and also the advantage of accounting for the unideal aspects of the world without compromising the divine character. It, furthermore, has the very considerable merit of providing a metaphysical basis for the Christian idea of sacrificial love and what looks like moral struggle in God. But it has the disadvantage of introducing into the divine consciousness a dualism that can hardly be regarded as satisfactory either religiously or intellectually. Two fundamental motives lie back of religion and of metaphysical philosophy. One is the need of a supreme good and the other the need of an ultimate unity. These two needs can find complete satisfaction only in an omnipotent Being who is able to reduce all multiplicity to unity and able to subdue

---

[31] From this statement of his position Professor Brightman dissents on the ground that "the divine purpose is eternal increase of value" and that so long as this increase is effected the divine purpose is not thwarted. But if the divine purpose aims merely at an increase of value and not at an ideal increase of value, it would seem to be ethically defective. Either the divine will exceeds achievement, or there must be divine acquiescence in the present imperfect order. And in the latter case there would seem to be no place left for the resisting "Given." Such a permanent resisting element in the divine nature, even though it leads to an eternal increase of value, seems to me to involve a permanent thwarting of the divine will and purpose.

all resisting forces to his own holy will. Without omnipotence there can be neither perfect unity nor perfect goodness. There might be perfect goodness of intention without omnipotence, but what religion seeks is an absolute objective goodness and this cannot exist even as an object of hope without an omnipotent will. To deny omnipotence to God is to deny to him also moral perfection. Absolute goodness presupposes absolute power.

Then, too, the theory in question seems to establish too sharp a distinction between the nature and will of God. We use these terms to denote different aspects of the divine life, but it is evident, when thought through, that they do not represent distinct elements within the Divine Being. One involves the other. The nature gives content to the will, and the will gives reality and validity to the nature. Neither could exist without the other. It is the union of the two that constitutes the divine personality. Or, rather, the divine personality comes first and nature and will are merely abstractions from it. The divine nature does not exist first, and then the divine will act upon it, as it were, *ab extra*. Rather does the divine nature exist only in and through the activity of the divine will, so that one might in a sense say with Spinoza that God is the cause of himself. To this Professor Brightman would readily assent, but he says nevertheless that "there is within God, in addition to his reason and his active creative will, a passive element which enters into every one of his conscious states," and this passive or given element he assigns to the divine nature. The divine will has apparently nothing to do with its production; and hence a kind of antithesis arises between them. At least we seem to have a portion of the divine nature which is not ratified by the divine will,[32] and this runs counter to the correlative relation of the two to each other just expressed. If the divine will is throughout the ground of the Divine Being, there would seem to be no place in the latter for such an imperfectly assimilated or subdued element as the "Given" of Professor Brightman's theory calls for.

## OMNIPRESENCE

The attribute of omnipresence, as we have already indicated, is a specification under that of omnipotence. It means that space constitutes no barrier or limitation to the divine power. The divine activity extends to all parts of the universe, and is as controlling in one part as in another.

This conception, like that of omnipotence and of monotheism in general, was, of course, a gradual development and in Scripture had a practical root. It grew out of a manifest need, the need of being assured of the divine help and fellowship wherever one might be and the need also of knowing that nothing can be hidden from the divine presence. At first this need in ancient Israel was so circumscribed geographically that it remained content with a national Deity, but with the rise of new international relationships, the broadening of outlook and the deepening of insight it burst its national bounds and in the eighth

[32] To this Professor Brightman would add: "but adequately and progressively utilized and spiritualized."

century B. C. asserted in unequivocal terms faith in the omnipresence of Jehovah. Not in captivity, nor in the depths of the sea, nor the yet greater depths of Sheol, could anyone, according to Amos (9. 1-4), escape his avenging hand. And, on the other hand, his mercy was as far-reaching as his justice. It extended to the ends of the earth. This was the moving theme of Deutero-Isaiah two centuries later; and from that time on the thought of the divine omnipresence was a basal one in Old Testament piety. The most impressive expression of it is found in Psa. 139. 7-12, where we are told that flight to the most distant place in space would not remove us from the divine care, nor would the blackest darkness hide us from the light of the Divine Presence. In the New Testament this conception of God is everywhere assumed. "In him," says Paul, "we live, and move, and have our being;" and again he declares that absolutely nothing can separate us from his love.

But while there is no question about the divine omnipresence from the biblical and practical points of view, how it should be conceived metaphysically is a problem. Some tell us that we ought to accept it as a religious truth and not attempt to form any clear philosophical conception of it. As thinking people, however, we can hardly adopt such a position. Some sort of notion of what is involved in omnipresence we must form. The idea of a "boundless bulk," a divine substance filling all space, is, of course, to be rejected. Such a view would be inconsistent with the divine unity. For whatever occupies space can be divided. Furthermore, a space-filling substance would be present in any particular place only part for part; it would not be *omni*present. To be omnipresent means to be "all there," to be present at every point with one's entire being. It was this idea that the scholastic mystics had in mind when they said that God has his center everywhere and his circumference nowhere. But such a conception manifestly has no meaning except on the personal plane. Only in and through an infinite self-consciousness could omnipresence in this sense of the term be realized. The very idea would be self-contradictory if applied to an impersonal or spatial being.

Infinite self-consciousness alone, however, does not constitute omnipresence. Presence in the world from the metaphysical point of view means something more than consciousness of it. It means immediate action in it. Immediate action extended to all things would, then, be omnipresence; and this is the sense in which the term should be understood. "God is in all things," said Thomas Aquinas,[33] "not, indeed, as part of their essence, nor as an accident, but as an agent is present to that upon which it works." Divine presence means, then, divine agency. This is the form under which we are to conceive the relation of God to the world. Under the Ptolemaic system God was supposed to have his home in heaven, a region beyond the stars, and to intervene in the world beneath, exercising a kind of control over it. To visualize the universe meant, therefore, in a sense to visualize God along with it. He formed a constituent part of it, so that he seemed as real to men as the world itself. But

[33] *Summa Theologica*, Pt. I, Qu. 8, Art. 1.

with the advent of the Copernican astronomy heaven was banished from the spatial universe, and with the establishment of the modern mechanistic and evolutionary world-view no place was left for divine intervention in the temporal order. Consequently, God seemed unnecessary to the world, and the sense of his reality declined among men. This holds true today, and if he is again to be made real in the human consciousness, it can be only by giving him an established place in our modern world-view. Such a place is accorded him, if we conceive of him as the sustaining cause of the world and identify the ultimate cosmic energy with his will.[34] In any case, it is in this sense that we are to understand his omnipresence.

## Eternity

The attribute of eternity is another specification under that of omnipotence. As omnipotence affirms that the divine power is not limited by space, so eternity affirms that it is not limited by time. As God is not a local being, so also he is not a temporal being in the sense of being confined to any particular period of time. In some way he spans all time, just as his activity extends to every point of space. But there are special difficulties connected with the idea of eternity that make it somewhat uncertain how it should be conceived.

First, however, a word should be said about its religious basis. Schleiermacher tells us that the idea of omnipresence "is a more living idea and has a more

[34] For an elaboration of this idea see Th. Steinmann, *Die Frage nach Gott*, pp. 18-77.

general currency," that it has been "more splendidly and more widely honored" in devotional literature, and that the idea of eternity "pervades the religious life to a lesser degree and is marked by a colder tone."[35] But this is by no means universally true. We, no doubt, live largely in the present and hence as a rule think of God in his present relation to us. But that he is omnipresent is an idea that hardly stands so close to our individual experience as does that of his eternity. Eternity stares us all in the face, but not so the distant points in space. The latter we may disregard altogether. And so we find that, while Israel only slowly arrived at the idea of the omnipresence of Jehovah, it seems to have grasped the idea of his eternity from the outset. Nowhere in the Old Testament is it stated or even hinted that Jehovah was not eternal. The close relation of this idea to religious experience may also be judged from the fact that "*eternal* life" became in New Testament times the standing expression for the highest good that religion brings to us. The eternity of God would thus seem to be grounded quite as directly and deeply in human need as his omnipresence.

But how to conceive of the divine eternity is a question that has puzzled thinkers since the days of Plato; and the same may also be said of time. "What is time? If no one asks me, I know: if I wish to explain it to one that asketh, I know not." These words of Augustine[36] have been echoed again and again through the centuries, and reflect the uncertain state

---

[35] *The Christian Faith*, Par. 53.
[36] *Confessions*, Bk. XI, 17.

of mind in which many still find themselves. What makes time a more difficult problem than that of space is that it enters into our inner life as space does not. Space is external to us. Our minds do not occupy space; they transcend it. And hence it is not difficult to think of God as superior to it and as omnipresent through the activity by means of which he grounds it. Whether we think of it as merely the form of external experience or as having some sort of independent reality, it is in any case an effect of the divine activity rather than an obstacle in its path. But with time the situation is different. The temporal relation applies to our inner as well as our outer experience. We cannot divest ourselves of it, and hence it is extremely difficult to conceive of a being that transcends it in the way that we think of God as transcending space.

Eternity may be understood in three different senses. It may denote (1) endless duration, or (2) timelessness, or (3) a combination of both. The first is the common view. According to it eternity differs from time only in extent. "From everlasting to everlasting thou art God." The thought is an impressive one, and not unworthy of the Absolute. But there are serious difficulties inherent in it. One may from this standpoint think of time in two different ways. One may regard it as an all-containing form filled out with the divine duration or as a law of the divine nature. In the former case time would be a kind of existence, external to God, conditioning his existence; indeed, destroying his inner unity. For a being in real time would be subject to division in the same way that a being in real space would. On the other hand, time as a law of the divine nature would make of God a changing and developing being and thus deprive him of that absoluteness without which he could not be the ultimate ground of change. An absolute, self-existent Being may initiate change, but he cannot be subject to the law of change. If he were, he would be a conditioned being, and as such would require for his explanation a higher being upon which he would be dependent. Mere endless duration does not, therefore, fill out the idea of eternity as ascribed to Deity.

Hence it became customary to oppose eternity to time and to interpret it as timelessness. This conception we owe to Plato and Aristotle. It is illustrated in the case of truth as a logical content. Ideas in their meaning are changeless. They remain the same, unaffected by the flow of time, and so are eternal. To them Plato apparently ascribed objective reality. Aristotle rejected his master's teaching at this point, but his own Prime Mover, defined as the thought of thought, was, as Bergson has pointed out,[37] simply Plato's Ideas, "pressed into each other and rolled up into a ball." Consequently, God to him had the unchangeability of ideas and was eternal in the same sense as they. But how such an abstract and timeless Deity could initiate the world of change and how any living content could be introduced into his own being is a problem that has never been solved and that has constituted an insuperable obstacle to religious thought. Eternity in the sense of timelessness be-

[37] *Creative Evolution*, pp. 321f.

comes an unmanageable conception the moment an effort is made to translate it from a logical abstraction into concrete reality. The living God cannot in his consciousness be the complete antithesis of time; he must somehow stand in a direct and appropriative relation to it.

The effort consequently has been made to interpret eternity in such a way as to make it inclusive of or at least consistent with the consciousness of time. Insofar as time involves development, growth, and decay, it is manifestly inconsistent with the divine eternity. There is also a large relative element in our temporal judgments, due to our physical and mental limitations, that cannot be ascribed to God. But that he is aware of our temporal experiences and that he by his creative energy sustains the temporal order is most emphatically affirmed in Christian teaching. It would seem, then, that there must be some sort of succession, some sort of before and after, in his consciousness and in his activity. It has been said that the succession in his thinking is logical, not chronological. But logical succession is not "real" succession, and hence does not properly reproduce the actual succession of the cosmic order. Strict timelessness cannot be attributed to a Creator-God. The moment we ascribe creative activity to the Deity he moves over into the temporal sphere, and his eternity becomes tinged with time. This also is what we should expect in view of the relation of the phenomenal to the real. It is through the phenomenal and the temporal that we arrive at the knowledge of the real and the eternal. Time does not, then, mask eternity. It is, as Dean Inge[38] says, "the symbol and sacrament" of it, and as such reveals it. The eternal consciousness is, therefore, to be regarded as in some sense embracing time while also transcending it.

The time-transcendence of Deity may be conceived in several different ways. The "specious present" of our human experience may be magnified into the "eternal now" of the divine. But such "a maximized consciousness of time," as Pringle-Pattison terms it,[39] does not quite fill out the idea of eternity. By the eternity of God we mean not only that he grasps in the sweep of his consciousness the entire temporal order, but that he sees the informing principle of the whole, that he keeps before his mind's eye the eternal goal of creation. It is in this unifying plan and purpose of the universe that the truly eternal element in the divine consciousness is to be found. The temporal facts appear in it, but only as symbols or vehicles of a larger meaning and value. It was this aspect of the divine eternity that Ritschl singled out as constitutive of it.

Another way of conceiving the eternity of God is to lay stress on the fact that intelligence implies a supertemporal element and that personality constitutes itself one and the same in spite of the multiplicity and change involved in its own consciousness and activity. Knowledge of the temporal flow would be impossible if there were not something in the intellect that stood apart from it and observed it. Then, too, personality knows itself as one and abiding.

---

[38] *The Philosophy of Plotinus*, II, p. 102.
[39] *The Idea of God*, p. 356.

Through the miraculous power of memory it rises above the flux of time and becomes in a sense supertemporal. So it is also with the divine consciousness. God constitutes himself forever the same, and herein lies his eternity. There is no divine stuff that persists through endless time. But above the stream of time, as its author and observer, stands the divine intelligence, forever renewing the consciousness of its own unity and identity. Such a conception of the divine eternity is entirely consistent with that concreteness and richness of experience which the religious nature insists on attributing to God. The eternity or timelessness of God does not exclude a knowledge, on his part, of our temporal experiences, nor does it necessarily exclude the temporal from his own experience. If it did, it would be, as Bishop McConnell[40] rightly insists, a limitation of the divine power.

We need to remember, however, that in the divine omnipotence, omnipresence, and eternity we have, after all, attributes that transcend all human power of understanding, that separate the divine from the human completely, and that set God on high as the "wholly Other," the Absolute, a Being to be worshiped and adored rather than fully understood.

---

[40] *Is God Limited?* Pp. 45-55.

## CHAPTER VIII

## THE PERSONALITY OF GOD

"Personality is the form in which the idea of God is given through Revelation." This statement by Ritschl[1] would perhaps not be seriously questioned by any one who admits the fact of revelation, and even one who denies it would hardly call in question the view that the God of the Christian Scriptures is a personal Deity. But whether and to what extent the personality of God is a distinctively biblical or Christian teaching, Ritschl does not say. It would probably be generally conceded that Christianity has laid more stress upon personality as applied to the Deity than any other religion,[2] and in this sense the doctrine might be said to be a "revealed" truth. But, on the other hand, it may justly be urged that revelation at this point is only the culmination of natural religion. There is, as we have already seen, a theistic bent in all religion. No doubt there have been religions without a personal God and, for that matter, without any God. But these were imperfect and undeveloped forms of religion. In its vital and unperverted form religion tends toward the belief in a per-

[1] *Justification and Reconciliation*, p. 237.

[2] Cf. C. C. J. Webb, *God and Personality*, pp. 61-88. Martineau speaks of the idea of personality as "the noblest gain of Christian thought" (*Types of Ethical Theory*, I, p. xxviii).

sonal God. Indeed, the earliest gods were personal beings. It was this that differentiated them from mere spirits or demons. What made them gods was their possession of personality. Absoluteness and perfect goodness were not ascribed to them, and could not be. Polytheism rules out the idea of absolute power and absolute goodness as inherent in any one being. Only monotheism makes possible the ascription of these attributes to Deity. This is worth noting, that God was personal before he was regarded as absolute or as perfectly good. Such was the case with Jehovah. It was not until after the lapse of centuries that omnipotence and absolute righteousness came to be attributed to him. Personality may, then, be said to be the earliest and most general characteristic of divine beings. "God" meant originally a personal God. It is only in a derived sense that the term has come to be applied to impersonal beings, though it is, of course, true that the line of demarcation between "personal" gods and "impersonal" spirits has not always been sharply drawn in popular thought.

In view of the importance of personality in the conception of God it is somewhat strange that the term did not come into general use, as applied to the Deity, until comparatively recent times. The word "person" figures prominently in the early Trinitarian and Christological controversies and in that connection received its first clear definition as a philosophical and theological term. "A person," said Boethius in a treatise written at the beginning of the sixth century, "is the individual subsistence of a rational nature."[3] In this sense Christ was a person, though possessed of two distinct natures. But the word "person" was not applied to God as a unitary Being; rather, was it said that there are three "persons" in the Godhead. Personality *in* God was thus the teaching of the church, and not the personality *of* God.[4] This continued to be the case till toward the close of the eighteenth century.

Several reasons for this use of the term "person" or "personality" may be noted. First, early Christian thought under the influence of Platonic realism tended to subordinate the individual to the universal. The general notion of being or essence seemed consequently a more ultimate idea than that of personality, which involves more or less individuation or limitation. A personal being may be the highest form in which the ultimate essence manifests itself, but in and of itself the essence, at least in idea, transcends personality by its unity and simplicity. As one and simple God is essence. As personal he is three, and hence in that respect not ultimate and absolute. This logically secondary and subordinate character of personality is suggested by the word *"substantia"* in Boethius' definition. The word is the Latin equivalent of the Greek *hypostasis,* and is rendered more precisely by the English word "subsistence" than by the word "substance." It denotes a distinction within the ultimate substance or reality rather than that reality itself. As the ultimate, simple, and unitary

---

[3] Persona est naturæ rationabilis individua substantia. *Liber de Persona et Duabus Naturis,* chap. III.

[4] Cf. C. C. J. Webb, *ibid.,* p. 65.

essence God is not a person. It is the three hypostatic distinctions within his being that are persons. To this conclusion early Christian thought was led by the metaphysical universalism of Greek philosophy.

Another aspect of Greek thought that contributed to the same end was the philosophical reaction against polytheism. The Greek gods were personal, too personal; and so the profounder and more earnest minds turned away from them and fixed their attention upon divinity in general. The Divine in the abstract and ideal seemed to them nobler and more adorable than the gods of popular belief. A kind of impersonal Divinity thus supplanted the personal divinities in the higher religious faith of the day; and this meant that in any fusion that might be attempted of personalism with impersonalism the primacy in worth as well as in logic would fall to the latter. The result was that the Græco-Roman idea of religious value combined with Platonic realism in preventing the complete personalization of the idea of God in Christian theology. Personality was regarded as an eternal and constituent element in Deity, but Deity itself was not thought of as personal.

A third and perhaps more serious difficulty in the way of a thoroughgoing theological personalism was its apparent bearing on the divinity of Christ and the Holy Spirit. If God himself in the innermost fiber of his being is a Person, the question would naturally arise as to whether the Son and the Holy Spirit may also be regarded as persons. The difficulty here might perhaps be said to be verbal rather than real, but in the early and medieval church it seemed real and significant. To have ascribed personality to the innermost essence of Deity at that time would have been to advocate a unitarian as opposed to a trinitarian type of Christianity. At any rate, it seemed then easier and more natural to protect the divinity of the Son and the Spirit by treating them as eternal persons within a larger divine whole than by regarding them as somehow included within an all-embracing divine personality. In other words, a trinitarian personalism with its impersonal background seemed more congenial to the historic faith than a thoroughgoing unitarian personalism. The latter view seemed to crowd out the unique and essential deity of the Son and the Spirit.

It was such considerations as the foregoing that kept Christian thinkers for upward of seventeen centuries from affirming the personality *of* God. They believed most emphatically in God as a personal and spiritual Being. Not for a moment did they belie the profound personalism of the Christian faith. But they did not look upon personality as so completely constitutive of the divine as to be identical with its essence. For them God was personal, but he was not personal to the very core of his being. Hence it did not seem fitting to speak of him in his unity and totality as a person. But in the latter part of the eighteenth century this reserve in mode of expression disappeared. Theologians now began to refer to God as a person and to lay stress upon his personality. William Paley, for instance, in his *Natural Theology,* published in 1802, had a chapter on "The Personality of the Deity." The argument of this chapter he concluded by saying that "after all the struggles of a reluctant philosophy the necessary resort is to a Deity. The marks of *design* are too strong to be got over. Design must have had a designer. That designer must have been a person. That person is God." Since Paley's day less stress has perhaps been laid upon the idea of design in connection with that of personality, but upon the idea of personality itself as applied to the Deity there has been a steadily increasing emphasis. The expression, the personality *of* God, is now commonly accepted as a proper formulation of a fundamental doctrine of the Christian faith.

For this change a number of reasons may be given. One was the new stress placed on the unity of the world and the consequent unity of its underlying cause, occasioned by the scientific theories with which the names of Copernicus and Newton are particularly connected. This emphasis tended to push into the background the Trinitarian distinctions which had engaged the thought of an earlier day, and to concentrate attention upon the divine unity. Not the personal distinctions within this unity, but the personal character of the unitary agent himself became thus the object of special interest. Then, too, the peril involved in the materialistic monism of the eighteenth century naturally led Christian thinkers to emphasize the personality of the world-ground.

Another factor contributing to the change was the revival of pantheistic modes of thought toward the close of the eighteenth and the beginning of the nineteenth century. The revival, taking its start from Spinoza, was reflected in the great idealistic movement represented by Fichte, Schelling and Hegel, and in the theology and philosophy of Schleiermacher. If these thinkers did not expressly reject the personality of God, they at least took an uncertain and hesitating attitude toward it, and, on the whole, seem to have been inclined toward an impersonal view of the Absolute. This was particularly true of some of the later Hegelian theologians such as Strauss and Biedermann. By way of reaction against this tendency, there consequently arose a conscious need of a new emphasis upon the personality of God. Christian thinkers, who previously had taken the doctrine for granted, now felt it incumbent upon them to make it central in their teaching.

At the same time there grew up, especially under the influence of Leibnitz, Berkeley, Kant, and Lotze, a new insight into the metaphysics of personality, which has given to theistic personalism a new vogue. It now came to be seen that personality does not stand in an adjectival relation to ultimate reality, nor is it a mere hypostatic distinction within it, but it is itself the key to ultimate reality and identical with it. Only in and through the personal can we arrive at an understanding of the Absolute. This insight made possible not only a more complete personalization of the idea of God than had been current in earlier times, but also a more adequate and convincing justification of it. Modern metaphysics thus co-operated with the monism of modern science and with the instinctive Christian reaction against modern materialism and pantheism in establishing and giving currency to the belief in the unitary personality of God.

## The Meaning of Personality

Thus far we have used the words person and personality as though their meaning was self-evident and such it no doubt is in a general way. But before we proceed further we need to define their meaning more precisely.

Personality is known to us directly only in its human form; and here it is always associated with a body. Consequently, we might conclude that corporeality is essential to personality. Indeed, this is the view which men at first instinctively and almost inevitably adopt. In early religious thought it was reflected in the belief in the resurrection of the body and in the worship of images. The gods were supposed to have bodies or something akin to them. But with the rise of ethical monotheism in Israel Deity was detached from material form of every kind; and this conclusion, reached through religious insight, was later ratified by speculative thought. In the case of Deity personality was thus separated from corporeality, and the possibility of a similar separation in the case of human personality was taught by Plato and later by Christian theology. There have been, however, and still are two streams of thought that have resisted this conclusion—the materialistic, or naturalistic, and the pantheistic. Both of these types of philosophy have maintained that personality is indissolubly bound up with a material organism, and that with the disappearance of the latter human personality vanishes. Materialistic naturalism, furthermore, denies the independent existence of spirit altogether, while pantheism denies to the absolute Spirit personality. The fact that God does not have a body as we do is supposed to exclude his being a Person. This linking up of personality with corporeality lies at the basis of one of the most common criticisms directed against theism since the time of Xenophanes. The response to it is found in the fact that the body is not an analytically necessary factor of our mental life. Our inner personal life might conceivably go on apart from its present material organism. Personality as such does not necessarily imply corporeality.

In its essence personality is, then, psychical and spiritual. It is necessary to affirm this because there has been of late a tendency to ascribe personality to God in a nonpsychical sense. A German writer[5] has, for instance, distinguished between "psychical" and "spiritual" personality. The former may be subdivided into "natural" and "cultural" personality, but in principle it remains the same in both forms. Stress is here laid on the unity and identity of the self and on the principle of self-preservation. These are the fundamental factors constitutive of psychical personality. It is personality in this sense of the term that is attributed to the gods on the polytheistic plane. They are simply magnified men, and the method employed in ascribing existence to them is the "mythological." It is the unbridled fancy that

[5] Th. Steinmann, *Die Frage nach Gott*, pp. 78-142.

gives to them their being. To the one God personality in its "psychical" sense is not, then, to be ascribed.

Spiritual personality, on the other hand, is characterized by devotion to social and ideal ends. Not self-preservation, but the fulfillment of tasks and duties is its ruling aim. Struggle and achievement are thus inherent in the very idea of spiritual personality. To be a person in this sense means to be in the process of becoming one. At least this is true of men. Human personality is incomplete and always remains such, an ideal to be attained; and so the poet speaks of

> ". . . . progress, man's distinctive mark alone,
> Not God's, and not the beasts': God is, they are,
> Man partly is and wholly hopes to be."

This quotation from Browning[6] answers in advance the question we were about to ask as to whether spiritual personality in its human form may be ascribed to God; and the answer is a negative one. God is not a struggling and developing Being; he is "complete." It is consequently, according to Steinmann, only symbolically that personality is to be affirmed of him. He is personal in the sense that he stands in a "causal" relation to our higher spiritual life. By virtue of this relationship he may himself be said to be spiritual. But his spirituality does not consist in a flexible adjustment on his part to our changing needs. It is, rather, to be found in the firmness and faithfulness with which he adheres to his saving purpose, in the unchangeable steadiness of his holy will. What it

[6] *A Death in the Desert.*

implies beyond that we cannot say. To attempt to define the divine personality more precisely is to forsake the firm ground of religious experience and conviction and fall back upon an illusory "knowledge" derived from human tradition and human desire.

A somewhat similar, though more extreme view, was expounded a few years ago in a book that had considerable vogue in America.[7] In it we were warned against "psychologizing the consciousness of God." Just what "consciousness" could possibly mean if every psychical element were eliminated from it, it would be difficult to say. We were told that "self-consciousness" and "the power to know" do not hold true of God in any sense which these words bear in our human experience and speech." From this the only conclusion would seem to be that as applied to the Deity they have no intelligible meaning whatsoever. And if so, one would naturally suppose that the only consistent thing would be to deny personality to him. But this, the author, who was a teacher of theology, did not have the hardihood to do. So he told us that his conception of the personality of God did not rest on a theory of the divine consciousness, but on the character of the ends disclosed in the universe. "Ends," however, are as meaningless without consciousness as "consciousness" is without the psychical. What we call ends in nature would be simply effects, results, without a purposing intelligence. To talk about "ends" and "consciousness" and "personality" as though they did not imply such psychological elements as willing and knowing is merely to befog

[7] *The Idea of God*, by C. A. Beckwith.

oneself and one's readers. Personality as applied to God must mean more or less of what we understand by the term when applied to ourselves, or it is a misleading symbol.

But while personality must be construed in psychological terms, it does not necessarily imply limitations and imperfections such as those incident to the growth and development of the human spirit. If it did, we should either have to transform God into a finite and developing being or deny personality to him. Neither of these alternatives is necessary. The objections to the first we considered in the preceding chapter, and a little later we shall deal more fully with the question as to whether the idea of absoluteness excludes that of personality. Here we wish simply to point out that the essential psychical elements in personality do not in and of themselves involve the kind of finitude to which we have just referred. These elements, as commonly given, are knowing, willing and feeling; or, if we wish to combine the last two, we may designate them as self-consciousness, self-knowledge, or the power to know, on the one hand, and self-control or self-direction, on the other, "control" and "direction" containing an implicit reference to feeling. In none of these is there any implication of dependent limitation. Indeed, the lack of any of these powers, the power to know or to will or to feel, would itself be a limitation. We are ourselves dependent beings and in us these powers necessarily manifest themselves in an imperfect and limited way, but there is no reason why they should not be possessed by an absolute Being and in him manifest themselves in a perfect form. The particular methods by which we acquire self-knowledge and self-control are not essential to such knowledge and control in and of themselves. They may quite conceivably exist as eternal possessions of an Infinite Spirit. And wherever we find them in any being, we have a person. Personality in its essence means "self-hood, self-knowledge and self-direction,"[8] and in these respects it may be either finite or infinite.

Yet another point relative to the meaning of personality remains to be noted. This has to do with the idea of selfhood and the relation of selves to each other. Some lay stress upon the exclusiveness and isolation of the self. "Personality," said D. F. Strauss,[9] "is that selfhood which shuts itself up against everything else, excluding it thereby from itself." In a passage which he says he has since had occasion to regret putting in that form, Pringle-Pattison declared that "each self is a unique existence, which is perfectly impervious . . . to other selves—impervious in a fashion of which the impenetrability of matter is a faint analogue. . . . The self is in truth the very apex of separation and differentiation. . . . Though the self is in knowledge a principle of unification, it is in existence or metaphysically a principle of isolation."[10] In this view there is no doubt a large element of truth, but it is only a half-truth. Personality is also social. It implies reciprocal intercourse with other persons. A completely

---

[8] B. P. Bowne, *Theism*, p. 162.

[9] *Die Christliche Glaubenslehre*, I, p. 504.

[10] *Hegelianism and Personality*, 1887, pp. 216f.

isolated person would not be a person in the full sense of the term. For this reason the god of Aristotle does not measure up to what we mean by a "personal God." He is a self-conscious individuality, but his activity is directed wholly upon himself, upon his own thinking. He does not have that forth-going energy which we associate with self-control or self-direction and which is suggested by the idea of a personal will. He is a shining ideal which attracts the world, and in this sense the world loves him, but he does not love the world. He stands aloof from it. There is no reciprocal intercourse between him and men. He lacks that warmth and intimacy which we connect with personal relationships, and hence is not himself truly personal. What we especially have in mind when from the religious point of view we speak of the personality of God, is the thought of fellowship with him. He is a Being who knows us and loves us and whom we can trust. It is because the personality of God implies all this that we regard it as so vital to religion.

In addition, then, to self-knowledge and self-control we need to emphasize in personality the thought of communion with others. This communion is ethical, not metaphysical. It presupposes selfhood and the general psychical functions of knowing, willing, and feeling; without these there could be no communion. But there must also be something more, if there is to be true communion. There must be mutual trust and mutual goodwill. In the case of God and man these feelings naturally take a different form from what they do in the relation of equals to each other, but in principle they are the same. They rest on an ethical basis. It is the appropriate ethical attitude of two or more persons to each other that alone makes true fellowship possible; and this attitude is one of mutual regard based on a mutual recognition of worth. Hence if fellowship or reciprocal intercourse is essential to a complete personality, we must regard worth or dignity as a constituent element in it. In other words, personality must be viewed as an end in itself.

Summing up, we may say that personality does not necessarily imply either corporeality or dependent limitation. In its essence it is selfhood, self-knowledge and self-control; or, more concretely, a person is one who thinks and feels and wills. Such a being by his very nature seeks communion with others. He does so because only in this way can his own true self and his own intrinsic worth, and the like self and worth of others, come to full expression and realization.

## Personality and the Absolute

In the preceding paragraph and elsewhere we have already pointed out that dependent limitation is not a necessary implication of personality. A being might be personal, and yet might conceivably be free from all dependent limitation, or, in other words, be absolute. Between absoluteness and the essence of personality there is no inconsistency. This, we believe, has been made reasonably clear. But the contrary view has so frequently been maintained that the subject calls for more extended discussion.

To some extent the controversy at this point has

been merely one about words. It has been argued that "personality" naturally and almost inevitably suggests human limitation of some kind and that to apply it to Deity is a piece of anthropomorphism that ought to be avoided. The Absolute is spirit and as such embraces all that is of value in personality, but it is not itself personal; it is "superpersonal." If this means that Deity represents a higher type of consciousness and will than that represented by human personality, it simply states what has not only been conceded, but maintained by all theistic personalists. The "name *person,*" said Thomas Aquinas, "is fittingly applied to God; not, however, as it is applied to creatures, but in a more excellent way (*via eminentiae*)." Human personality is, then, a symbol rather than a mirror of the inner life of God. What that life is we cannot fully understand. It transcends us. But if it is a life of free intelligence, it does not matter whether we have any further understanding of it or not, nor does it matter whether we call it personal or not. So long as free intelligence of any kind whatsoever is ascribed to the Absolute, the difference between the personalist and the "superpersonalist" is only one of words.

But in the dispute over the word "person" and its applicability to the Absolute something far more significant is usually at stake than the mere meaning of the term. The real point at issue is as to whether the Absolute is to be thought of as a self-conscious and self-directing Being. Those who deny personality to him or it usually mean that he is not a Being to whom intelligence and freedom may be ascribed. He is pure will without intellect, as Schopenhauer taught, or unconscious intelligence, as Hartmann held, or blind force, as has often been maintained. It is this view of the world-ground as unintelligent that alone gives significance to the contention that personality is inconsistent with absoluteness. Personality does not stand opposed to a higher type of divine intelligence, but to nonintelligence. To deny personality to the Absolute or world-ground means that it is not intelligent and free. The real question consequently is as to whether conscious and free intelligence is consistent with the idea of absoluteness.

In dealing with this question it is important that we distinguish the different senses in which the word "absolute" is used. We noted three in the preceding chapter: the agnostic, the logical and the causal. In its agnostic sense the absolute means the unrelated, and since nothing can be known except in its relations it follows that an absolute Being must be unknowable. Personality cannot be affirmed of it nor can anything else. But such a Being, as we have previously said, is not only unknowable, but also unaffirmable. It serves no purpose in the universe, and may be dismissed as a mere shadow of the mind's own throwing. The only rational ground for affirming an Absolute is that its existence helps us to explain the world of appearance, but if it is itself entirely unknowable, it manifestly cannot serve as a principle of explanation. A thoroughgoing agnosticism contradicts itself.

The "logical" Absolute is arrived at by the subordination of the individual to the universal. The assumption is that the highest universal is the ultimate reality. Such a universal transcends all finite modes of being and yet embraces them all. It may take the form of the all-inclusive *unity* of Neoplatonism, or the all-inclusive *substance* of Spinoza, or the all-inclusive *spirit* of Hegel. In any case it is a transcendent reality which cannot be identified with any concrete mode of being. It expresses itself in and through the finite, but nothing finite expresses its essential nature. We cannot, therefore, attribute consciousness or personality to it. For that would be to limit it to one mode of being, and to do so would be to destroy its universality and its absoluteness. Personality, it is urged, is only one of many forms of existence, and not only that, it is a form of existence which bears in itself the stamp of finitude. We have already quoted Strauss as saying that "personality is that selfhood which shuts itself up against everything else, which it thereby excludes from itself." To this he added that "the Absolute, on the other hand, is the comprehensive, the unlimited, which excludes nothing from itself but just the exclusivity which lies in the conception of personality."[11]

Again, it is argued that there is a necessary duality in personality which implies its finitude. "Can an infinite reason and an infinite will," asked Schleiermacher in a letter to Jacobi, "really be anything more than empty words, when reason and will, by differing from each other, also necessarily limit each other? And if you attempt to annul the distinction between reason and will, is not the conception of personality

[11] *Die Christliche Glaubenslehre*, I, p. 504.

destroyed by the very attempt?"[12] The assumption here is that ultimate reality lies beyond all differences. It is pure unity or pure identity.

Another and more common method of trying to prove the necessary finitude of personality is to say that consciousness implies a distinction between subject and object or between ego and non-ego, and hence is impossible to an absolute Being who embraces all reality. Such a Being can have no object, for there is nothing external to itself, nor can there be a non-ego standing apart from it. It cannot, therefore, be a conscious Being. But this line of argument, as has often been pointed out, confuses a logical or psychological form with an ontological otherness.[13] The Absolute might make himself his own object; and being absolute there would, of course, be no need of a non-ego to condition the development of his consciousness, as is the case with us.

The fundamental objection, however, to the foregoing attempts to establish an antithesis between personality and absoluteness is the abstract way in which they conceive of the Absolute. For them the Absolute is a logical universal. Its existence is arrived at by a process of logical subordination. The individual is subordinated to the class to which it belongs, and this class to the class above it, until finally the ultimate universal is reached which embraces all finite beings. Throughout the process the fiction is maintained of supposing that the broader

---

[12] *The Life of Schleiermacher*, as unfolded in his autobiography and letters. Translated by Frederica Rowan. Vol. II, p. 283.

[13] Cf. B. P. Bowne, *Metaphysics* (Rev. ed.), p. 117; *Theism*, pp. 164f.

the universal the greater the depth and richness of its being. But this is the reverse of the truth. Only the individual is real. The universal is a concept, and the more inclusive it is the more barren it is of content. The ultimate universal is thus the emptiest of all terms; and this the Absolute becomes when it is arrived at by a process of logical subordination and is identified with universal being. When conceived of as pure unity or pure substance or pure spirit it is a mere abstraction. It has no analogue in concrete reality. It transcends all forms of finite being and is the all-embracing and indefinable element common to them all. As such it is necessarily nonpersonal, but it is also devoid of any definite character whatsoever, and may be set aside as a fiction of conceptual thought.

If the idea of a metaphysical Absolute is to be retained, it should be in the causal sense of the term; and in this sense there is no inconsistency between it and the idea of personality. From the causal point of view the Absolute is the independent ground or cause of the universe. It is dependent upon nothing outside of itself; but it is not completely unrelated and unlimited. It stands in relation to the world and is to some extent limited by it. But the limitation is one that is self-imposed. The Absolute is not itself the All nor is it the Unknowable. Its causal relation to the world makes it to some degree knowable, and its creative activity makes it possible for us to distinguish between it and its work. Everything is dependent upon it for its existence; and it is this that constitutes its absoluteness. But absoluteness thus understood does not exclude self-limitation. Indeed, not to have this power would itself be a limitation. And the same is to be said of the power to know and the power of self-control. These powers, which are the essential constituents of personality, are also essential to the Absolute, if he be regarded as absolute in power. The power to know is certainly not a limitation, nor is the power of self-control. The only limitation connected with them is to be found in the degree in which they are possessed by finite beings. We have these powers only to a limited extent; and hence it is proper to say that we represent personality only in an imperfect form. If we had perfect knowledge and perfect self-control, we would be more truly personal than we now are.

The common judgment must, then, be reversed. Instead of saying that personality is inconsistent with absoluteness, we must say, rather, that perfect personality is possible only in the Absolute. The contrary view rests upon a mistaken conception of what metaphysical absoluteness is.[14]

## Religious and Philosophical Value

The real ground, however, for holding to the personality of God must be found, not in its consistency with the idea of absoluteness, but in its positive religious and philosophical value. These values have already been incidentally noted, but it may be well at this point to summarize them.

There are two fundamental religious values. One

[14] Cf. H. Lotze, *Microcosmus*, II, pp. 685ff.; B. P. Bowne, *Theism*, pp. 167f.

is fellowship with God, the other is trust in his goodness; and both of these imply his personality. No fellowship is possible without freedom and intelligence. There may be interactions between impersonal beings, both organic and inorganic. But true communion can exist only between beings who know each other and take an emotional and volitional attitude toward each other. If God were pure intellect, as Aristotle conceived him to be, no communion with him would be possible. And the same would be true of him if he were made on the Epicurean model and sat apart

> "Where never falls the least white star of snow,
> Where never lowest sound of thunder rolls,
> Nor sigh of human sorrow mounts to mar
> His sacred, everlasting calm."

Fellowship requires something more than thought, something more than power to know; it requires an outgoing of feeling and will. This it is that underlies that moving word of Scripture, the "*living*" God. Life, as applied to God, does not mean something less than intelligence; it means something more. It means that in God there are a heart and will, responsive to human need, an attitude of mind that both evokes and answers prayer. This is perhaps the aspect of personality that is most characteristic of it. Personality stresses will even more emphatically than it does intelligence. And here it is that we have the difference between intellectualism and personalism. The former, representing the classical tradition, puts the stress on the theoretical reason; the latter, reflecting biblical teaching, lays the stress on the practical reason. It is the moral and emotional nature that forms the basis of that living fellowship with God which constitutes the essence of true religion.

Even on the impersonal plane religion seeks union with the Divine Being. But there is a vast difference between a mystical, metaphysical union with an impersonal Being and the kind of union with the Divine taught us in Scripture. Here we have to do not with the union of absorption, but with a union that grows out of reciprocal intercourse, a union of heart and will and intellect; and such a union is possible only between personal beings. Only the personality of God makes possible the union of communion with him.

His personality is also the presupposition of his goodness. There can be no goodness in the ethical sense of the term without freedom and intelligence. In other words, only a personal being can be good. Things and subpersonal beings may be useful, but they are not morally good. Goodness is an attribute of personality and apart from it is a mere abstraction. All those religious values consequently that are bound up with the belief in the divine righteousness and love are dependent for their very being on a personalistic view of the world. Providence with all that it implies would be meaningless without a personal God, and so would prayer. The very heart of our prophetic and Christian religion would vanish without him. It is, then, no erring instinct and no theological aberration that has led to the insistence on the personality of God which has been characteristic of Christian thought. The basic values of Christian experience are wrapped up in it.

Another religious value that attaches to the personalistic conception of Deity is the bearing that it has on our conception of man. In emphasizing the personality of God we affirm, not the likeness of God to man, but, rather, the likeness of man to God. We declare that man is made in the image of God, and in so doing we affirm not only the high dignity of man, but also the love of God. For the divine love would not be the highest form of love if it did not lead God to communicate his own life and his own likeness to his creatures.[15] The personality of God means, then, that he has imparted his own self to men and has thus exhibited his love to us. So his personality is not only a metaphysical presupposition of his love, it is itself an affirmation of our kinship to him and his loving relation to us.

The *philosophical* value of the idea of personality as applied to God has been slower in coming to recognition. The word "person" as used in the doctrine of the Trinity was a source of embarrassment to reason rather than otherwise. Augustine felt keenly its inadequacy, and said that the answer "three persons" was given to the inquirer "not that it might be spoken, but that it might not be left unspoken."[16] Later, under the influence of Albertus Magnus and Thomas Aquinas, the doctrine of the Trinity was lifted above the plane of rational justification alto-

---

[15] Cf. H. H. Wendt, *System der Christlichen Lehre*, p. 102.

[16] *On the Trinity*, Bk. V, Chap. IX. English translation by A. W. Haddan, p. 156.

gether and based exclusively on the authority of revelation. But with the advent of the modern era and the new direction given to philosophy by Descartes a new importance came to be attached to the idea of personality and eventually it came to be applied to the entire Godhead.

Two considerations in particular have tended to give to the idea added metaphysical significance. One is the concrete character of personality, the fact that it is given in experience. Every attempt to transcend personality leads to some form of abstractionism or agnosticism. A type of reality that is not revealed to us in experience is either entirely incapable of definition or is constituted by some general idea and is devoid of concrete content. It is in experience that all true reality is revealed. What reality might be apart from experience we cannot say. If there is a superempirical principle or reality in the objective world, it must be construed in personal terms or handed over to complete nescience, for it is in self-experience, and there only, that we have insight into the true inwardness of things.[17] We know the self as we know nothing else. This truth Augustine and Descartes made irrefutably clear, and in so doing not only established a permanent bulwark against thoroughgoing skepticism, but laid the foundation of a sound empirical metaphysics. In personality we have the only empirical key to ultimate reality; and that as a metaphysical principle it has a decided advan-

---

[17] For an excellent statement of this position in its relation to current philosophical theories see an article by Professor G. A. Wilson on "The Search for the Concrete" in the *Monist*, 1929, pp. 80-98.

tage over the abstract essences of all types of impersonal philosophy has been made increasingly clear by the course of modern thought.

The decided advantage consists not only in the fact that personality is a concrete and empirical reality, but also in the further fact that it contains in itself a solution of the fundamental problems of metaphysics such as no impersonal principle or essence does or can. This is the second consideration above referred to, that has militated to the advantage of personalism. Kant stated the underlying principle as follows: "One may therefore say of the thinking I (the soul), which represents itself as substance, simple, numerically identical in all time, and as the correlative of all existence, from which, in fact, all other existence must be concluded, that it *does not know itself through the categories,* but knows the *categories* only, and through them all objects, in the absolute unity of apperception, *that is, through itself.*"[18] Bowne put it more simply by saying that the categories do not explain intelligence, but are explained by it. If we wish to know what the categories of unity, identity and causality mean, we must go to our experience of free intelligence and find the answer there. If we wish to know how unity can be harmonized with plurality, and identity with change, we must seek the solution not in some transcendental and unknowable *xyz,* but in our own conscious and free agency. We know ourselves one and yet we do many things. We are constantly changing and yet we

[18] *The Critique of the Pure Reason,* 1st ed., p. 402; Max Müller's translation, p. 324.

constitute ourselves one and the same with our past selves. How this is possible, we do not know. But the fact is sun-clear, and it is inherent in personality itself. Here, then, in our free intelligence, and there alone, we have the solution of the age-old problems of metaphysics. The solution is empirical, not theoretical, but that makes it none the less valuable.

Philosophical insight has thus combined with religious appreciation to make personality an all-important category in the conception of Deity. Personality, however, is itself complex. It implies unity, identity, self-consciousness and self-control: four attributes, the last three of which, when applied to the Supreme Person, may perhaps better be designated as immutability, omniscience, and freedom. These three attributes together with that of the divine unity we shall, therefore, consider here in connection with the personality of God, just as we considered his omnipotence, omnipresence, and eternity under the head of his absoluteness.

## Unity

The unity of God has a double meaning. It means that he is indivisible and that he is only. Both of these ideas were developed in the Old Testament and became permanent elements in prophetic and Christian theism.[19] The indivisibility of God was emphasized by way of contrast with the polybaalism and polyyahwism current in ancient Israel, and the onliness of God was emphasized by way of contrast with ancient polytheism in general. Both ideas received

[19] See my *Religious Teaching of the Old Testament*, pp. 68-92.

their classical expression in the famous saying of Deut. 6. 4, "Hear, O Israel: The Lord our God is one Lord." Over against the multiplicity of Baals it was here affirmed that there is but one Lord or Jehovah, and over against the many gods of heathenism it was affirmed that there is but one God. Jehovah was here declared to be, not a vague pantheistic sort of being that differentiated himself or itself into a number of local Jehovahs, but a unitary and indivisible being, a *Person* in essentially the modern sense of the term. He was also here declared to be the sole Deity. The latter idea was a later development than the former, but it was bound up with and organically related to it. Jehovah in his universality remained as unitary and individual a being as he was when regarded as merely the God of Israel. This rigid unity of the Old Testament God tended to keep him on a high moral plane. It saved him from the degrading effects of sexual differentiation and from the almost equally degrading effects of differentiation into a number of local deities. It linked him up with the higher interests of the nation as a whole and with the universal interests of mankind. At the same time it established a bond of union with the intellectual demand for a fundamental monism and thus prepared the way for an alliance with Greek philosophy. It was the common need of a basal unity that brought Hebrew and Greek thought together. And to this day the need of such a unity is equally imperative in the field of religion and of philosophy.

But what we are here concerned with is not the history and the grounds of the belief in the divine unity, but the way in which this unity is to be conceived. A homogeneous substance or force pervading all space and extending through all time would perhaps be the form under which spontaneous thought would at first be inclined to think of the unitary ground of the world. But since unity excludes divisibility, this view is manifestly untenable. For both space and time are infinitely divisible. No matter how homogeneous a thing might be, it could have no unity if it were in metaphysical space or time; only a being that transcends space and time can be a true unit. This holds for both the finite and the infinite. The divine unity cannot, then, be found in any space-filling and permanently enduring substance or force. Such a substance or force would be divisible into an infinite number of parts each external to the other, and these parts would again be infinitely divisible, so that not only all unity, but all abiding reality would be dissolved away.

If unity is to be ascribed to the world-ground, it must be lifted to a superspatial and supertemporal level. This has been generally recognized by speculative thinkers. But how it is to be done, has not been always clear. A common method has been to identify the world-ground with the highest universal, with bare being, and then define its nature as pure simplicity. As such it transcends all the plurality and all the differences of finite existence. It is not mind, nor is it matter. It is something above them both. But what it is, aside from the fact that it is one and simple, we cannot say. We can, according to Schleiermacher, form no "real conception" of it.

It lies beyond reason and will, and beyond nature and consciousness. So far as our articulate experience is concerned, it is a mere blank. We can assimilate it to nothing that we know; and as a concept it serves no function in a rational system, for an absolutely simple being cannot differentiate itself. Nothing can be deduced from it. It can explain nothing. In logic there is no way of passing from the simple to the complex or from bare unity to plurality; and if God be thought of as a unitary being in this sense of the term, he could not account for the world as we know it. He would be reduced to "a rigid and lifeless stare."

It is only on the plane of free intelligence that true unity can be realized, and it is from this standpoint alone that the divine unity can be properly construed. In the case of an intelligent agent unity does not consist in any simplicity of being or of substance, but in consciousness itself, in the ability of the agent to originate activity, to posit plurality, and to maintain his own unity and identity over against the changing many. How this is possible we do not know, but it is a fact of our own experience; and what holds true of us in a limited degree we are warranted in ascribing to God in an unlimited degree. In any case this is the only intelligible and self-consistent form under which the divine unity can be conceived. God knows himself as one over against the changing world which he posits and maintains through his own free creative activity.

### Immutability

As unity denies divisibility, so immutability denies change. But change may be of various kinds. It may be either metaphysical or ethical, and it may be due either to internal or external causes. It is usually the latter one has in mind in thinking of change. Hence to ascribe immutability to Deity is often equivalent to asserting his independence and eternity. There is no external being or beings upon which he is dependent and which have the power to produce changes in him. The fact that he is unchangeable means, then, that he is self-existent and eternal. He is not a dependent and perishing being as are the things of the world. "They shall be changed; but thou art the same" (Psa. 102. 26f.). The sameness, however, does not simply look outward, and contrast the eternity of God with the transitoriness of the world. It also looks inward and affirms an identity of being within God himself. It is this that in the stricter sense of the term constitutes his metaphysical immutability. Neither internal nor external causes alter the inner essence of his being. "I, the Lord, change not" (Mal. 3. 6).

In Scripture it is chiefly the ethical unchangeability of God that is affirmed, though his metaphysical immutability in the twofold sense just indicated is everywhere assumed. This holds true of the words just quoted from Malachi, and also of the characterization of God in James 1. 17 as "the Father of lights, with whom can be no variation, neither shadow that is cast by turning." The various passages that deny that God repents (for example, Num. 23. 19) and that declare that his counsel stands forever (for example, Psa. 33. 11; 19. 21; Isa. 46. 10) are also to be so construed. This stress on the ethical constancy of God is in keeping with the practical nature of biblical teaching, and has to do with his "goodness," which is the subject of the next chapter.

We are here more particularly concerned with the way in which the metaphysical immutability of God should be conceived. As unity has been conceived as pure simplicity, so immutability has been conceived as rigid sameness of being. The fundamental difficulty in the two cases is the same. Just as there is no way of passing from simplicity to complexity or from unity to plurality, so there is no way of passing from identity to change or from immutability to motion. If God be thought of as changeless substance, there would be no way of accounting for the advancing cosmic movement. Changes in the world must be due to changes in its underlying cause. An unchanging cause could produce only an unchanging effect. And the changelessness of such a cause and such an effect would lie not in any rigid monotony of being, but, rather, in the constancy of the law that governed its activity or its states. A law, however, no matter how constant it may be, has no ontological existence. For a truly real and immutable principle we must, then, go beyond the idea of an unchanging substance and that of a constant law. We must ascend to the personal plane and find it in the unique power of self-consciousness by means of which the mind differentiates itself from its states and activities and constitutes itself one and the same. It is in this marvelous capacity of self-identity, characteristic of free intelligence, that we have the key, and only key, to the divine immutability. Such self-identity is entirely compatible with change. Indeed, it is only through changing activity that it is realized. Immutability is thus completely dissociated from immobility.

### Omniscience

Personality is characterized by unity, self-identity, and the power to know. The last-named in the case of Deity is commonly supposed to take the form of omniscience. That the power to know is not incompatible with absoluteness, has already been made clear. Rather would the lack of this power be a limitation. But whether omniscience implies a knowledge of everything without any exception whatsoever is a question that has been much debated.

So far as faith itself is concerned, all that it requires is that God know all that he needs to know as moral Governor of the universe. He needs to know the hearts of all his free creatures that he may judge them aright. He needs to know all the forces of the universe, all his created beings good and evil, so that he may guide them toward the realization of his ultimate goal and so that he may direct the affairs of the world in such a way that men may place implicit confidence in him. He needs to know all that is involved in the task of caring for his creatures and in that of redeeming those who place their trust in him. Nothing can, therefore, be hidden from him which pertains to the welfare of his children. Such are the motives that lie back of the scriptural assertions relative to the range of the divine knowledge. "The very hairs of your head are all numbered" (Matt. 10. 30). "All things are naked and laid open before the eyes of him with whom we have to do" (Heb. 4. 13). "The eyes of the Lord are in every place, keeping watch upon the evil and the good" (Prov. 15. 3). "Sheol and Abaddon are before the Lord: How much more then the hearts of the children of men!" (Prov. 15. 11). "O Lord, thou hast searched me and known me. Thou knowest my downsitting and mine uprising, thou understandest my thought afar off" (Psa. 139. 1-2). "Great is our Lord, and mighty in power; his understanding is infinite" (Psa. 147. 5). "The darkness and the light are both alike" to him (Psa. 139. 11). He declareth "the end from the beginning, and from ancient times things that are not yet done" (Isa. 46. 10). "O the depth of the riches both of the wisdom and the knowledge of God!" (Rom. 11. 33.)

In all these passages the divine knowledge is viewed from the standpoint of its relation to the moral government of the world and to human redemption. It is from this point of view alone that faith is interested in the divine omniscience. But while it is only a practical omniscience that faith affirms, the difficulties involved in conceiving it are virtually the same as those involved in absolute omniscience. They have to do chiefly with two points: the divine knowledge of our finite experiences and the divine foreknowledge of free acts.

Faith would seem to require that God have a direct knowledge of our physical pain and suffering and other experiences that we cannot ascribe to him as an infinite and purely spiritual Being. We understand these experiences in others, because we ourselves have had them. But apart from our own experience of them, we could not know them. The contents of the sense of sight would be entirely unknowable to us if we ourselves did not have organs of vision. And the same holds true of sense-experience in general. How, then, can we ascribe a knowledge of such experiences to God? The only way would seem to be to attribute to him modes of knowing that we cannot comprehend. To say that our experiences are also his and that he consequently knows them, would be to fall into a pantheistic confusion of the divine with the human that would befuddle rather than clarify thought. On the other hand, to deny to God a knowledge of our finite experiences and to say with Spinoza[20] that there is about as much correspondence between divine and human knowledge as there is between the constellation *Dog* and the barking animal by that name would be to establish a gulf between the human and the divine that would make God of very little religious value. Faith requires a Divine Being who is touched with a feeling of our infirmities; and that we do not understand how he comes to know these infirmities is no reason for rejecting the belief that he has such knowledge.

The divine foreknowledge of free acts does not stand so vitally related to faith as does the divine knowledge of our finite experiences. Foreknowledge of an evil act, for instance, would not be of much value unless it should lead to an effort to prevent it, and in that case it would not be foreknowledge. To deny to God foreknowledge of free acts, would not

[20] *Ethics*, I, p. 17, Scholium.

necessarily be inconsistent with his omniscience. For as omnipotence does not imply the power to do the nondoable, so omniscience does not imply the power to know the unknowable. If foreknowledge of free acts is a self-contradictory conception, there is no reason why such knowledge should be ascribed to God. But that it is a contradiction cannot be proved. All that can be shown is that we do not know how such foreknowledge is possible. We can know the future only on the basis of its connection with the present. But a free act is a totally new beginning, and as such is not represented by anything before it occurs. Hence we have no way of foreknowing it. But that it is absolutely incapable of being foreknown would be an unwarranted assertion. God may have a way we do not understand of foreknowing free acts just as we believe he has a way of knowing our inner experiences although he has not experienced them.

Some Calvinistic writers have sought to relieve the difficulty connected with the divine foreknowledge by maintaining that "an act may be certain as to its occurrence and yet free as to the mode of its occurrence."[21] In other words, contingency is not essential to free agency. An act may be rendered certain by a divine decree and yet may be voluntarily wrought by a free agent. But how God could render an act certain without necessitating it is as much of a metaphysical mystery, indeed, a greater one than that involved in the foreknowledge of free acts. If Calvin is right in saying that God "foresees future events

[21] Charles Hodge, *Systematic Theology*, I, p. 401.

only in consequence of his decree that they should happen,"[22] it would seem that the decree must carry with it a causal efficiency that excludes free agency in their production. Objective certainty cannot, so far as we can see, be combined with true freedom.

Still, in spite of the difficulties connected with the divine foreknowledge of free acts, it has been customary to affirm it. But the reasons for the affirmation are not altogether convincing. The one on which chief reliance was placed in the past was that drawn from the predictive element in Scripture. But this argument has been greatly weakened, if not completely undermined, by biblical criticism. There is hardly a specific prediction in the Bible that requires divine foreknowledge of free acts for its explanation. Another consideration urged in favor of such foreknowledge is the greater security it gives the believer. If God foreknows everything, he will never be taken by surprise, not even by the acts of evil men. Hence we may trust him all the more securely. But while there may be some religious value in this line of thought, the margin within which human freedom moves is so limited that, even though its acts cannot be positively foreknown, to infinite insight it is hardly possible that they should contain much in the way of surprise, and certainly to one possessed of infinite resources of wisdom and power their unexpectedness would constitute no serious practical problem nor would there be in it any valid ground for appreciably lessening one's confidence in him.

---

[22] *Institutes*, Bk. III, Chap. 23, Par. 6; English translation, Vol. II, pp. 169f.

A somewhat more substantial consideration in support of divine foreknowledge is found in the impressiveness of the conception and in the relativity of time. That all reality, future as well as present and past, is open to the divine gaze, that time is relative to the knowing mind, that it offers no barrier to the divine knowledge, but is itself dependent for its existence upon the divine consciousness and will—this is a view that seems more unified and more acceptable to faith than one that withdraws a considerable tract of the future from the range of the divine vision. But how a knowledge of the contingent future is possible, we cannot say, no matter whether we hold to the ideality or reality of time. All that we can say is that God may have an intuitive grasp of the future that transcends our human ways of knowing. Future, past, and present may for him constitute a kind of "eternal now"; but, if he thus knows the future, he must nevertheless know it as future and not as present.

### Freedom

In addition to unity, self-identity, and the power to know, personality is characterized by freedom or self-determination. Freedom is sometimes identified with spontaneity, and in this sense it would necessarily be an attribute of the Absolute insofar as it is active, for the Absolute by its very nature is independent and acts from within itself. But personal freedom means something more than this. It means the power of contrary choice, it means conscious and purposive action. It means that God stands in no necessary relation to the present world, that its creation was a voluntary act, that he might have created some other kind of a world in its stead. Here it is that we have the dividing line between theism and pantheism. According to pantheism the world is a part of God or a necessary consequence of his nature. According to theism God is a free Being and might have willed not to create such a world as this. Freedom in this sense is involved in the idea of the divine personality.

A difficulty, however, arises when we attempt to conceive the relation of the divine will to the divine omniscience. Does not omniscience in a perfect being exclude the power of contrary choice? Would not such a being be determined in his every act by his knowledge of the outcome, since his character would require him to choose the line of action which would yield the greatest good? This difficulty, says John Miley,[23] "is far deeper than the usual question of consistency between foreknowledge and freedom, which concerns only the relation of foreknowledge in God to freedom in man, while the question in hand concerns the consistency of omniscience and freedom, both being in God himself."

In meeting this difficulty it should be noted that omniscience is not a passive mirroring of an objective reality, that it is an achievement and as such implies free agency. Without the divine will there would be no divine knowledge. Fundamentally, omniscience and freedom involve each other rather than otherwise. Then, again, it should be noted that as a motive-power the outcome of a line of action is dependent

[23] *Systematic Theology*, I, pp. 189f.

not only upon knowledge, but also upon appreciation, and appreciation is dependent upon the will and affections rather than upon the intellect. The fact is that we cannot estimate the value of any particular thing apart from the co-operation of our entire nature. It is, then, a mistake to suppose that God has a pure foreknowledge of the future and its possible values, apart from the activity of his will, and that this foreknowledge necessarily determines his action. Appreciative foreknowledge is impossible without the co-operation of the will and the affections. In such a case, consequently, the intellect does not determine the will any more than the will the intellect. Furthermore, the eternity of the divine foreknowledge or omniscience does not condemn the divine will to rigidity. The content of an omniscient mind may in a sense perhaps remain the same. But such a mind must distinguish between the future and the present; it must take account of the changing world order, and insofar as it does this it leaves the way open to such free, plastic, and living adjustments of the divine will to human need as are implied in the doctrine of the divine Fatherhood. Between freedom and omniscience we find, therefore, no antithesis. The two imply each other and are essential attributes of the one absolute Person.

## CHAPTER IX

## THE GOODNESS OF GOD

THUS far we have dealt for the most part with the philosophical presuppositions of the Christian doctrine of God rather than with the doctrine itself. Christianity assumes that God exists, that he is absolute, and that he is a personal Being, but it is primarily interested in his ethical character; and this holds true also of religion in general. The bare absoluteness of God might awaken the sense of wonder and his metaphysical personality might elicit a spirit of inquiry with reference to the ultimate meaning of life; but these mental states belong only to the antechamber of religion. In its essence religion is trust in the goodness of God. If God were a nonmoral Being, either intelligent or nonintelligent, he would not be a proper object of religious faith. It is only insofar as he is morally good, and so worthy of being trusted, that he is truly God in the religious sense of the term. At first the idea of divinity probably had very little ethical content; the gods were feared more than they were trusted. But they were never entirely devoid of ethical character. If they had been, they would not properly have been classed as divine beings. For it is characteristic of gods as distinguished from demons and spirits that they are to some degree dependable and that they evoke from the human heart more or less confidence. If they had not had this characteristic, religion would never have been born, or at least would never have taken on a theistic form.

Faith in the responsiveness of the superworld to human need has always been the heart of religion, and the development of religion through the ages has consisted largely in the increasing clearness and thoroughness with which men have moralized this responsiveness. The first great step in the process was the more definite personalizing of the superhuman world through animistic influences—a change that laid the foundation of a more distinctly ethical relation between the human and the divine. The second great step was the rise of ethical monotheism in Israel and the ascription of moral absoluteness to God. This advance was due to the prophets, who thus created a new ethical and spiritual atmosphere in which the Jewish-Christian religion has since lived and moved and had its being. Here it is that we have the essence of "revealed" religion. The biblical revelation was in its essential and distinctive nature a revelation of the moral character of God, a revelation of his righteousness and love, or, in the broader sense of the term, a revelation of his goodness.

## Biblical Teaching

Historical evidence favors the view that there was a distinct ethical element in the conception of Jehovah from the beginning of Israel's history. Whether the Decalogue came from Moses or not, there are still good grounds for holding that he looked upon Jehovah as a God of right and law and that he inculcated absolute loyalty and devotion to him on the part of his people. It was, indeed, the intensity and sustained power of this devotion that constituted the distinctive factor in the early religion of Israel and that led to its unique development.[1] But while there was a moral element in the Mosaic and early Israelitic conception of Jehovah, this element did not become absolutely dominant and controlling until the eighth century B. C. It was the great prophets, Amos, Hosea, Isaiah, and Micah, who first completely moralized the conception of Jehovah and identified him with the moral principle of the universe. In his name they condemned the traditional ceremonialism and every degrading feature of the contemporary worship. In his name they denounced unrighteousness and inhumanity of every kind, and insisted on moral obedience as the only way of winning the divine favor. "Let justice," they cried, "roll down as waters and righteousness as a mighty stream." "What," they asked, "doth the Lord require of thee, but to do justly, and to love mercy, and to walk humbly with thy God?"[2] But even more significant was their announcement of an imminent day of the Lord, a day when all iniquity and evil would be overwhelmed and an eternal kingdom of righteousness would be inaugurated. Before the bar of this impending event, this marvelous manifestation of the divine power and will, they summoned the people of their day, and thus lifted them to a new level of insight by disclosing Jehovah to them as the absolute moral ideal. Hence-

[1] See my *Religious Teaching of the Old Testament*, pp. 79ff., 157ff.

[2] Amos 5. 24; Mic. 6. 8.

forth transcendent perfection was linked with his name, and moral absoluteness was bound up with the thought of Deity.

In expounding the moral ideal represented by Jehovah the prophets and their successors laid stress on the commonly accepted virtues. Jehovah was righteous, just, holy. He punished the wicked and rewarded the righteous. On the other hand, he was also loving, merciful, longsuffering, faithful, forgiving. He did not deal with erring men according to their sins nor reward them according to their iniquities. As the heaven is high above the earth, so great was his mercy toward them that feared him. He thus maintained an even balance between kindness and severity. He was "a just God and a Saviour,"[3] as merciful as he was just and as just as he was merciful. One prophet or psalmist might stress one aspect of his being, and another might stress another. But the total Old Testament conception of his character was that of a well-rounded ethical ideal.

There was, however, this general limitation, that he was thought of predominantly as King or Sovereign; and this tended to interfere with the highest and completest moralization of his character. A king is usually more or less capricious; his attitude toward his subjects is official rather than personal; and it is not customary to think of him as sacrificing himself for the good of others. He symbolizes the state; and the state has never represented a high degree of ethical development. It stands for power rather than for goodness of heart. Thinking of God chiefly as

[3] Isa. 45. 21.

king, therefore, as the ancient Jews did, tended to obscure those intimate personal and lofty ethical qualities in which alone absolute confidence can be placed. Unlimited power was ascribed to Jehovah and also perfect holiness, but still there was more or less of a feeling of uncertainty concerning him. The Old Testament saint complained of the way in which both the nation and the individual were at times treated.[4] He could not escape the feeling that God was more or less arbitrary in his dealings with men.[5] This arbitrariness was regarded as inherent in his sovereignty and not as a moral shortcoming, but it was on that account none the less a fact that needed to be reckoned with. It introduced a disturbing factor into Old Testament faith. It left the believer with a feeling of insecurity. He did not know with certainty what God might do, and this was inevitable so long as he was thought of primarily as King or Judge. Belief in the divine Kingship had its ethical and religious value for the ancient Israelite. It meant the deification of law and the common conscience, and in that respect it marked a most significant advance beyond the earlier nature-religions. But it also meant a one-sided and imperfect moralization of Deity, and in this respect it fell short of the Christian conception of the divine goodness.

It has recently been argued that Jesus' idea of God was wholly Jewish, that it represented no advance beyond the view held by his contemporaries. Nothing, we are told, could be more erroneous than

---

[4] Isa. 40. 17; Hab. 1. 13; Jer. 15. 18; 20. 7ff., 14ff.

[5] Job 38-42, esp. 40. 2ff.

the notion that Jesus went beyond his countrymen in preaching the love and forgiveness of God and in emphasizing his Fatherhood. The novel element in the Christian conception of God came through Paul and was due to his extending the category of Deity so as to include Christ. The idea of a self-sacrificing God formed no part of Jesus' own teaching. In his life and death, however, he illustrated the sacrificial principle in a supreme way, and hence, when he was deified by Paul and the early Christians, the idea of self-sacrifice was carried up into the thought of God himself. The characteristic element in the Christian conception of God thus did not originate with Jesus, but grew up after his death as the result of his deification.[6]

In this radical theory there is no doubt a grain of truth. It was the personality of Jesus rather than his teaching that exercised the profoundest influence upon his disciples. But while this is freely conceded, it by no means follows that there was a contrast between the two and that what Jesus taught concerning the character of God did not square with his own ethical ideal. That in his own life Jesus represented a moral ideal far in advance of that which he attributed to God, is certainly inherently improbable. He who bade his disciples be as perfect as their heavenly Father (Matt. 5. 48) would surely not ascribe to the Father a moral standard below that which he regarded as obligatory upon himself and others. There is every reason to believe that he regarded the spirit

[6] Arthur C. McGiffert, *The God of the Early Christians*, pp. 1-40.

which led him to the cross as the spirit of God. Indeed, he said to Peter, who was seeking to turn him away from the path that led to suffering and death, "Be gone, thou Satan, for thy thoughts are man's, not God's." It could hardly be more plainly and emphatically stated than in these words of Jesus that the divine way is not the way of shrinking from self-sacrifice.

But more important than this specific statement was Jesus' teaching concerning the divine Fatherhood. God is called "Father" a number of times in the Old Testament,[7] and the term was in common use among Jesus' contemporaries. But it is generally held by New Testament scholars that its use by Jesus had a new and distinctive character.[8] He made the idea of fatherhood the unifying principle in his conception of God, giving to it "a position of sole and sovereign authority," as had not been done before. And this he did, not because of any reasoned conclusion to which he had come with reference to the divine nature, but because his own religious experience took the form of a conscious filial relation to God. No doubt he had been taught by his mother to call God "Father," but this formal address had in his case been translated into a vivid personal consciousness, so that he spoke of God not simply as "Father,"

---

[7] Jer. 3. 14, 19; 31. 9; Isa. 63. 16; 64. 8; Deut. 32. 6; 2 Sam. 7. 14; Psa. 68. 5; 89. 27; Mal. 1. 6; 2. 10. See my *Religious Teaching of the Old Testament*, pp. 182-84.

[8] H. H. Wendt, *The Teaching of Jesus*, I, pp. 191ff.; J. Scott Lidgett, *The Fatherhood of God*, pp. 50ff.; James Moffatt, *The Theology of the Gospels*, pp. 85-126; John W. Buckham, *The Humanity of God*, pp. 44ff.; Adolf Deissmann, *The Religion of Jesus and the Faith of Paul* pp. 54, 68, 86.

but as "*my* Father."[9] Indeed, this was one of the most characteristic things in his teaching, that God appears in it not simply as the Father of men in general, but as *his* Father. Instinctively he cried "Abba" in his prayers, and "the 'Abba' of the praying Jesus," as Deissmann says, "resounded as far as Galatia and Rome[10] and is found to-day in all the languages in which the Bible is translated."[11] This fact alone is convincing evidence of the new intimacy and moving power which Jesus gave to the word "Father."

It was, however, not only its personal and experiential basis that gave uniqueness to Jesus' conception of the divine Fatherhood, but also its content. In the Old Testament God is usually called Father in the kindly and affectionate sense of the term, but the idea of fatherhood was not lifted up distinctly to the plane of self-sacrificing love, nor was such love clearly and definitely attributed to God. In one instance[12] it is said of him that "in all their afflictions he was afflicted," but the text is here corrupt and the original reading was quite different.[13] In Hosea suffering love is ascribed to Jehovah, and in Isaiah 53 vicarious suffering is exalted in such a way that one would naturally expect it to be predicated of Deity. But Old Testament thought did not rise to that level nor did later pre-Christian Judaism. In the Old Testament a man might suffer in spite of his

[9] Matt. 7. 21; 10. 32f.; 11. 27; 12. 50; 15. 13; 16. 17; 18. 10; 19. 35; 25. 34; Luke 2. 49; 10. 22; 22. 29; 24. 49; etc.

[10] Gal. 4. 6; Rom. 8. 15.

[11] *The Religion of Jesus and the Faith of Paul*, p. 54.

[12] Isa. 63. 9.

[13] Cf. my *Religious Teaching of the Old Testament*, p. 303.

being just, but in the New Testament suffering is a *necessity* for one who is in perfect fellowship with God. In other words, self-sacrifice is inherent in perfect love. And this thought Jesus introduced into his conception of God. For him God was love, self-sacrificing love. He was not only a forgiving God, but one whose love went in search of the sinner. And so we read of Jesus that *sinners drew near to him.* "Surely," says a distinguished Jewish scholar, "this is a new note, something which we have not yet heard in the Old Testament or of *its* heroes, something which we do not hear in the Talmud or of *its* heroes. . . . The virtues of repentance are gloriously praised in the rabbinical literature, but this direct search for and appeal to the sinner are new and moving notes of high import and significance."[14] In this new element in the ministry of Jesus we do not have a mere personal idiosyncrasy nor do we merely have the expression of a new human ideal; we have the reflection of a new conception of the divine Fatherhood.

Jesus' view of God was not, then, "wholly Jewish." It transcended the Old Testament and Jewish standpoint in its emphasis on self-sacrificing love. This emphasis is the distinctive characteristic of the Christian conception of God and would remain such even if it owed its origin to Paul rather than to Jesus. But there is, as we have seen, ample ground for holding the traditional view. Jesus and after him Paul linked up religion with the *uncommon* conscience,

---

[14] C. G. Montefiore, *The Synoptic Gospels*, first ed., II, p. 985. See also I, pp. lxxviii, 86; II, p. 574, and *Some Elements of the Religious Teaching of Jesus*, p. 57.

with the heroic and sacrificial spirit, as had not been done before, and carried this idea up into the thought of God himself. In so doing they did not break with prophetic and Jewish teaching, but they did transform it into something higher and nobler. For them God remained a God of righteousness and mercy, but these traditional attributes were lifted to a new level and transfigured by the overshadowing sense of the divine sacrificial love. This higher thought of God did not, however, obliterate the distinction between the divine righteousness and grace. God continued to be regarded as "good" in the twofold sense of being just and loving; and about these two foci the ellipse of Christian thought relative to the divine character was drawn.

Before we proceed to a discussion of these two aspects of the divine character we need to consider briefly the more important ethical terms applied to the Deity in Scripture. We have just referred in the preceding paragraph to his goodness, his righteousness, his justice, his love, his mercy and his grace. To these should be added his holiness, his truth, and his faithfulness. Other ethical terms such as compassion, pity, longsuffering, indignation, anger, and wrath may be subsumed under those just mentioned. All of these terms fall readily into one or the other of two groups, in the first of which is expressed the divine embodiment of and regard for the moral law as such and in the other of which is expressed the divine regard for other spiritual beings. Some of them, however, are at times used in a comprehensive sense to express the entire ethical character of God. Goodness, for instance, may denote simply benevolence or kindness and is often so used by theologians, but it may also denote moral rectitude in general, and it is in this sense that it is used in the title of the present chapter. The goodness of God includes what he is in himself as well as what he is in his relation to others. In a word, it covers his whole moral life. The terms "holiness" and "righteousness" are also at times used in the same comprehensive sense. God, it is said, would not be truly holy or righteous unless he were also a God of love. And it is also claimed that he would not be love in the proper sense of the term unless he were also holy and righteous. But while each of these terms may be stretched so as to designate the whole moral character of God, the term "goodness" is most naturally given this meaning. The other terms are best used to denote a particular aspect of the divine character.

Righteousness, justice, truth and holiness express different phases of the divine perfection insofar as it has to do with the moral law and the moral ideal. Of these the most distinctively religious term is "holiness." Originally the Hebrew word for "holy" (*kadosh*), as we have previously pointed out, had no direct ethical connotation. It denoted that mysterious, indefinable, fear-inspiring quality that differentiates divinity from humanity. But in the course of time under prophetic influence the term was moralized. "God the Holy One," said Isaiah, "is sanctified in righteousness."[15] This change not only lifted holi-

[15] Isa. 5. 16.

ness to a higher plane, it also lifted morality or righteousness to a higher level. Holiness became now not only the equivalent of righteousness, it became transfigured righteousness, it became righteousness raised to its highest power, it became righteousness completely divinized. It might thus be said to be the crowning ethical attribute of Deity. Indeed, it has been described as "nothing less than the sum of his goodness, the glorious fullness of his moral excellence."[16] It implies stainless purity and the perfect realization of the moral ideal conceived actively as well as passively. It, consequently, includes righteousness, justice, veracity, and even love itself, since all of these belong to the moral ideal. But it is customary to associate holiness with rectitude of will rather than with warmth of affection and hence to think of it as characteristic of the divine love rather than *inclusive* of it. That it embraces the other three attributes is evident, though each has its own special meaning.

The attribute of *righteousness* brings out the thought that God is the ultimate source and ground of moral distinctions and that in him we have the perfect standard of right. The *justice* of God involves the same general idea, but directs special attention to the activity of the divine will in apportioning good and ill to men according to their deserts. This retributive aspect of the divine justice will come up for further discussion a little later. The attribute of *truth* differs from the preceding attributes in that it takes special cognizance of God as Revealer. He

[16] W. N. Clarke, *The Christian Doctrine of God*, p. 101.

is righteous, just and holy in himself and in the execution of his laws, but in addition to this he is truthful in the revelation he has made of himself. He "is not a man, that he should lie." His "word is truth"; it "endureth forever."[17] Whether spoken through nature or through man it is trustworthy. The heavens, that declare the glory of God, do not deceive us. The universe is veracious. It is on this assumption that all knowledge is based; and it is on the further assumption that the divine word spoken through seers and saints is equally veracious that all the higher forms of religion are based.

Of the ethical attributes expressive of the divine benevolence and governed more by the idea of the good than by that of abstract right, love is generally conceded to be supreme. In Scripture we find the categorical statement that God is love;[18] he has no higher attribute. By love in its human form is meant a craving and also a giving impulse. Both impulses are essential to true love. As a mere craving, a mere desire to possess its object, love would be selfish and would contradict its own ethical nature. On the other hand, love does not consist merely in giving. One might, according to Paul, bestow all one's goods to feed the poor and give one's body to be burned, and yet not have love. In true love there must be the warmth of personal interest as well as the sacrificial spirit. Each of these finds its necessary ethical complement in the other. So it is on the human plane. And what holds true of man may properly be re-

---

[17] Num. 23. 19; John 17. 17; 1 Pet. 1. 25.
[18] 1 John 4. 8.

garded as holding true also of God. The divine love should probably be thought of as primarily good will, the love of benevolence. It is objective, it seeks the welfare, the redemption of all men. In this respect, in the purity of its altruism, it transcends everything human. It is the prototype, the pattern, the standard of human love.[19] At the same time there must be in it more or less of the love of complacency, the love which takes pleasure in men and seeks fellowship with them. This is implied in the idea of the divine Fatherhood. God the Father looks with favor on his children and seeks to reclaim those that have gone astray. Here we have the climax of all human and inspired thought relative to the divine character. All other terms expressive of the divine benevolence are but specifications under the general conception of fatherhood or love.

*Mercy* and *grace,* for instance, are both manifestations of the divine love insofar as it is directed toward the redemption of the sinful, while *faithfulness* is a manifestation of the divine love when directed toward those who are obedient and submissive to the divine will. Mercy is commonly used as a synonym of grace, but, strictly taken, it is a broader term. It has reference to the general misery of sin, while grace is concerned with the more specific evil of guilt. Mercy is extended to sinful men insofar as they are wretched; grace is granted them insofar as they are culpable. But in ordinary usage this distinction is not observed. The two terms are, as a rule, employed interchangeably. Faithfulness expresses the attitude

---

[19] See Hosea 2. 3, and Matt. 5. 43-48.

of God toward those who in turn are faithful to him. It signifies that his love toward them is constant and that it will manifest itself in ever new forms of redemptive activity. But since even the most faithful among men are at the best unprofitable servants, without merit of their own and without claim upon the divine favor, it is evident that the divine faithfulness toward them is, after all, only a form of the divine grace. "We have all sinned," and hence the divine love directed toward us must in every instance be a love of the sinful. But inasmuch as we do distinguish between believers and unbelievers and between the misery and the guilt of sin, the above distinction between the mercy, grace, and faithfulness of God is warranted. All three are specific expressions of the divine love.

### Righteousness and Love

That love is the proper term to designate one side of the divine character is then admitted by all. But what term should be used to express the other side is a matter of difference of opinion. Some prefer the term "holiness," others "righteousness," and still others "justice." But since holiness and justice have certain specific connotations, due to their history, which righteousness does not have, it seems best to use the latter term. The question consequently arises as to the relation of righteousness and love to each other.

So far as actual usage goes, righteousness and love may be described as overlapping circles with circumferences so elastic that either one can be stretched so as to include the other. Perfect righteousness, for instance, would commonly be understood to include love,[20] and perfect love would generally be understood to include righteousness. But while the two terms thus stand closely related to each other, they still have different associations and different connotations. Righteousness is primarily concerned with moral excellence as an ideal, while love is primarily concerned with the happiness of other sentient beings. Righteousness, as ordinarily understood, has to do with the common virtues recognized in the larger social groups, while love in its higher form has to do with the morality of self-sacrifice realized especially in the family. Righteousness, again, fixes its attention on the act, while love has to do with the underlying motive. A greater inwardness, depth, and self-effacement thus belong to love than to righteousness.

This difference appears clearly in the contrast between the Old and New Testament conceptions of God. Taken by and in the large, the God of the Old Testament was a God of righteousness. What gave historic significance to the prophetic teaching concerning Jehovah was the ascription of moral rectitude to him in a more absolute way than had heretofore been done. He was now declared to be interested, not in rites and ceremonies nor in feasts and sacrifices, but in social justice. Righteousness and humanity were declared to be his one great concern.

---

[20] Cf. Ritschl, *Justification and Reconciliation*, pp. 473f.: "God's righteousness is his self-consistent and undeviating action in behalf of the salvation of the members of his community; in essence it is identical with his grace."

Religion was thus linked up with the elemental virtues more completely than ever before, and the holiness of Jehovah became the mainstay of social order and the guarantee of social progress. His ethical interest, it is true, did not confine itself to the external virtues; it penetrated also the inner life of the individual. But on the whole it was in the maintenance and the execution of the objective moral law that his ethical character manifested itself most distinctly. Righteousness and justice were the signature of his being.

The tendency in the later Old Testament period, however, was for the social passion connected with the earliest enunciation of the divine righteousness to degenerate into a barren legalism. Prophetism tended to give way to Pharisaism. Instead of being the leader in a mighty moral crusade God now became a glorified martinet, demanding meticulous obedience to law, but without the inspiration of a great spiritual enterprise. The result was that religion became cold, formal, and legalistic. The common man was, to a large extent, shut out from its comforts. To him God seemed distant, the upholder of a more or less arbitrary law, and without any deep significance for his own personal life. To right this evil Jesus appeared on the scene with a new vision of God, with a God who had not been imposed upon by human respectability, a God of the Fourth Estate, a God who was eager to save the lost and ready to sacrifice himself in order to achieve their salvation, a God of redemptive love. This was the distinctive element in the Christian conception of God, and under its influence religion became again a vital and inspiring power. The older prophetic idea of the divine righteousness was retained; indeed, it was the presupposition of the Christian conception of the divine love. It was because God was holy and just that the proclamation of his love had such a wondrous and subduing power. Love as a natural and nonmoral passion is no doubt wonderfully appealing to the human heart, but it is not divine love. The love of God is holy love, a love that redeems from sin as well as from loneliness. There is, therefore, no antithesis between the divine holiness and the divine love. The two go together. Love does not annul the divine justice, it fulfills it. Such is the teaching of Jesus and of the New Testament as a whole.

But in the course of the development of Christian theology the conviction arose that the divine righteousness and the divine love are logically opposed to each other and that the real genius of Christianity lies in the way in which this opposition was overcome in the interest of the divine love. Righteousness, it was argued, implies distributive justice, and distributive justice forbids any departure from the strict law of reward and punishment as determined by one's deserts. There can, therefore, be no forgiveness of sins until the demands of justice have been met. These demands were, however, met by the death of Christ, and thus a new era of divine grace was inaugurated. This theory will naturally come up for more complete discussion in connection with the work of Christ, which will be dealt with in a later volume, but it has an important bearing on one's conception of the divine righteousness and in that respect calls for consideration here. The question it raises is as to whether righteousness necessarily implies strict distributive and more particularly retributive justice. Does God regard and especially does he punish men in strict accordance with their deserts? If so, there would seem to be a conflict in his own nature between his righteousness and his love. One would seem to exclude the other.

A common method of explaining away this conflict is to say that the divine justice is always actuated by love. "Punishment is for the good of the offender and for the prevention of evil."[21] This view has been widely held in the church; but there has also been strenuous objection to it. It has been stoutly maintained that punitive justice is not benevolence.[22] It is an expression of the divine wrath, not of the divine love. To merge justice in benevolence is to misunderstand its essential nature. "Justice is the *exact* distribution of reward or of punishment," and as such may be regarded as self-operative for an omniscient Being. In its remunerative aspect it no doubt aims at the promotion of righteousness and in its retributive aspect at the destruction of sin, but in and of itself it is guided by the demand of the moral law and by that alone. Punishment is not inflicted simply for the purpose of reforming the offender and of preventing further evil. It is inflicted because it is required by the divine righteousness. Holiness is an

---

[21] Clement of Alexandria, *Paedagogus*, I, p. viii.

[22] W. G. T. Shedd, *Dogmatic Theology*, I, pp. 364-85; Charles Hodge, *Systematic Theology*, I, pp. 416-27.

end of the divine action quite as much as happiness. Indeed, it is the more fundamental end of the two, and because it is such its demands cannot be subordinated to the promotion of well-being. Sin must be punished regardless of its bearing on human happiness. The divine justice requires it. Love and justice cannot, therefore, be merged together by subordinating the latter to the former. The two must be retained intact as more or less disparate attributes of the Divine Being.

For this view not a little support can be found in Scripture. The retributive justice of God is there asserted again and again,[23] and much is also said about the divine wrath.[24] But how much doctrinal significance should be attributed to these utterances is a question. That God is righteous in the sense that he is not indifferent to moral distinctions and does not treat the upright and the wicked alike, and in the further sense that he betrays no favoritism in dealing with men, would be generally accepted as an essential part of Christian teaching. But that his righteousness requires him to mete out rewards and punishments to men in exact proportion to their deserts is quite another matter.

Such a view of God would make of him an unfeeling Judge and would reduce his relation to men to a purely ethico-legal basis. It would obscure his redemptive purpose and put in its stead a heartless calculation of merit and demerit. This was the ten-

---

[23] Gen. 2. 17; Exod. 34. 7; Deut. 27. 26; Ezek. 18. 4; Rom. 1. 32; 2. 8; 6. 23; 12. 19; Gal. 3. 10; 2 Thess. 1. 8; etc.

[24] Ezra. 8. 22; Psa. 20. 9; 106. 40; Isa. 9. 19; Rom. 1. 18; Eph. 5. 6; Col. 3. 6; etc.

dency in Pharisaism, and it was against it that the main polemic, if such it may be called, of Jesus' teaching was directed. He represented God as a Father, whose love welcomes back the undeserving prodigal son and who freely bestows his gifts upon all who ask.[25] The legalistic objection to such an attitude on God's part as unfair and unjust he expressly rejected as invalid,[26] and set forth the highest form of the divine love as that which manifests itself in disregard of the principle of exact distributive justice.[27] Love does not, of course, exclude remuneration and retribution from the principles operative in God's dealings with men. It recognizes both as valid and manifests itself to some degree in and through them. But forgiving love cannot be bound by them. It transcends the law of merit and demerit. It bestows favors on men in spite of their demerit. In so doing it does not altogether disregard their moral qualities. But the qualities it most prizes are those associated with the consciousness of demerit rather than those associated with the consciousness of merit. The consciousness of demerit may, it is true, be in a certain sense meritorious, but not in the sense that it can claim the divine grace as its right. The divine love is not attracted simply by human merit. If it were, it would be seriously curtailed in its operations, and would fall far short of what is implied in the divine Fatherhood. There would seem, then, to be no principle in the divine nature that requires that rewards

[25] Luke 15. 11ff.; 11. 9-13.
[26] Luke 15. 25-32; Matt. 20. 8-15.
[27] Matt. 5. 44-48; 18. 21-35.

and punishments be meted out to men in strict accordance with their deserts. The divine righteousness, in other words, does not involve strict retributive justice. No atonement in the ordinary sense of the term is necessary before the forgiving love of God can become operative. This is a point of decisive importance in the Christian conception of the divine character.

The wrath of God, which figures so prominently in both the Old and New Testaments, stands closely related to the divine holiness and may be regarded as the emotional expression of it occasioned by sin. As a just and holy Being God looks with approval upon right conduct, but wrongdoing awakens in him indignation and wrath. At first human analogy suggests that we have here two antithetical states of mind. One is directed toward the welfare of men, the other apparently toward their injury; and the two states may alternate in the divine attitude toward the same individual. The question consequently has arisen as to whether wrath may properly be attributed to God, and, if so, how it should be construed. Some theologians have rejected it as an unworthy anthropomorphism on the ground that it is inconsistent with the divine love and would, if real, require us to ascribe to God a change of will that in turn would be inconsistent with his eternity. Ritschl,[28] for instance, says that "according to the New Testament, God's wrath signifies his determination to destroy those who definitely set themselves against redemption and the final end of the kingdom of God." It thus stands

[28] *Justification and Reconciliation*, p. 323.

opposed to his eternal redemptive will; and hence "from the point of view of theology no validity can be assigned" to it. But the term "wrath" in the New Testament is not used exclusively in the eschatological sense as stated by Ritschl,[29] and even if it were, it would not need to be so construed by us. The more general meaning of indignation at wrongdoing would be quite permissible, and in this sense the divine wrath would stand in the same general relation to the divine love that the divine righteousness does. It would be viewed either as a co-ordinate and independent aspect of the divine character or as included within the divine love as a modified form of it.

According to the latter view, wrath is a "restrained manifestation of love." It is "holy love itself, feeling itself so far hindered because *they* have turned away from its blessed influence whom it would have received into its fellowship."[30] There is in the divine wrath, therefore, nothing of the vindictive or vengeful. It stands closer to grief and compassion; but it differs from them in that it expresses the sacredness of the moral law and the divine hostility to sin. There is in thwarted love a militant element and this on the moral plane finds vent in indignation. The love of righteousness implies hatred of sin. Between the wrath of God and his love there is, consequently, no antithesis. Both serve the same holy purpose, and if love be the proper designation of this purpose, then wrath is an instrument of love or an altered form of it.

---

[29] See Rom. 1. 18; Eph. 2. 3; John 3. 36.

[30] H. Martensen, *Christian Dogmatics*, p. 303.

To this it is objected that such an interpretation of the divine wrath does violence to linguistic usage. Wrath is not love, nor is justice love. Justice and wrath represent an independent aspect of the divine nature that cannot be fused with love. In God there is a deep-seated dualism, a dualism that in practice can be overcome only by an act of atonement. This view in the past commended itself to a large part of the church, and is still held by many. Indeed, it may be regarded as almost inevitable so long as we distinguish sharply between happiness and holiness and between the love of men and the love of righteousness. If human welfare and moral excellence represent two independent and ultimate values, there would seem to be no way of avoiding a conflict in the divine nature between love and justice. The former would seek the well-being of men, while the latter would guard the interests of absolute rectitude; and between the two there could be no harmony until the demands of justice were somehow met by an atoning act. But the assumption of such a fundamental antinomy is unnecessary, and is possible only so long as we remain on the natural plane. Our idea of happiness needs to be moralized and our idea of holiness needs to be personalized. The two ideas need to be brought together in the concrete conception of the kingdom of God, and when this is done the antinomy vanishes. Instead of two divine ends we now have one. The moral ideal and human well-being are fused together, and in God we no longer have justice and love at variance with each other, but one holy and loving will seeking the moral redemption of men. A moral monism thus takes the place of the older dualism. God is no longer righteousness and love, but righteous or holy love.

### Love and Personality

It is customary to say that God loves the sinner and hates the sin. In this way provision is made in the nature of God for hatred or wrath in the ordinary sense of these terms, and that without any conflict with the divine love. The love of God toward men is eternal. It never changes, is never succeeded by wrath. His wrath is directed against sin, is eternally directed against it, and coexists with the love of the sinner. In this distinction between sin and the sinner there is an element of truth. But it is not a distinction made by Scripture, nor is it one that can be accepted as ultimately valid. Love is properly directed only toward persons, and the same is true of hate insofar as it is the ethical antithesis of love. It is only in an accommodated sense that we speak of loving and hating *things.* The proper objects alike of love and hate are personal beings. It is not, then, strictly correct to distinguish between the divine love and the divine hate by making the object of the one personal and the object of the other impersonal. Indeed, sin apart from personality is an abstraction. It is only free intelligence that can give moral quality to an act. Condemnation of an act as sinful means, therefore, condemnation of its author also. We cannot completely separate the two. We cannot at one and the same time disapprove the act and approve the agent.

And yet there is a sense in which we may think of

God as hating the sin and loving the sinner. Only in very extreme cases, if at all, does the sinner completely identify himself with his sin. The sin is not a complete expression of his personality. Something of good remains within him and this good makes him redeemable. Toward him as the subject of redemption the divine love in the sense of benevolence is, consequently, directed. Sin, on the other hand, is by its very nature evil. It has nothing good in it, and hence upon it the divine wrath or hatred is properly vented. Its destruction is the necessary condition of the salvation of the sinner. In fact, to hate it means to love the moral agent who is seeking to free himself from bondage to it. Hatred of sin and love of the sinner thus imply each other; they are but two sides of the divine redemptive purpose, a purpose directed toward personal beings and meaningless apart from them.

The question has been raised as to whether love or personality is the more essential and significant element in the Christian conception of God. Ritschl decided emphatically in favor of love. "There is," he said, "no other conception of equal worth beside this which need be taken into account." It is "the only adequate conception of God." "Even the recognition of the personality of God does not imply independent knowledge apart from our defining him as loving Will."[31] It simply determines the *form* under which the real *content* of his being, his loving will, is conceived. Theodore Haering also takes essentially the same view. "The statement, 'God is love,' " he says,

---

[31] *Justification and Reconciliation*, pp. 273f.

"is the whole Christian doctrine of God." If we were required to choose between thinking of God as Absolute Personality and as Love, we should decide immediately in favor of the latter. As Christians "we believe in the (supramundane, unconditioned) personal love, not in the loving (supramundane, unconditioned) personality."[32] Julius Kaftan, on the other hand, assigns the precedence to the idea of *personality* on the ground that love consists in self-communication and that apart from a self or personality to communicate it would lose its deepest and most characteristic content.[33] As mere benevolence it might still exist, but without self-impartation it would fall short of what true love should be.

The situation here is similar to that which obtains in the relation of love and righteousness to each other. From one point of view love is the more ultimate term and from another point of view righteousness, but both imply each other; and so it is with personality and love. From the metaphysical point of view personality is the profounder attribute, but it needs love in order to complete itself. Without a loving will it would lack direction and also an ultimate and worthy goal. From the practical point of view, however, love is manifestly the more important attribute. It is the divine love that forms the basis of religious faith. But apart from personality love would be a mere abstraction, it would be like the smile of the Cheshire cat without the cat, of which we read in *Alice in Wonderland.* Love owes both its being and

---

[32] *The Christian Faith,* I, p. 323.
[33] *Dogmatik,* pp. 200-03.

its content to the personal agent who both possesses and expresses it. It is, then, a mistake to think of the divine love and the divine personality as in any sense opposed to each other or as rival claimants for the hegemony among the divine attributes. Personality is incomplete without love, and love without personality is nonexistent. Nor can it be truly said that "personal love" expresses the divine nature more correctly than a "loving personality." From one standpoint we may properly emphasize the divine love and from another the divine personality. As over against a legalistic but theistic Pharisaism we would naturally say that God is personal *love,* but as over against an impersonal naturalism we would more fittingly say that God is a loving Person. At bottom the two expressions have virtually the same meaning.

There is, however, a point of difference between them that should not be overlooked. If personality is put in an adjectival relation to love, there is danger that their organic and structural relation to each other may be obscured. The divine love may, for instance, be objectified and thought of as so exclusively expressed in the relation of men to each other and to the world that it can be known only through the practical exercise of love and through triumph over the world. This tendency we find in Ritschl, and no doubt it expresses an important truth, but it curtails the divine love insofar as it fails to bring out adequately the thought of a direct relation to God and of immediate fellowship with him. If, on the other hand, personality is made primary, provision is made for the love of self-communication as well as for the love of objectified benevolence. If God be first of all a Person, then love will mean not only good will, but also the communication of his life and his spirit to men; and this is clearly the teaching of Scripture. There is thus a genuine religious as well as a philosophical reason for affirming that God is pre-eminently a "loving Person." It is because he is such that he is also "personal love."

It remains to be pointed out that the attributes of personality and love agree in fixing attention on the volitional, as distinguished from the intellectual, side of the divine nature. The fundamental thing in personality is will, and this also is true of love. In emphasizing these two attributes and making them basal in its conception of God Christianity consequently differentiates itself sharply from the intellectualism of Greek philosophy. For Aristotle God was thought, a thinking on thinking; and this has been true of various forms of modern as well as ancient idealism. The causal, volitional, and emotional elements in the Divine Being did not come to adequate recognition in them. In its stress on these factors we have the most distinctive feature in the Christian conception of God. For Christianity God is intelligence, wisdom, reason, but he is also, and more fundamentally, will, purpose, benevolence. This viewpoint it is that we have in mind when we ascribe central importance to either the personality or the love of God. Both attributes have a common volitional rootage and both in their spiritual form tend to merge into each other.

## Philosophical Basis

Thus far we have dealt chiefly with the biblical doctrine of the divine goodness and its treatment in the history of theology, and have not raised the question as to its philosophical basis. In Chapter VI we expounded briefly the moral argument for the existence of God, devoting particular attention to the Kantian formulation of it. But the special reasons for affirming the goodness of God we have not yet considered. These reasons may be reduced to three: the analogical, the empirical, and the aprioristic.

By the "analogical" I mean the reason based on the analogy of the human spirit insofar as the latter implies a union of the intellectual and the ethical. It is true that there is no way of logically deducing the ethical character of God from his metaphysical attributes. These attributes are "ethically barren." The omnipotence, omnipresence, eternity, unity, identity, omniscience, and even freedom of God are conceivable without reference to the idea of moral obligation. We might have adequate rational grounds for believing in the existence of a being endowed with these various attributes and yet be under no logical compulsion to ascribe to him a moral character. But while this is true, it is also true that the analogy of the human spirit suggests with almost irresistible cogency that where we have free intelligence there we will also have moral responsibility. If, then, God is omniscient and free, there is every reason to believe that he is also a moral Being. He might conceivably be malevolent in nature. There are evil human beings. But on the same basis we might ascribe irrationality to the Deity. If we are warranted in thinking of him as rational, we are equally warranted in thinking of him as good. The same logic holds in both instances. Personality binds reason and conscience together so that the existence of one justifies our inferring the existence of the other. Consequently, on the basis of human analogy we may argue from the omniscience and freedom of God to his goodness. Indeed, so inevitable has this connection seemed that in the history of theism it has commonly been thought sufficient to establish the intelligence of God and then to assume that this carried with it his ethical character.

The empirical argument for the divine goodness is based on the moral nature of man, on the moral structure of human society, and on the moral principles operative in human history. The moral nature, it is urged, requires for its explanation a moral author. Man is organic to nature and owes his capacities to the power that lies back of nature. This back-lying Power must, as cause, be at least equal to the human spirit which it produces. He that formed the capacity for righteousness, shall he not himself be righteous? To ask the question is to answer it. Yet numerous efforts have been made to derive the moral from the nonmoral. It has been argued that man's ethical nature developed out of various animal impulses and requires no other account of its origin. But this naturalistic theory confuses temporal antecedence with metaphysical causation, and fails, furthermore, to recognize the unique character of the moral life. Between the "natural" and the "moral" there is a gulf which no logic can bridge. If an adequate cause of man's moral nature is, therefore, to be found, it must be in a world-ground that is itself moral. This line of reasoning is as sound in principle as it is convincing to spontaneous thought.

It might in a similar way be argued that human society also has a moral character and that as such it too points to a moral author. But in dealing with the ethical element in society and in the course of history it is customary to lay stress, not on its transcendent source, but on its reality as a revelation of an immanent divine power. Society, it is urged, is so constructed that it makes the way of the transgressor hard and encourages a life of moral obedience. This holds true not only of the individual, but of social groups. A righteous nation is exalted, but doom awaits the wicked. This, we are told, is the one great lesson of human history. There is a power, not ourselves, that makes for righteousness.

If this were manifestly so, if right were clearly regnant in human society and human history, it would point strongly to a moral governor of the world. But is it so? "There is the rub." One can by picking his facts make quite a showing in favor of the view that right reigns in the world. But over against these facts stand others of a contrary character. The righteous suffer while the wicked spread themselves as the green bay tree. Justice and humanity are trodden under foot, while cruelty and brute force sit regnant on the throne. How often have tyrannical and oppressive governments held sway in the world! How unequal and disproportionate is the allotment of outward fortune to the sons of men! How great is the load of suffering that weighs down upon unnumbered thousands, and even millions, of men through no conscious fault of their own! When one dwells upon such facts as these, the moral story of life is seen to be a complex and bewildering one. Instead of the simple and monotonous lesson of Hebrew history, we are confronted with an ambiguous oracle. Whether the unsifted facts of life speak for or against the reign of right, one can hardly say. Often they seem to present a moral chaos rather than the well-ordered system one would expect under a moral government.

The empirical appeal to history thus fails us. If we had no other source of light than the outward facts of life, we would hardly know what to say concerning the character of God. Certainly, we would have no adequate ground for a confident faith in his goodness. If such a faith had come to us from some other source, we might find here and there in the external course of events illustrations and confirmations of it, but nothing approaching a scientific proof. All that a study of the objective moral facts of life can do is to show that these facts do not negate faith in the goodness of God. They do not ground it, but they also do not contradict it. They simply leave the door open to it. This is as far as the social and historical argument can go.

The real strength of the argument for the goodness of God is to be found in its aprioristic form. Here we are not concerned with the outward experiences of men, nor with the ultimate source of our moral nature, but with our moral nature itself, its validity and its implications. The contention is that our moral consciousness stands in its own right, that in this sense it is absolute, and that it "carries with it a demand that reality shall be in accordance with it."[34] It matters not how we describe this demand or the doctrine implied in it. We may with Sorley speak of the objectivity of values, or with Troeltsch of a religious *a priori,* or with Bowne of an implicit faith in the reality of the ideal, or with Kant of the moral necessity of religion. At bottom they all amount to about the same thing. We begin with the assumption of the absoluteness of the moral law. The sense of "ought" is one that we cannot escape. Duty stands above us with a sway we cannot break. This is an ultimate fact which each must recognize for himself and one which, when recognized, justifies itself. But however valid and authoritative the subjective law of right may be, it is theoretically possible that we may have in it simply a personal idiosyncrasy or a mere reflection of the authority of society. As such it would still have its value, a value, however, that would be purely æsthetic or practical. It would ground no objective belief. The next point consequently to be noted is that the absolute moral law would not be absolute if it did not contain "an authentic intimation of the nature of the system to which we belong."[35] When we say "I must," we mean that the nature of things demands that we do it. Not my own ego, not society, but the larger realm of reality stands back of the moral law. This assump-

[34] W. R. Sorley, *Moral Values and the Idea of God,* p. 336.
[35] John Baillie, *The Interpretation of Religion,* p. 352.

tion is implicit in the sense of duty, and it is this fact that gives to duty its absolute character. To affirm the absoluteness of the moral law means, then, to affirm its objective validity or, in other words, the moral character of the universe.

It is only translating the same thought into other terms when we insist on the objectivity of values, or on a religious *a priori*, or on the fundamental and inevitable character of our faith in the reality of the ideal. Value-judgments, we say, have an objective reference. They would be meaningless without it. The affirmation of value means the affirmation of an objective order that has value. No purely subjective interpretation of value would be true to what we have in mind when we talk about values and particularly moral or ideal values. In the very conception of these values their objectivity is implied. If there were no existence corresponding to them, they would not be values. Valuation carries with it objectification. We are so constituted that this is inevitable, and hence there is a certain warrant in speaking of a religious *a priori*. By this expression we mean that religion is an autonomous validity, that the idealizing process involved in it is structural in the human reason, that there is an inner logic within the practical reason that leads to religious faith. There is, in other words, a kind of rational or moral impossibility about denying value to reality or, what is practically the same thing, denying reality to our ideals. Our mental life begins with an implicit faith in these ideals. We may describe this faith as an objectification of our ideals or as a religious *a priori*, but however described, it is an ultimate fact of our nature, a kind of moral necessity. And it is on this necessity that we rest our case for religion and for the belief in the goodness of God. Other considerations, rational and empirical, may lend support to it, but in the last analysis belief in the divine righteousness rests on the self-evidencing power of our instinctive and irrepressible faith in the ideal.

### Goodness and Absoluteness

Assuming the general trustworthiness of Scripture and the validity of the inference from what *ought* to be to what *is,* we may confidently affirm that God is good. But while from the human side this may seem clear, difficulties arise when we think of goodness in its relation to absoluteness.

There is an ethical as well as a metaphysical absoluteness. The latter we discussed in Chapter VII. It receives its most definite and most fundamental expression in the attribute of omnipotence. The human spirit in its quest after life meets with resistance. This resistance at first seems to come from many independent sources, but eventually the mind rises to the thought of one ultimate and irresistible power, upon which everything depends, the eternal Whence and Whither of our own being and of all that is. Science joins with religion in enforcing this thought of a dynamic Absolute. But the human spirit not only meets with resistance, it seeks peace and satisfaction. This satisfaction it cannot find in itself, nor can it find it in the various objects round about it. Hence it rises to the thought of an ultimate and highest good, a good in which the restless soul finds rest and out of which no new and unsatisfied desire arises. An ethical Absolute thus takes its place alongside of the dynamic or metaphysical Absolute, and the two are fused together by faith. Indeed, it is not certain but the belief in the ethical Absolute was historically the source of the belief in the metaphysical Absolute. It has at any rate been maintained that it was the prophetic faith in the moral absoluteness of Jehovah that led to the belief in his omnipotence. It was because the prophets looked upon the moral law as universal and absolute that they assumed or asserted the unlimited power of Jehovah, whom they regarded as its living embodiment. This theory may or may not be correct; but whether correct or not, it can hardly be doubted that in the history of thought the sense of moral necessity has co-operated with that of causal necessity in producing the idea of the Absolute. In the Absolute we have a conjunction of the moral and theoretical ideals, a union of the highest good with the highest power.

But while the main stream of speculative thought since the time of Plato has not hesitated to combine moral with metaphysical absoluteness in its conception of God, several scruples have from time to time arisen with reference to the validity of this combination. Three of these scruples call for brief consideration. The first has to do with the supposed incompatibility of omnipotence and perfect goodness, the second with the assumed inconsistency between morality and absoluteness, and the third with the apparent contradiction between the implications of love and a fundamental monism.

The difficulty involved in the conception of God as both good and all-powerful is of long standing,[36] but it did not become acute in Western thought until toward the close of the seventeenth and the beginning of the eighteenth century. Previous to that time several factors tended to keep it in abeyance. One was the belief in the immediate sovereignty of God, another the doctrine of original sin, and yet another the vividness of the eschatological hope. These beliefs contained a relatively simple solution of the problem of evil. Since an almighty God is the direct author of all that occurs, humility would suggest that men accept the ills of life without complaint. But if they did not, it was sufficient to remind them that these ills are traceable to original sin; and then, if this did not altogether quiet their protest, it could be and was added as an effective ground of consolation that these ills are only temporary and serve as a means of attaining to life eternal. With the rise, however, of modern rationalism, humanism, and a more impersonal view of the world this simple solution proved inadequate, and the problem of evil be-

---

[36] Lactantius in expounding the view of Epicurus put the difficulty as follows: "God either wishes to take away evils, and is unable; or he is able, and is unwilling; or he is neither willing nor able, or he is both willing and able. If he is willing and is unable, he is feeble, which is not in accordance with the character of God; if he is able and unwilling, he is envious, which is equally at variance with God; if he is neither willing nor able, he is both envious and feeble, and therefore not God; if he is both willing and able, which alone is suitable to God, from what source then are evils? or why does he not remove them?" *A Treatise on the Anger of God*, Chap. XIII.

came the hot spot of theological interest. It was Pierre Bayle (1647–1706) who by his radical criticism first projected the problem into philosophy and made it a subject of vital concern in the field of religious thought.[37] He sought to show that the traditional conception of God and his relation to the world was shot through and through with inconsistencies and that in particular his power and his goodness could not be harmonized with each other. In taking this position he himself professed to aim at strengthening the cause of revealed religion as over against rationalism, and in this he may have been sincere. But the actual effect of his criticism was to call in question the very right of religion to exist. It was generally felt that he had made a formidable attack upon religious faith itself and that the attack must somehow be met if faith was to maintain itself in the modern world.

By far the most significant and influential response was that made by Leibnitz (1646–1716), to whom we owe the application of the term "theodicy" to the problem. It was his contention that both physical and moral evil are due to metaphysical imperfection, and that metaphysical imperfection follows with logical necessity from the very concept of a world. The world, therefore, could not exist without suffering and sin, and hence in spite of these evils we may regard it as the best possible world; and if it be such there is, of course, no conflict between the divine goodness and

[37] Dr. Otto Lempp, *Das Problem der Theodicee in der Philosophie und Literatur des 18 Jahrhunderts bis auf Kant und Schiller*, pp. 1-32.

the divine power. In maintaining this view Leibnitz fell into numerous inconsistencies; but his main thesis that evil is a rational necessity and consequently no reflection upon the divine goodness, was for a time widely accepted as an adequate reply to the criticism of Bayle and as a satisfactory apology for religious belief in general.[38]

To us the Leibnitzian and whole eighteenth-century treatment of the problem of theodicy seems abstract and artificial. The idea of a best possible world, which necessarily involves more or less of the quantitative if carefully thought through, is a contradictory conception like that of a highest possible number. The present world, furthermore, does not admit of deduction from any necessary truths of reason. The evils of life are not logical necessities. They are contingent events and might conceivably have been either nonexistent or quite different from what they are. Whether in their present form they are consistent with the divine goodness is not a question that can be settled by invoking the abstract idea of a perfect world. The perfection or goodness of the world is dependent upon the end that it is supposed to serve, and this end does not admit of logical demonstration. If it be mere enjoyment, we may pass one judgment upon the world; if it be the development of character, we may pass another; and if it be some nonhuman end, our judgment would probably be still different. There is no commonly accepted standard by which the world can be judged, nor is there any abstract ideal which enables us to determine whether its evils

[38] Otto Lempp, *id.*, pp. 33-64.

are consistent with creative goodness or not. The whole question of theodicy needs to be taken out of the abstract realm in which it, to a large extent, moved in the eighteenth century and carried over into the realm of actual experience. Whether life is worth living or not depends on the kind of life lived. Apart from living experience itself the question cannot be settled. And so it is with the problem of the divine goodness. Only life itself can solve it. We cannot prove that this is the best possible world, nor can we prove that it is even a good world. On the other hand, we cannot prove the contrary. The facts of life, taken logically and abstractly, are ambiguous. They permit faith in the divine goodness, but do not require it. The question admits, therefore, only of a *practical* solution, and this is something that can be arrived at only through the living experience of each individual.[39]

But while the tendency during the past century has been to transfer the problem of theodicy from the theoretical to the practical realm, the old scruple with reference to the possibility of harmonizing the goodness of God with his omnipotence has lingered, and in recent years has given rise to the theory of a finite God. This theory we considered at some length in Chapter VII. In its more extreme form we rejected it as both religiously and philosophically untenable. And even in its more moderate form, as represented by Professor Brightman, we found it open to rather serious objections. It is freely admitted that, if we limit the power of God, we to that

[39] See B. P. Bowne, *Theism*, pp. 263-90.

extent reduce his responsibility for the evils of the world and thus render belief in his subjective goodness easier. But at the same time we limit what may be called his objective goodness and thus weaken the grounds of faith. From the purely theoretical or rationalistic standpoint there may be a certain advantage in seeking to save the divine goodness at the expense of the divine power. By so doing the gulf between the world and God is to some degree narrowed. But there is, in my opinion, a more excellent way, and that is frankly to recognize the limitations of human knowledge when it comes to evaluating the varied experiences of life, and to hold that if we knew all, as God does, the unideal aspects of the world would not seem so entirely out of harmony with an absolute and holy love as they now do. This, it is true, does not solve the problem, but it is quite as tenable an hypothesis as that of "a resisting and retarding element" in the divine nature, and it has the distinct advantage of being more congenial to religious faith. In the last analysis all faith in God rests on faith in the ideal, and nothing short of the highest will satisfy this faith. If the existence of evil requires us to affirm either the divine impotence or human ignorance, and if one theory is logically as tenable as the other, faith will have no hesitancy in making its choice in favor of the latter.

The second scruple, above referred to, had to do with the idea of the Absolute and its relation to that of moral goodness. There is a notion in certain circles that morality is relative to man and that it cannot properly be affirmed of the Infinite. This conclusion is supported by two lines of thought. First, it is said that morality implies the coexistence of good and evil, and that the Absolute is the unity or identity beyond all differences, so that for him or it no moral distinctions can exist. He must be regarded, therefore, as "supermoral." This view is akin to that of a "superpersonal" Being. In discussing the latter conception we pointed out that the word "superpersonal" is ambiguous. It may denote a higher type of personality than that represented by man, or it may denote a type of existence that completely transcends personality and is exclusive of it. The same ambiguity appears in the use of the term "supermoral." The word may simply denote a higher type of morality than that represented by the human consciousness or it may denote a type of Being that transcends the moral altogether and excludes it. With reference to the first of these interpretations there is no dispute. All theists not only admit, but affirm that if personality and morality are attributed to the Absolute, it must be in a form that transcends their limited realization in human life. It is the second interpretation that is the cause of debate and that alone gives significance to the insistence on the "supermoral" and "superpersonal" character of the Infinite. In this sense, however, the terms imply an "agnostic" or "logical" conception of the Absolute which we have found ample ground for rejecting as invalid. The true view of the Absolute is that which regards it as the unconditioned ground or cause of the world, and when so understood there is no conflict between it and the idea of goodness. Indeed, the *cause* of man's capacity for goodness must, it would seem, also be good.

Still, it is urged that from the religious point of view evil as well as good is referred to God, and that we must, therefore, think of him as sharing in neither and as beyond both. But this confuses moral with natural evil. The latter we ascribe to God, but not the former. Some theological theories have held God ultimately responsible for sin, but this view runs counter to one of the most fundamental characteristics of religion, namely, its instinctive or *a priori* alliance with moral idealism. The unsophisticated as well as the enlightened religious consciousness has always repudiated the idea that God is the cause of sin as he is of goodness. To ascribe moral neutrality to him is as obnoxious to our religious as it is to our ethical nature.[40]

But while this may be true of God in his relation to the world, the situation, we are told, is different when we think of him as a self-existent and independent Being. It is here that the third difficulty, above mentioned, emerges. How, it is asked, can love be predicated of a Being who has no ontological other? A similar problem exists in connection with knowledge, but there the solution is relatively easy. For the knower may make himself his object. But not so the lover. He must have an object other than himself. How, then, can love be ascribed to the Absolute, in and of himself, apart from the beings whom he has created? One might look upon creation as an eternal

---

[40] Cf. Hastings Rashdall, *The Theory of Good and Evil,* II, pp. 268-91.

and necessary consequence of the divine nature and so hold that there have always been beings toward whom the divine love could be directed. But this would lead to pantheism. Another suggestion is that we deny to the Absolute love in our sense of the term and content ourselves with affirming his free personal self-determination without attempting to define more precisely the concrete content of his moral consciousness.[41] But this does not seem altogether satisfactory. It has, consequently, been maintained that the true solution of the problem is to be found in the Christian doctrine of the Trinity. Here personal distinctions are introduced into the absolute consciousness which make possible an eternal love-life within the Deity himself. This doctrine, as we shall see in the next chapter, is not free from serious difficulties, but in its relation to the problem under consideration it has not a little speculative value. One may perhaps achieve essentially the same end by holding that creation is eternal, yet free and actuated by love. In this way love would be made an eternal attribute of Deity and there would also be eternally for him objects of love. But however that may be, the important thing religiously is not the love that may exist within the Godhead itself, nor the divine love toward prehuman or angelic beings, but the love of God toward men. And this we may affirm, regardless of the other possible expressions of his good will. There is nothing in his absoluteness, correctly conceived, that is inconsistent with his righteous and loving attitude toward the world.

[41] So E. Troeltsch, *Glaubenslehre*, p. 187.

## CHAPTER X

## THE TRINITY

The biblical conception of God may be defined in a general way as ethical personalism; and the distinctive element in the New Testament conception, as we have seen, is its stress on sacrificial love. If the latter idea had been communicated to the world simply through verbal instruction, Christian teaching would probably not have advanced beyond strict monotheism. But the revelation of the divine love was not made merely nor primarily in word, but in deed, and particularly in the life, death, and resurrection of Jesus Christ. This method of revelation imparted to the divine love a new and vital quality that it would not otherwise have had; but it also did more, it extended the divine love and with it the divine essence beyond the strictly monotheistic limits to which it had previously been confined. Deity as a result took on a new range; a new name came to be linked with it. Jesus as well as the traditional God came to be regarded as divine; and out of this expanded idea of Deity there grew eventually the doctrine of the Trinity.

### Origin of the Doctrine

The Trinity is the specific Christian doctrine of God. There are or have been numerous ethnic "trinities" or triads; such as Osiris, Isis, and Horus among the Egyptians; Anu, Enlil, and Ea among the Sumerians; Sin, Shamash, and Ishtar among the early Babylonians; Demeter, Kore, and a variable male deity among the Eleusinians; Uranos, Kronos, and Zeus among the Romans; and Vishnu, Siva, and Brahma among the Hindus. These triads were all polytheistic, and hence differ radically from the Christian Trinity, which is fundamentally monotheistic. Only the last-named, the Hindu Trimurti, as it is called, bears a certain resemblance to the Christian doctrine: Brahma, Vishnu, and Siva are treated as different manifestations or revelations of one and the same divine essence, the impersonal Brahman. But the resemblance is superficial. Between the two types of triadic monism there is a vast difference, and neither owed its origin to the other. What we have in the Hindu Trimurti is "a method of reconciling the claims of rival monotheistic religions with one another and with a traditional philosophy."[1] The triad is probably not very old, and has never had any considerable religious significance.

Nathan Söderblom[2] has pointed out that besides the many polytheistic triads in the history of religion there are also nonpolytheistic triads. Of the latter the most important is the Buddhistic *"triratna,"* or three jewels, consisting of Buddha, his Doctrine, and his Order. According to Söderblom it is here that we have the closest ethnic analogy to the Christian

---

[1] George F. Moore, *History of Religions*, I, p. 345.

[2] *Vater, Sohn und Geist unter den heiligen Dreiheiten und vor der religiösen Denkweise der Gegenwart*, 1909.

Trinity. The *triratna* has played a rôle in the history of Buddhism comparable in importance to that of the Trinity in the history of Christianity; and in both we have the same general scheme. The three factors in each are constituted by the *content* of the revelation, its *mediator,* and its *realizing agency* in the world. The content is in the one case the "Doctrine" and in the other God; the mediator is in the one case Buddha and in the other Jesus Christ; the realizing agency is in the one case the Order and in the other the Holy Spirit. But this correspondence is manifestly purely formal in character. So far as the content and inner structure of the two "trinities" are concerned, there is no real parallel between them. The one is theistic, the other nontheistic. The one has to do with distinctions within the Godhead, the other with different factors in an historic movement unrelated to the Deity. That one was not derived from the other, and particularly that the Christian Trinity was not derived from the Buddhistic *triratna,* is thus evident.

Still, there [illegible] a feeling that there must be some connection between the Christian Trinity and the numerous ethnic triads. One writer[3] has, for instance, argued that there was a primitive Semitic triad of Gods and that this triad, handed down by a continuous tradition, though now and then hidden from the view of the historian, came to new life in what he calls the "tritheistic" teaching of the New Testament. The original triad consisted of Father, Mother, and

[3] Ditlef Nielsen, *Der dreieinige Gott in religionshistorischer Beleuchtung,* 1922.

Son, who were somehow connected with or represented by the Moon, the Sun, and Venus. But the existence of such a primitive "trinity" is open to serious question, and that it in any case lost its religious significance both among the northern and southern Semites in pre-Christian times is conceded by the author. The theory may, consequently, be dismissed as a fanciful speculation. It throws no light on thc origin of the Christian Trinity.

Another writer[4] has propounded the theory that among primitive peoples three was the highest number in their arithmetical system and that it hence came to be used as an expression of completeness or totality. Three objects stood for a large group or for a rounded whole, and so it became customary to put the names of three gods together as a designation of the entire superworld. It was in this way that the many ethnic triads arose, and to this motive also the origin of the Christian Trinity is traced. But whatever truth may attach to the theory, so far as it relates to the significance of the number three, it fails to account for what is distinctive in the Christian Trinity. The ethnic triads were made up of relatively independent deities and had a polytheistic background. The gods composing them were not bound together by any metaphysical or other ties. Their union was more or less "accidental," and hence in their case the idea of totality suggested by the number three may have been an important factor in combining them into triads. But with the Christian Trinity the situation is different. There we have a monotheistic back-

[4] Hermann Usener, *Dreiheit*, 1903.

ground, and surely the idea of completeness and totality is expressed as effectively by the number one as by the number three. In any case, in view of the known facts, it would be highly absurd to attribute the rise of the Trinitarian doctrine to the magical influence of a number. No doubt the Trinitarian formula has seemed to Christian people a more adequate expression of the idea of Deity than Jewish monotheism, but the reason is hardly to be found in the fact that it is composed of three parts.

A third writer has attempted to account for the doctrine of the Trinity by tracing its origin to what he regards as the threefold root of religion.[5] One of these roots is found in the worship of nature, another in the cult of the dead, and a third in the belief in a supremely good Being. The last of these is the most important, but the other two support and corroborate it, and together they constitute the source of religion. The fact that the source is threefold explains the numerous triadic and trinitarian formulæ that have appeared in the course of religious history, for in these formulæ the effort is made to sum up the essential elements in religious faith. But however true the latter statement may be, it is extremely dubious whether religion has just three roots, and it is still more dubious whether the three roots are those above mentioned. The fact is that the worship of nature and the cult of the dead are incidental expressions of reli-

[5] Leop. v. Schröder, *Beiträge zur Weiterentwicklung der Christlichen Religion* (1905), pp. 1-39; *Arische Religion* (1914), I, pp. 48-138.

gion rather than its sources, and the belief in a supremely good Being is a late development in religious history. The account given of the genesis and nature of religion is thus seriously defective. But apart from that it is very doubtful if there are three, and only three, sources of religion or fundamental elements in it. Georg Wobbermin,[6] who criticizes the foregoing theories, maintains that there are three fundamental religious feelings—the feeling of dependence, the feeling of protectedness (*Geborgenheitsgefühl*), and the feeling of longing or aspiration—and that these feelings receive their "specific Christian stamp" and their "highest conceivable unfolding" in trinitarian monotheism. But while the latter part of this contention may be true, it by no means follows that a correct analysis of religion necessarily takes a threefold form, nor does it follow that such a threefold analysis had any significant influence in the development of the doctrine of the Trinity. Certainly, the framers of the doctrine were guided by very different considerations. The truth is that religion is a highly complex phenomenon and is capable of analysis into many different elements or feelings. No threefold analysis could command general assent. Religion is not in any strict sense triadic in structure, nor can it be made such. There is nothing, therefore, in its essential nature that necessarily leads to the Trinitarian doctrine. This doctrine cannot with any stringency be psychologically deduced, nor was any attempt made to do so in the period of its formation. No doubt religious feeling had much to

[6] *Wesen und Wahrheit des Christentums*, pp. 419-34.

do with the development of the doctrine, and after its formulation its three component elements each met a fundamental religious need. But it was no triad of religious needs or feelings that gave rise to the doctrine. Other forces of a historical rather than a psychological nature were there determinative.

A trinity that stood closer to the Christian doctrine than any of the ethnic triads mentioned above was that of the Neoplatonic philosophy. According to Plotinus there were three hypostases or divine principles: the One or the Good, Intelligence or Spirit (*nous*), and the World-Soul. The first was the Godhead in the absolute sense of the term, the second was an emanation from it, and the third an emanation from the second. How such "emanations" were possible we do not know. Indeed, they were not emanations in the strict sense of the term. They did not arise by a division of the divine substance. They were, rather, "overflowing by-products" which left the ultimate substance unchanged, though they proceeded from it by a necessity of its essence. They represented lower orders of reality, but they belonged still to the sphere of the Divine and found their ground and unity in the One, so that together they constituted a real triunity. Plotinus himself thought that this trinity could be found in Plato, and Socinus held that the church derived its Trinitarian doctrine from him. Both were mistaken, though there was more truth in Plotinus' contention than in that of Socinus. Plato did express ideas that later furnished a basis for the Neoplatonic trinity. But neither he nor Plotinus nor Greek philosophy in general was in a similar way the source of the Christian doctrine. It has been maintained by an influential school that the doctrine of the Trinity was the result of the importation of Greek metaphysics into Christian theology. And it is no doubt true that not only this particular doctrine, but the whole theological movement in the early church was stimulated and guided by the Greek spirit of inquiry and was cast in molds of thought borrowed from Greek philosophy. But the essential content of the Trinitarian doctrine and the impelling motives behind it were not borrowed from Greek speculation, but were embedded deep in Christian history and Christian experience. It was the fact of Christ and the fact of a new life in and through him that constituted the real basis of the doctrine. These facts called for explanation and in the process of evolving an adequate explanation metaphysics necessarily played an important part; and more or less unconsciously the analysis of religious experience may also have had considerable influence. But the moving force in the whole process was its factual basis, and this was distinctively Christian.

There is, however, an important truth connected with the attempts at both a psychological and a speculative derivation of the Trinitarian doctrine. In both of them it is assumed, and correctly, that the doctrine stands in an organic relation to reason and to religious experience. This is a fact that needs to be emphasized in view of the tendency in the past to lay so much stress upon the mysterious character of the doctrine as to deny to it any rational or empirical basis. Since the time of Thomas Aquinas it has been customary in orthodox theology to separate the Trinity from the doctrine of God and treat it as a pure mystery, a superrational truth of revelation. It may, we are told, be grounded in the *divine* reason, but so far as man is concerned, it lies entirely beyond the range of rational justification. The only basis on which we are warranted in accepting it is the authority of Scripture. "Faith in the Trinity and its cognate doctrines," said Miner Raymond, "must be founded on an unquestionable 'thus saith the Lord,' or it is a mere superstition."[7] With the Christian doctrine of God, however, it is different. It is a "mixed article," based both on reason and revelation, and hence admits of rational support and exposition, such as has been given it in the preceding chapters.

This sharp cleavage between the idea of God as a unitary Being and the doctrine of the Trinity owed its origin to the influence of the Aristotelian philosophy which became dominant in the church in the thirteenth century. Previous to that time the difficulties involved in the Trinitarian doctrine were, of course, recognized, but they were not regarded as essentially different from those connected with the general idea of God. Again and again the early church Fathers declared that God in his essential nature lay beyond the reach of the human understanding. "That God is, I know," said Basil,[8] "but what his essence is, I hold to be above reason; . . . faith is competent to know that God is, not what he

[7] *Systematic Theology,* I, p. 125.
[8] *Adversus Eunomium,* I, p. 12.

is." "It is not," said John of Damascus, "within our capacity to say anything about God, or even to think of him, beyond the things which have been divinely revealed to us. It is plain that there is a God. But what he is in his essence and nature is absolutely incomprehensible and unknowable."[9] The being of God itself was thus thought of as representing the extreme of mystery. Between it and the Trinity there was in that respect no difference. Both were on the same plane. They were what Lotze would have called "limit notions." From the side of the facts they were simple enough; they were rational constructions, interpretations of facts. But when taken by themselves and viewed from the standpoint of their intrinsic rationality they faded into dimness and unintelligibility. This was as true of "the unity of the essence" as of "the distinction of the persons." The two were equally mysterious, and each involved the other. The Trinity was not a kind of revelational appendix to an otherwise rational self-consistent idea of God. It was the fuller unfolding of the Christian view of Deity itself, its completer explication. However mysterious it may have been from the point of view of the finite reason, it was not uniquely so. It was arrived at by logical processes and stood vitally and organically related to the general Christian conception of God. What the latter implied was most clearly exhibited in the doctrine of the Trinity. Trinitarianism was the ripe fruit of Christian theism.

This view of the Trinity has been expounded at

---

[9] *De Fide Orthodoxa*, I, pp. 2, 4.

length from the religious standpoint by Georg Wobbermin in the third volume of his *Systematische Theologie.* He there maintains that the decisive difference between Christianity and Judaism is to be found in their conceptions of God. The Christian conception is more thoroughly personalistic and more absolutely monotheistic. Its personalism was deeper and more sharply defined because of the new stress placed upon the thought of eternal fellowship with God. Christ was raised from the dead in order to enter upon this fellowship and in order to lead others into it. This gave to the personal character of God a depth and inwardness that it had previously lacked. It also carried with it the idea of his absoluteness in a new and more exclusive sense. The older nationalistic particularism was completely transcended, and the Divine Father came to be regarded as absolute from both the metaphysical and the ethical points of view. "No one is good," said Jesus, "no one but God himself."[10] It is worthy of note that this remark was made in response to a question that had to do with the attainment of eternal life. In the light of this goal Jesus declared God to be alone good and to be the only God. In other words, God was for him the end as well as the beginning, the Omega as well as the Alpha, the Redeemer as well as the Creator. These two were essential moments in the early Christian view of God, and their vital union represented a distinct advance beyond the Old Testament. But there was a third and even more significant factor. Between creation and redemption there is a long period,

[10] Mark 10. 18.

and during it God was regarded as regnant in nature and history, a history that reached its religious climax in Christ. A God immanent in history, especially religious history, who was also Creator and Redeemer—such was then the God of the early Christians, and he was, as the foregoing analysis shows, a triune God.[11]

Several variations of this triple analysis appear in Wobbermin's book. He, for instance, says that the Christian God is (1) transcendent, (2) personal, and (3) immanent.[12] He is also (1) a God of creation, (2) a God of redemption, and (3) a God of sanctification.[13] Again, he is (1) the All-ruler, (2) the immanent God of history, and (3) a spiritual-personal God.[14] To this objective Trinity Wobbermin, furthermore, finds a corresponding subjective or ethical trinity, consisting of faith, love, and hope.[15] And yet again he points out that there is a parallel between the three elements in the Christian conception of God and the three fundamental religious feelings—the feeling of dependence, the feeling of "protectedness," and the feeling of longing.[16] In these different trinities it may be noted that transcendence, creation, universal rule, faith and the feeling of dependence go together and have reference to the "Father." Redemption, spiritual-personality, hope, and the feeling of longing likewise stand related to each other

---

[11] Georg Wobbermin, *Systematische Theologie*, III, pp. 77-80.
[12] *Systematische Theologie*, III, pp. 175ff.
[13] *Ibid.*, pp. 179f.
[14] *Ibid.*, p. 238.
[15] *Ibid.*, pp. 156, 241ff., 389.
[16] *Ibid.*, pp. 414f.

and point to the second principle in the divine nature, the "Son." Immanence, sanctification, love, and the feeling of "protectedness" constitute the third group and find their parallel in the "Holy Spirit." This correspondence of the various "trinities," mentioned by Wobbermin, with each other and with the ecclesiastical Trinity is not exact; but the relation between them is sufficiently close to bring out rather impressively the fact that the Christian idea of God can be analyzed into three basal elements and that there are three analogous elements in our empirical response to them.

For the analysis presented by Wobbermin there is not a little scriptural support. He himself lays special stress upon Rom. 11. 36. There we read that "from him and through him and unto him are all things." God is the Creator of the world, the source of all that is. *From* him comes everything. Everything also exists *through* him. He is the immanent ground of the world. In him we live and move and have our being, and by him human history is guided toward its ultimate goal. This goal is found in God himself. So *unto* him also are all things. Everything ends in him. He thus fulfills a threefold function. He is the Whence and the Whither of life and its sustaining Ground.

That this triple formula was taken seriously by Paul and had something more than a merely literary or æsthetic significance would seem to be indicated by the other passages where it occurs. In 1 Cor. 8. 6 the apostle says: "To us there is one God, the Father, *from* whom are all things, and we *unto* him; and one

Lord Jesus Christ, *through* whom are all things, and we *through* him." Here again we have God referred to as both the Whence and the Whither of life, its Creator and Redeemer. But instead of his being also designated as the immanent ground of the world and of history, Jesus Christ appears as the one *through* whom are all things and we *through* him. This does not mean that Christ is only another name for the immanent activity of God. He is rather represented as a distinct Being, the Mediator of creation and redemption. Mediatorship, however, does not exclude divine activity; it presupposes it. There is, therefore, in the mediatorial activity of Christ an implied reference to the third factor in the early Christian view of God; and this reference assumes that the immanent activity of God in history reached its climax in Christ Jesus. The same assumption underlies Col. 1. 15-17. Here we read of Christ that "all things have been created *through* him and *unto* him." But back of his creative activity lay the original creative power of the Father (v. 12), *from* whom all things came and who reveals himself in the work of Christ. In this passage also we thus have in the background of the apostle's thought the triple formula: from God, through God, unto God.

Some have maintained that this formula is not specifically Christian, that it was borrowed from Stoicism, and that it is interpreted most naturally in a pantheistic sense. Hence no such fundamental significance can be attached to it as does Wobbermin. He, however, rightly replies that, while a similar formula occurs in Marcus Aurelius and may have been common in Stoic circles, and while Paul may have derived it from that source, he gives to it an entirely new and distinctively Christian content. The various contexts in which it occurs make this evident. Consequently, there is no inherent reason why it should not be equated with the trinitarian benediction in 2 Cor. 13, 14: "The grace of the Lord Jesus Christ, and the love of God, and the communion of the Holy Spirit be with you all." It has been argued that there was no connection between the two in the apostle's mind; but in Eph. 4. 4-6 the essential ideas expressed by both are bound up immediately with each other. We there read of the "one Spirit," the "one Lord," and then the "one God and Father of all," who, in conformity with Rom. 11. 36, "is over all, and through all, and in all." Another significant passage is that in 1 Cor. 12. 4-6, which is the earliest clear-cut and unquestioned formulation of the Trinitarian doctrine. It speaks of "one and the same Spirit," of "one and the same Lord," and of "one and the same God," adding of the last named that he "worketh all things in all," a clause that suggests Rom. 11. 36.

There are many other Trinitarian passages in the New Testament[17] or passages that suggest the Trinitarian formula;[18] but those cited suffice to illustrate the view that the Christian conception of God was from the outset Trinitarian in form. Whether Wobbermin's analysis was consciously in the mind of Paul

[17] For example, Matt. 28. 19; John 14. 16f., 26; 15. 26; 16. 7-13; 2 Thess. 2. 13f.; 1 Thess. 5. 9f.; 1 Pet. 1. 1f.; Jude 20f.; Eph. 2. 18.

[18] For example, 1 John 1. 3; 2. 22; 3. 23f.; Col. 3. 4; Mark 8. 38; Matt. 16. 27; Luke 9. 26.

and the early Christians or not, it brings out the three essential elements in their thought of God; and these elements have through the ages been the vital source of Trinitarian speculation. The doctrine of the Trinity was not, then, superimposed upon the doctrine of God as a more or less alien addition and as a unique mystery completely transcending the human reason. No doubt many mysterious and contradictory things have been said about the Trinity, so that there is more or less justification for Doctor South's warning that "as he that denies this fundamental article of the Christian religion may lose his soul, so he that much strives to understand it may lose his wits."[19] But the difficulties in the doctrine have grown out of later speculative elaborations of it rather than out of the religious ideas expressed by it. It has always been the latter that have been the generating and sustaining source of the doctrine and they are inherent in the Christian view of God. It is to them and the historic facts with which they were associated in New Testament times that Christian Trinitarianism owes its origin. The particular form taken by it in later times was due in considerable measure to ideas borrowed from Greek philosophy, but the spirit that inspired it was always Christian. In the Trinity we have simply an explication of the primitive Christian faith in God.

## Development of the Doctrine

In the development of the Trinitarian doctrine

[19] Quoted by W. G. T. Shedd, *Dogmatic Theology*, I, p. 250, from *Sermon XLIII.*

there were two main periods. The first was marked by the recognition of a unique presence of God in Christ—a presence that called forth and warranted a worshipful attitude toward him. The second was characterized by the identification of this presence with a distinct and eternal mode of being within the divine essence itself. Between these two periods there was no sharp line of demarcation. The first passed gradually over into the second. Roughly speaking, it may be said that the first was represented by the New Testament. The second reached its climax at the Council of Nicæa in 325, but extended a full century beyond that date.

In both periods it should be noted that interest centered in the person of Christ. It was not God the Creator, nor God the sanctifying Spirit, nor was it the idea of threeness[20] in the Godhead with which the doctrine of the Trinity was primarily concerned. Its fundamental concern was with God the Son or God in Christ. The divinity of Christ carried with it the idea of a Divine Creator and of a Divine Spirit and thus grounded the idea of a Divine Trinity. But it was not the Trinity as such toward which the attention of the early church was especially directed, nor was it the Creator or Holy Spirit; it was God incarnate in Christ. This was the great creative idea in the life and thought of the church. It may have had

[20] Note the following statement by Basil: "In delivering the formula of the Father, the Son, and the Holy Spirit, our Lord did not connect the gift with number. He did not say, 'into First, Second and Third,' nor yet 'into One, Two and Three,' but he gave us the boon of the knowledge of faith which leads to salvation, by means of holy names" (*De Spiritu Sancto*, 44).

as its background such a Trinitarian conception of God as that expounded by Wobbermin. But this conception was itself due to the influence of Christ. It was he who by his life and death put the redemptive activity of God on a par with his creative activity and made vital the idea of his immanent activity in the world—an activity that reached its religious culmination in his own Messiahship and was perpetuated in the church by the work of the Holy Spirit. The Trinity represented by the creative, redemptive, and immanent activity of God, as it was conceived by Paul and others in the apostolic age, was the direct result of the life and teaching of Christ. Indeed, it might be said to be an inference from the impression made by his personality. It was in him and his sacrificial death that God was most fully revealed as Redeemer, and it was in the sanctifying work of the Spirit that his immanence was made most manifest to men. Apart from these concrete manifestations of the redemptive and immanent activity of God, the Trinity of creation, redemption and immanence would probably not have been thought of in Jewish circles and certainly would have been devoid of the power necessary to found a universal church. It was Christ and the Holy Spirit, not the abstract ideas of the redemptive and creative activity of God, that laid hold of the minds and the hearts of Christian believers. Hence the Trinitarian formula, adopted by the church, spontaneously took the form of a confession of faith, not in three aspects of the divine activity, but in the Father, the Son, and the Holy Spirit.

The starting point of Christian Trinitarianism was

the belief in what may be called the unique divinity of Christ. How this belief arose is one of the most mooted questions in the history of religion. Its rise in a polytheistic faith would not have been especially strange, but that it should have sprung up in connection with a clear-cut monotheism creates a perplexing problem. Two groups of theories may be distinguished. One traces the source of the belief to the actual impression made by Jesus upon his disciples and to its logical and consistent development. The other group finds its origin in some contemporary myth such as that of a dying Saviour current in the non-Christian mystery cults of the day. Some have gone so far as to argue that Jesus never existed and that the gospel figure was that of a cult-god, clothed in historical dress.[21] Others hold that, while a Jewish rabbi by the name of Jesus existed, no real importance would ever have attached to him but for the fact that a mystery cult with its mythical deity came somehow to be grafted upon his surviving memory. Still others look upon Jesus as a religious genius of transcendent significance, but they insist that he was only a man and that the later association of his name with Deity was not only at variance with his own teaching, but a perversion of Christianity that has cursed the whole subsequent history of the church. According to this view we must distinguish sharply between the religion *of* Jesus and the religion *about* Jesus, and between the Jesus of history and the Christ of faith. Occasionally the distinction is spoken of as one between Jesus

[21] For example, Arthur Drews, *The Christ Myth*.

and Paul or one between Palestinian and Hellenistic Christianity. But however it is phrased, the meaning is essentially the same. The real Jesus, the Jesus of history, was a mere man, to whom divinity could not in any proper sense of the term be attributed. It was the creative imagination of the early church and the influence of the mystery cults that translated him into an object of worship. Paul, in particular, was responsible for the change.

This theory and the others related to it seek to fit Jesus into the frame of a semideistic Jewish monotheism, and in so doing necessarily deny to him the unique position accorded him by the Christian faith. From their point of view there is a gulf between the human and the divine which cannot be bridged except by mythology. There may have been such a man as Jesus or there may not, he may have been a very remarkable man or he may not; but in any case there could have been no unique divine element in him. The ascription of divinity to him was due to the mythmaking faculty. There was no historical or empirical basis for it. The later Trinitarian and Christological doctrines were simply rationalizations of a myth. It was, we are frankly told, a myth that conquered the world.

Opposed to theories of this type stands the New Testament conviction that "God was in Christ" in a real and unique sense. How this conviction arose we cannot say with certainty, nor is it altogether clear how the Divine Presence in Christ was conceived by the New Testament writers. But that they regarded it as a fact is evident, and it is equally evident to

Christian faith that this conviction was no foreign importation, but was due to the direct impression made by Christ himself upon his disciples.

The factors and considerations that led the early disciples to set Jesus apart from other men and to ascribe to him more or less of a divine character were no doubt numerous. We may distinguish five. For one thing there must have been something about the personality of Jesus that awakened the sense of the "numinous" or the superhuman. Rudolf Otto[22] directs special attention to Mark 10. 32, where we read that, as Jesus went before his disciples on the way to Jerusalem, "they were amazed, and as they followed they were afraid." The feeling here referred to, we are told, was that of the numinous, and "no artistry of characterization" could express it "so powerfully as these few masterly and pregnant words." Akin to this verse is Luke 5. 8, where it is said of Peter that he "fell down at Jesus' knees, saying, Depart from me, for I am a sinful man, O Lord," and also Matt. 8. 8, where the centurion is reported as saying, "O Lord, I am not worthy that thou shouldest come under my roof." In addition to these, it is probable that there were many unrecorded instances of a similar kind. Only on this supposition would it seem possible to account for the depth of attachment to Christ implied in the founding of a religious community in his name.

A second factor that contributed to the same end was Jesus' Messianic consciousness or his consciousness of a unique filial relation to God. Of these two

[22] *The Idea of the Holy*, pp. 162f.

the latter was the more basal. It was Jesus' consciousness of divine Sonship that led to his Messianic consciousness rather than the reverse. It has, it is true, been denied that Jesus thought of himself either as the Messiah or as standing in a unique relation to God; but the grounds on which this conclusion is based have not commended themselves to the great body of New Testament critics. It is also true that there is considerable difference of opinion as to the exact meaning of the Sonship and Messiahship which Jesus in all probability claimed for himself. But that these terms carried with them the idea of an altogether unique mission can hardly be doubted. They denoted someone greater than a prophet. This is evident from Matt. 11. 27 and 16. 15-17. In the first of these passages we have that most self-revealing of all Jesus' words, "No one knoweth the Son, save the Father; neither doth any know the Father, save the Son, and he to whomsoever the Son willeth to reveal him." In the second we have Peter's confession of Jesus' Messiahship, "Thou art the Christ, the Son of the living God." This insight, it is worthy of note, Jesus attributed to an immediate experience on Peter's part, an experience of the numinous or intuitional type. "Flesh and blood," he said to him, "hath not revealed it unto thee, but my Father which is in heaven." The important thing, however, was not the way the disciples arrived at their belief in Jesus' Messiahship, but the fact that they derived it directly from him. It was his own self-consciousness that awakened in them the belief. Either he told them of his inner conviction or they sensed it,

In any case he stood apart from all others as the bearer of a "superprophetic consciousness, the consciousness of the accomplisher to whose person the flight of the ages and the whole destiny of his followers is linked";[23] and this fact led naturally to his being called "Lord" in the religious as well as the merely honorific sense of the term.

A third fact that tended to lift Jesus above the common human plane was his exalted moral character, his embodiment of the principle of sacrificial love. This received its supreme expression in his death, but it must have radiated from his entire life. It is significant, as John Baillie[24] points out, that the affirmation that "No man hath seen God at any time," which occurs twice in the New Testament,[25] is in one instance followed by the statement that we nevertheless see him in the love we show one another, while in the other instance it is followed by the statement that we see him in Jesus. Between these two statements there is no contradiction, nor do they represent two different findings of God. It was the perfect love in the soul of Christ that led men to recognize in him the unique and unalloyed presence of God.

A fourth element that had much to do with the finding of God in Jesus was the belief in his resurrection. However this belief may have originated, it led inevitably to the view that he was in some special sense divine. As Paul put it, it was by the resurrection of the dead that he was declared to be the Son

---

[23] W. Bousset, *Jesus*, p. 179.
[24] *The Place of Jesus Christ in Modern Christianity*, p. 119.
[25] 1 John 4. 12; John 1. 18.

of God with power.[26] The word "power" may refer to the miraculous method of the declaration, as Sanday[27] holds, but it may also refer to the new accession of strength that came to the risen Christ. The latter thought was anticipated by Jesus himself (Luke 12. 49f.) and was assumed in the life and beliefs of the early church. Certainly, it was the risen Christ that Paul thought of as operative in the hearts of believers. To them to live was Christ. It was this experience of the risen Christ that was the source of all living interest in him, and the risen Christ thus experienced must have been looked upon as essentially divine. Between him and God there could have been no perceptible difference. The *agape* that constituted the soul of the early Christian fellowship was the love both of Christ and of God. The love bearing these two names was not two loves but one.

A fifth consideration that must have tended to give rise to and confirm the belief that "God was in Christ" was the deep-seated religious conviction that all history is rooted in God. To one holding this conviction it must have seemed inevitable that "the unsearchable riches" discovered in Christ were primarily and fundamentally a divine gift to men. Jesus was no doubt the ideal man, and the ideal he attained was in one sense an achievement; his life was a quest after God, an instance of perfect obedience and of perfect faith. But it was much more than that. It was "a self-disclosure of Deity," a quest of God after man, a supreme

[26] Rom. 1. 4.
[27] *The Epistle to the Romans*, in the International Critical Commentary, p. 9.

instance of divine grace. In and through Christ God imparted himself to men, he *did* something for them. To this conclusion we are driven by the Christian conception of God's relation to the world as well as by the intuitions of experience and the testimony of Scripture.

In view of the foregoing facts and considerations we are warranted in deriving the higher view of Christ from the impression made by his personality upon his disciples instead of from an alien and mythical source. But the higher view is not clearly defined in the New Testament. Christ is treated as an object of worship; but there is apparently no consciousness of a conflict between this attitude toward him and monotheism, and no direct effort is made to reconcile the two. Christ is also thought of as in some sense divine; but the relation of the divine element in him to the eternal God, on the one hand, and to the human element in his own being, on the other, is not made a subject of speculation. Problems of this kind were left for a later date. What the New Testament writers were concerned about was to find a designation of Christ that would do justice to the supreme religious and spiritual value they found in him. Such terms as "Messiah," "Lord," and in Greek circles "Logos" lay close at hand, and were used. But they were more or less ambiguous terms and did not define in a precise way the relation of the person of Christ either to God or man. They served, rather, a practical religious purpose, and their use formed part of the problem bequeathed to later generations.

It would, however, be a mistake to suppose that

the apostolic age had no interest in the speculative questions connected with the person of Christ. The beginnings of such speculation are observable in the account of the baptism and in the story of the virgin birth; and a bold invasion of the speculative field is represented by the doctrine of Christ's pre-existence taught by Paul and by the authors of the Epistle to the Hebrews and the Gospel of John. In Col. 1. 15-17 and later in Heb. 1. 3 and John 1. 1-18 cosmic significance is attributed to Christ; he is declared to be the Mediator of creation. This has been characterized as "one of the most daring leaps of imagination that have ever been made by the mind of man" and as "the intellectual miracle of the apostolic age."[28] And such it may seem to us who do not know its historical antecedents. But more remarkable than the idea itself was the fact that, so far as we know, it went unchallenged when first announced by Paul. This would seem to indicate either that the idea was not original with him or that it was accepted as a natural inference from the view of Christ previously held. So closely had Christ already been identified with Deity that it imposed no strain upon the Christian imagination to ascribe creative activity to him. But for our purpose the point of special interest is that Paul conceived of the pre-existent Christ as a kind of archangelic being, distinct from God, and fully personal.[29] In what relation the incarnate personality stood to the pre-existent personality, except that it was somehow a continuation of it, he does not tell us; nor does

---

[29] Phil. 2. 5-11; 2 Cor. 8. 9.
[28] H. T. Andrews in *The Lord of Life*, p. 108.

he harmonize this conception of the incarnation with the statement that "God was in Christ." In speaking of "God" in the latter connection he may have had in mind the pre-existent Christ, but more likely the statement was a general one that took no account of the pre-existent state. Indeed, it might have been said of the pre-existent as well as the incarnate Christ that God was in him. The mystery of the unique presence of God is not solved by the theory of pre-existence, and Paul's particular theory of pre-existence was not accepted as adequate by later Christian theologians. It owed its origin to contemporary modes of thought, and for a time served as an effective expression of what Christ meant in Christian experience. But later and profounder thought demanded a more intimate relation between the divine element in Christ or his pre-existent state and God himself, and this prepared the way for the second period in the development of the Trinitarian doctrine.

In the first period, represented by the New Testament, there was a clear conviction that "God was in Christ," but there was no uniform or adequate theory of the nature of this unique divine presence. The fact of it led naturally to a more immanental view of Deity, but this did not solve the special problem created by the person of Christ. At first the current angelology suggested a solution, and this was later supplemented in Hebrews and the Prologue to John's Gospel by ideas borrowed from Greek philosophy. But the idea of an archangelic being, whether called the Son or the Logos, did not, when thought through, prove satisfactory either to faith or reason. A more complete deification than that represented by such a being was needed, and so in the second period of Trinitarian thought the divine principle in Christ was identified with a mode of being within God himself.

The process by which this identification was brought about was a gradual one. We may note five stages in its unfolding.[30] The first marked what seems but a slight advance beyond the New Testament. It consisted in the equating of Christ with the Logos by the Apologists of the second century. What differentiated their position from that of the Prologue to the fourth Gospel was the fact that they were adherents of the Platonic-Stoic philosophy and that the idea of the Logos was fundamental in their theory of reality. Consequently, they made it basal also in their Christology. The fourth Gospel subordinated the idea of the Logos to that of the Son, but the Apologists reversed the order, and in so doing took what Harnack has called "the most important step that was ever taken in the domain of Christian doctrine."[31] This new step was not altogether free from evil consequences, but it had its distinct advantages. The very fact that Greek philosophers saw in Christ an incarnation of the Logos was itself a striking testimony to the extraordinary impression produced upon them by his personality. But what is more significant, the identifying of Christ with the Logos gave to the belief in him a rational status that it had not had before. It lifted the pre-existent and exalted Christ out of the realm of Jewish fancy and trans-

---

[30] Cf. W. A. Brown, *Christian Theology in Outline*, pp. 142-45.
[31] *What Is Christianity?* Pp. 217f.

formed him from a semi-mythical archangelic being into a "rational Power," a Power or Being that had its established place in the philosophical world-view of the day. Such a view naturally had an "intoxicating effect" upon Christian believers in intellectual circles. Then, too, it brought Christ into closer relation to the absolute Deity. The term "Logos" was an elastic one and was used in various senses. It denoted the Mediator of creation, the immanent Divine Reason, and the world of Ideas rooted in God. But however conceived, the Being designated by the term stood in a more organic and "essential" relation to Deity than did the transcendent Christ of earlier Christian thought. To define exactly this relation was not an easy task. According to the Apologists the Logos-Christ was not a "creation," nor was he an "emanation." In some nonquantitative way he shared in the being of God and yet was dependent upon him. "Generation" seemed the most satisfactory term to designate this dependence, but it was manifestly figurative, and whether the process indicated by it referred to the divine will or the divine nature was not made clear. It was also left uncertain whether "generation" implied that the Logos had an absolute beginning. Some statements would seem to favor this view, and yet it was held by Justin, for instance, that "potentially" the Logos was "eternally in God."[32] The very fact that he was the Reason of God and that God was never devoid of reason seemed to point to such a conclusion.

In view of this uncertainty a new stage in the de-

[32] J. A. Dorner, *The Doctrine of the Person of Christ*, I, p. 272.

velopment of the doctrine of the Trinity was introduced by Origen when he plainly and emphatically taught the "eternal generation" of the Logos-Son. This teaching ran parallel in his mind with the idea of the eternal creation of the world, but was not derived from it. It "owed its origin, in the last instance, to the transformation of the conception of God brought about by the ethical appearance of Christ."[33] In advocating it Origen was actuated by two apparently contradictory motives. He wished, on the one hand, to identify Christ more closely with the Father than the Apologists had done and, on the other hand, to distinguish him more clearly from him. In holding to the temporal generation of the Son the Apologists and other writers such as Tertullian reduced him, so far as his own *hypostatic* being was concerned, to a finite and temporal plane and thus shut him out "too much from the essence and sphere of the Father." Origen consequently affirmed his *eternal* generation, and by so doing lifted him out of the temporal sphere and made him share more completely in the nature and being of God. That this formula came nearer to expressing the living Christian faith of the day is evident from the eager way in which it was received and from the fact that it became "a corner stone in the doctrinal edifice of the church." It stood as a permanent support of the higher view of Christ. But while Origen was thus concerned with bringing the Son and the Father closer together he was also deeply interested in establishing a clear distinction between them. The

[33] J. A. Dorner, *ibid.*, II, p. 113.

Apologists had ascribed a kind of existence to the Logos before his "generation," but this existence was hardly distinguishable from that of the absolute Deity; and others, such as the Patripassians and Sabellians, completely identified the Son with the Father. Against this tendency Origen resolutely set himself in the interest of the reality of the incarnation and the distinct personality of Christ, but here he went further than the faith of the church was willing to follow. "Generation," he held, implied subordination. The Son was, therefore, not God in the full sense of the term. He was *theos,* but only the Father was *ho theos.*[34] Absolute Deity belonged only to the latter. There were then degrees of Godhood, and the Son, while the image of the Father, was subordinate to him. He was "of a nature midway between that of the uncreated and that of all creatures." While sharing to some extent in the being of the Father he was not completely *homoousios,* of the same substance, with him. Only by taking this position did it seem possible to Origen to maintain the necessary distinction between the Son and the Father.

The church, however, thought otherwise. It retained the distinction between Father and Son, but it felt the need of a Son or Redeemer in whom dwelt "all the fullness of the Godhead bodily," a Redeemer who was of the same divine essence as the Father and hence could mediate immortal life to men. To this great affirmation Trinitarian thought in its *third* stage, consequently, devoted itself. The affirmation was made officially at the Council of Nicæa. Its im-

[34] See John 1. 1-2.

mediate occasion was the heresy of Arius; but apart from that the doctrine it formulated must have come eventually to definitive expression, for it was the logical outcome of the conviction of the early church. This Athanasius, the leader and hero of the new movement, made abundantly clear. He showed that the divine unity required that the Logos, or Son, should be *homoousios* with the Father, that only such a Son was worthy of worship, and that only the incarnation of such a fully divine Being could make possible human redemption. If Christ were less than God, union with him would not be union with God and so there would be no salvation for those who trusted in him. The very heart of the gospel, according to Athanasius, consisted in the belief that in Christ God "was made man that we might be made God." Hence the only consistent view to take of the Son was that of the Nicene creed, where he is said to be "very God of very God, begotten, not made, being of one substance with the Father." Indeed, God would not be Father unless he were also Son. The two belong logically together in the divine unity.

With the attainment of this insight the chief motive underlying the doctrine of the Trinity came to its full development. The monotheistic idea was now so enlarged as to take up into itself the new elements contributed by the person and work of Christ. But formally the Trinitarian doctrine was not yet complete. It was dyadic rather than triadic. Then, too, more explicit statements were needed with reference to the personal distinctions within the Deity and also with reference to the nature of the divine unity. To these problems the Cappadocian theologians and Augustine devoted themselves. The former—Basil of Cæsarea, Gregory of Nazianzum, and Gregory of Nyssa—belonged to the latter half of the fourth century, and represent the *fourth* stage in the development of Trinitarianism. To them, and especially to Gregory of Nyssa, we owe a sharp distinction between the terms *ousia* and *hypostasis.* In the Nicene creed these terms were used synonymously, but now "hypostasis" was differentiated from "essence" and applied to what was distinctive in the Father and the Son. At the same time the Holy Spirit was definitely recognized as a third hypostasis, thus giving rise to the full Trinitarian doctrine with its one essence and three hypostases.

The hypostatizing of the Spirit followed naturally that of the Son and had no special doctrinal significance. It would perhaps have been possible to think of the Spirit as a mere influence emanating from the Father and the Son, but biblical and ecclesiastical usage was on the whole against such a view. In the baptismal formula and in the apostolic benediction the Spirit was co-ordinated with the Son in such a way that, if the Son was regarded as a divine hypostasis, it was almost inevitable that the Spirit should be also. It was said of the Spirit that it *proceeded* from the Father instead of being *begotten* by him as was the Son. This difference of terminology may suggest a more personal view of the Son than of the Spirit, but otherwise no distinguishable meaning can be attached to the two terms. Both seem to indicate a certain subordination to the Father, and this was the prevailing view in the Eastern church. The Father was looked upon as the center of the divine unity, the principal seat of divinity. From him the Son and Spirit derived their being. Not only was he the logical commencement of the trinitarian process, he was the unifying principle in it, the root and source of all Deity. In assigning him this position the intention was not to attribute to the other hypostases a lower form of divinity, but, rather, to provide within the Godhead a ground of unity so that it would not be necessary to make of the common divine essence a fourth principle and thus fall into Tetradism.

By an "hypostasis" the Cappadocian Fathers understood a mode of being midway between a substance and an attribute. Like an attribute it presupposed a substance and like a substance it had attributes. But what it was beyond that it was difficult to say. The translation of the term by the Latin "persona" led to much confusion and misunderstanding. That the Cappadocian Divines meant by "hypostasis" something less than what we mean by "person" is generally conceded. They were seeking to guard the doctrine of the Trinity against Sabellianism on the one hand and Tritheism on the other. Hence they maintained that Father, Son, and Spirit were more than divine attributes, more than successive and temporary phases of the divine self-revelation. On the other hand, they were not independent centers of self-consciousness and self-determination. They were "hypostases," eternal distinctions within a larger divine unity.

But how was this unity to be conceived? Logically,

there would seem to be need of a unitary divine essence, immanent in the three hypostases, which constituted each of them divine. But this would have led to Tetradism. Hence the tendency was, as we have seen, to find the source of the divine unity in the Father. This, however, involved a subordination of the Son and the Spirit which by implication, at least, denied divinity to them in the highest sense of the term and which to that extent seemed out of harmony with the unqualified affirmation of faith that "*God* was in Christ." Consequently, Trinitarian thought did not rest content until it had removed the last trace of subordination on the part of the Son and the Spirit. This was done by Augustine, whose work *"On the Trinity"* marks the *fifth* and concluding stage in the development of the Trinitarian doctrine. It was under the influence of his teaching that the so-called "Athanasian Creed" was written, in which the absolute equality of the three Persons of the Trinity is declared to be "the Catholic Faith, which except a man believe faithfully, he cannot be saved."

According to Augustine, each Person, or Hypostasis, was totally and absolutely God. The terms "begotten" and "proceeding" were still used of the Son and the Spirit, but they were divested of every element of subordination, and to indicate this it was said that the Spirit proceeded from the Father *and the Son* (*filioque*). Formally this still left the Spirit in an apparently subordinate relation to the Father and the Son, but it was only formally and apparently so. Actually everything positive that was said of the Father and the Son was also said of the Spirit, and each was equated with the total Deity. "In that highest Trinity," said Augustine, "one is as much as the three together, nor are two anything more than one. And they are infinite in themselves. So both each are in each and all in each, and each in all, and all in all, and all are one."[35] Some indication of what was meant by such a statement as this may be gathered from the unity of consciousness. The subject is completely present in each one of his states or acts; and so it is with God. That is what we mean by his omnipresence. And what Augustine and the Athanasian creed did, was to apply the attribute of omnipresence to the inner being of the Trinitarian God. Only from this point of view can any intelligible meaning be given to their paradoxical utterances. God is present in each Hypostasis in some such way as the self is in each of its states, except that his presence is not limited to one Hypostasis at a time. He is simultaneously and completely present in them all by virtue of his self-consciousness; and it is this consciousness that constitutes his unity. In no other way can his unity be rationally conceived.

The dogmatic theologians sought to explain the inner unity of the triune God by the theory of "circumincession" or "perichoresis." According to this theory, there is a "living reciprocal interpenetration of the three hypostases." They are in ceaseless interaction and intercommunion with each other. They are bound together by "an immanent circulation in the Divine Nature—an unceasing and eternal *move-*

---

[35] *On the Trinity*, VI, p. 12.

*ment* in the Godhead, whereby each Person coinheres in the others, and the others in each."[36] This conception of an eternal process in the divine life has the advantage of ascribing to God a vital and dynamic character that he lacked in non-Trinitarian thought, and it no doubt has value also as a metaphysical interpretation of the terms "generation" and "procession," but it hardly solves the problem of the divine unity. It rather forms a part of it. "Process" does not constitute nor explain metaphysical unity; it presupposes it. If we are to understand the divine unity, we must rise above the plane of mere "process" or "essence" and lay hold of the idea of self-consciousness. Only in it do we have the key to real unity. This, however, is an insight to which the ancient world did not attain. It adhered to the idea of an underlying or immanent substance or essence as the ground of unity. This was true both of the mental life and of things. But it is interesting and significant that at this point Augustine noted a distinction between the activities of the mind and the Hypostases of the Trinity. "Whereas," he said, "memory, understanding, and will are not the soul, but only exist in the soul, the Trinity does not exist in God but is God."[37] Here it is implied that the divine unity is not distinguishable from the three Hypostases, but is realized only in and through them. They are bound together by an interacting and interpenetrating process which in a sense constitutes them one as well as three.

[36] W. G. T. Shedd, *A History of Christian Doctrine*, I, p. 348.

[37] Epist. CLXIX. Quoted by H. C. Sheldon, *History of Christian Doctrine*, I, p. 215.

But this process can be truly unified only in the form of an all-embracing consciousness, and to such a conception the theory of circumincession may be regarded as pointing forward.

With this theory and with the Athanasian creed the development of the doctrine of the Trinity came virtually to an end. Since then the doctrine has been elaborated and refined by Thomas Aquinas[38] and other theologians, but in its essential features it has remained the same. For a long time it has been subjected to a steady stream of criticism and numerous efforts have been made to modify it or dispense with it altogether, but thus far these efforts have failed. The doctrine in its traditional form still maintains itself, and to a brief consideration of its elements of strength and weakness we now turn.

### Traditional Form of the Doctrine

The doctrine of the Trinity owed its origin, as we have seen, to the deep-seated conviction of the early church that God was in Christ in a way and to a degree that justified his being made an object of worship. This conviction led to an enlargement of the idea of God. The enlargement took two different forms, that of external addition and that of internal expansion and enrichment. The first of these was embodied in the Adoptionist theology represented by such men as Theodotus, active in Rome between 189 and 199, and Paul of Samosata, bishop of Antioch from 260 to 269. These men are commonly known as Dynamic Monarchians, because they insisted on the

[38] *Summa Theologica*, Part I, Qu. XXVII-XLIII.

older unitarian or monarchic view of God and looked upon Jesus as a man in whom a unique divine power (*dynamis*) dwelt, but who was not an incarnation of Deity. They did, however, hold that through his own perfect obedience and through divine grace he attained to divinity and after his resurrection was invested with divine rank. He thus became a proper object of worship and, insofar as there was anything distinctive in his being, supplemented to that extent the idea of Deity heretofore current. But such a method of enlarging the conception of God had more in common with polytheism and mythology than with the Christian faith, though there are some passages in the New Testament that may seem to support it.[39] A deified man or any being who might conceivably achieve deity or have deity thrust upon him would not be God in the Christian sense of the term. Such a being might have angelic or even archangelic status, but he would still be external to essential Deity. No real enrichment of the idea of God can come through the adoptionist method. This the early church clearly saw and so rejected it as heretical.

The other method of interpreting the divine presence in Christ was that represented by the doctrines of the incarnation and the Trinity. This was the method adopted by the church; but within it there were three possibilities. One might think of the incarnated Being as the one God, or as a subordinate and created Being, or as an eternal mode of being within the one God. The first view was advocated toward the close of the second and the early part of

[39] For example, Acts 2. 32-36; 5. 30-31.

the third century by Praxeas, Noetus, and Sabellius, from the last of whom the movement later took its name. These men were called *Patripassians,* because they held that it was the Father himself who suffered in Christ, and *modalistic Monarchians,* because they maintained that the so-called "persons" in the Trinity were merely successive and temporary modes of manifestation on the part of the one Father-God. To this type of theology there were three main objections. It was out of harmony with the distinct personality ascribed to Christ in the New Testament; it denied the existence of the Divine Christ after his ascension and thus ran counter to a vital element in Christian experience; and in the third place it was in a state of unstable equilibrium in its view of God, tending to attribute to him either a "heathen mutability" on the one hand or an extreme deistic transcendence on the other. The church, consequently, put it under the ban at a Synod held in the year 261.

The second possible view above referred to, which conceives of the preincarnate Christ as a temporal and created being, was represented by Arianism. According to it, the Holy Spirit was another created Being second to the Son. The Trinity was thus dissolved into a triad, consisting of the omnipotent God and two creatures. To this view also three important objections were raised. For one thing it presupposed an extreme form of the divine transcendence which excluded the self-communication of God to the world and living communion with him. Then in its conception of the Son and the Spirit it introduced into Christianity a mythological element, closely akin to that of heathen polytheism. And in the third place it was religiously barren. Sabellianism stood close to the fundamental Christian conviction that "God was in Christ"; but Arianism substituted for the living, indwelling God an intermediate Being, a demi-God, who on examination turned out to be hardly more than a cosmological principle and hence could not serve as an adequate ground for the redemptive experience of the Christian believer. It was for this reason that Athanasius so vigorously and persistently opposed it and eventually triumphed over it.

There remained, consequently, as the only view acceptable to the Christian faith the third one above mentioned, which identified the divine life incarnate in Christ with an Hypostasis or mode of being within the one God. How this view developed through various stages until it reached virtually its final form in the teaching of Augustine and the Athanasian creed, we have already shown. Here we are concerned with its merits and defects. We begin with the former.

Traditional or orthodox Trinitarianism has this primary advantage over all deistic forms of monarchianism or unitarianism; it gives us a *living* God, and that in a twofold sense. He is living in the sense that his inner being is eternally active. The three Hypostases are in ceaseless interaction; they interpenetrate one another. There is a circular movement coursing through them, and this movement is not mechanical nor an "unearthly ballet of bloodless categories." It is vital, a form of spiritual communion. It is life and love. The Trinitarian God is also *living* in the sense that he is immanent in the world. He is no distant and self-inclosed deity of the Aristotelian type; he is a God active in the world and in history, a Being who has entered human life through Jesus Christ and through the sanctifying Spirit. The common idea that Trinitarianism gives us a peculiarly mysterious, unreal, and transcendent type of Deity is thus the reverse of the truth. The Trinitarian God is the living God of Christian experience, the God incarnate in Christ, the God operative in human redemption. He is the *near* God as opposed to the abstract and transcendent God of ancient philosophy. It was because of this fact that the early Christian theologians laid so much stress upon the Trinitarian idea. What they were concerned about was the union between man and God; only thus could redemption be effected. And such a union for Christian believers was possible only in case the incarnate Son was of the same substance with the Father. Only in case he was "very God of very God" could we have in Christ such a union of divinity with humanity as would make possible the "divinizing" and redemption of the Christian believer. God, it was said over and over again, became man that man might become God. No doubt it was a limited immanence that the Trinitarian theologians had in mind, but though limited it was vital. The God immanent in Christ and in Christian experience was a living God.

Another significant element in the doctrine of the Trinity is the provision it makes for the moral absoluteness of God. The highest affirmation concerning God is that he is love. But how can he be love, if in his essential nature he is one and alone? "Love consists in a union of different persons. Hence the I requires a Thou, the first a second person, the loving a beloved, without whom he could not love. God conceived of as only I, as a mere subject, would be absolute egoism, and thus the very reverse of love."[40] This conviction was one of the major motives in the development of the doctrine of the Trinity. Athanasius, for instance, in contending for the deity of the Son maintained that the divine Fatherhood implied the divine Sonship. Apart from the Son there could be no Father. The two terms were correlative; one involved the other. And this, of course, was true not only of the terms but of the ideas expressed by them. Athanasius was not basing his case on a mere exegesis of metaphors. What he meant was that the love of God implied an object, a Son, as well as a subject, a Father. Without both, an I and a Thou, there could be no love in the proper sense of the term. The deity of the Son was thus an implication of the divine Fatherhood. Without at least a duality of divine persons there could be no divine love. Later this thought was extended so as to apply to the three persons of the Godhead. "Thou dost see the Trinity," said Augustine, "if thou seest love." For in love "there are three things: He that loves, and that which is loved, and love."[41] This idea of a trinity of love was elaborated at length during the medieval period by Richard St. Victor in his six books *de Trinitate,* and in modern discussions of the subject it has fig-

[40] Ernest Sartorius, *The Doctrine of Divine Love,* pp. 8-9.
[41] *On the Trinity,* Bk. VIII, 12, 14.

ured prominently. It is at present, for instance, urged that personality is in its very nature social. It implies fellowship. There can, therefore, be no proper personality of God except on something like the Trinitarian basis. If it be objected that a unitarian God might be personal in the full social and ethical sense of the term by virtue of his relation to finite spirits, the answer is that this would make his personal and ethical self-realization dependent upon his creatures and would thus destroy his moral absoluteness. In and of himself he would in that case be only potentially moral. A community of personal life within his own being is essential to his being morally absolute. The very highest religious values associated with deity—personality and love—are, therefore, bound up with Trinitarianism.

A third important religious value in the traditional doctrine of the Trinity is found in the support that it lends to the doctrine of the incarnation. If the second Person of the Trinity freely renounced the glory that he had with the Father and assumed a human form with all its limitations and suffering in order to redeem men, we have in that fact the supreme manifestation of the divine love. In it the possibilities of grace are exhausted. Nothing beyond it is conceivable. Self-sacrifice in its sublimest form is now carried up into the very heart of God and he becomes the chief of burden-bearers. This thought lies at the very center of Christianity and constitutes its chief source of power. What has always stirred the human heart most profoundly has been the condescension, the self-renunciation of the Lord Jesus. "Though he was rich, yet for your sakes he became poor, that ye through his poverty might become rich." No belief is more distinctively Christian than this, and none has contributed more to the enrichment of the idea of God. That God at infinite cost to himself redeemed men is the most moving thought of Scripture; and it is this thought that lies at the basis of the doctrine of the Trinity and is the inspiring source of all vital faith in it.

A fourth element of strength in the Trinitarian doctrine is its philosophical value. This has manifested itself in two different ways. First, the doctrine saves philosophy from the impasse to which it has often been brought by the assumption of an ultimate simple and distinctionless unity. Such a unity has within itself no principle of movement. It is unable to differentiate itself into plurality and hence either leaves the concrete world unaccounted for or condemns it to a shadowy form of existence. As over against this sterile type of monism the Trinitarian theory gives us a differentiated unity which has within it the principle of action and which makes provision for creation and for the plural world of sense-experience. Furthermore, the distinctions within the Trinitarian unity have an analogy in human self-consciousness. We distinguish between feeling, willing and knowing, and also between the subject, the object and the union of the two. The latter has figured prominently in the triadic dialectic of the Hegelian philosophy. Whether in this form it has any metaphysical validity need not here concern us. What we should note is that in human personality or self-consciousness we have a concrete instance of differentiated unity and that we may regard it as a faint reflection of the infinite triune personality.

The other service which the Trinitarian doctrine has rendered philosophy is the protection it has afforded theism as over against deism on the one hand and pantheism on the other. We have already seen that by way of contrast with the remote and transcendent God of deism the Trinitarian Deity is an immanent and living God, a God forever linked up with humanity by the incarnation. But while immanent in the world he is distinct from it. He is himself absolutely self-sufficient. He does not need the world to complete himself, and hence there is no danger of identifying him in pantheistic fashion with the world. On any theory that denies to God complete self-sufficiency the latter is a very real peril. Trinitarianism by the provision it makes for both the moral and the metaphysical absoluteness of God, consequently, renders a very important service to theism by protecting it securely against the ever-recurring tendency toward pantheism.

But while the traditional doctrine of the Trinity has the very great merits that have been pointed out, there are serious difficulties in and objections to it that cannot be overlooked.

1. The most common objection is that the doctrine is tritheistic; and so long as each Person, or Hypostasis, is regarded as "having self-consciousness and making self-decision,"[42] it is difficult to see how the objection can be completely met. The usual way of

[42] O. A. Curtis, *The Christian Faith*, p. 492.

meeting it is to say that the three persons are not independent of each other as are human persons, but are bound together into an indissoluble unity. "Generation" and "procession," we are told, are necessary processes; they are due to the divine nature rather than the divine will. There is, therefore, no possibility of one Person detaching himself from the others. Necessity binds the three into unity, and in this sense we may say with Bowne that the doctrine of the Trinity is pantheism applied to the Godhead. But if this view be rigidly carried out, the distinction of persons would be virtually eliminated. We would in that case be left with one causal center. This center might be found in the Father, as Athanasius held and as Olin A. Curtis so vigorously maintained, or it might be found in a superpersonal essence immanent in the three persons, as Augustine and others have taught. But in either case the necessitating agency would leave no room for three distinct centers of self-decision. Real self-decision means independence, and independence is impossible where the underlying unity is of the necessitated type. There might, it is true, be an apparent independence, as is the case with human persons on the pantheistic theory, but the independence would be merely apparent. Actually, we are from the pantheistic point of view completely determined in all our thinking, feeling, and doing. And so it would also be with the persons of the Trinity if the pantheistic idea of unity be applied to the Godhead. There would be no independent self-decision on the part of the Son or the Spirit, or even on the part of the Father from the Augustinian standpoint. On the other hand, if a certain degree of independence is ascribed to the persons of the Trinity and if the existence of each is regarded as eternal and necessary, it cannot be denied that we have a form of tritheism. The only mitigating consideration would be that the independence of each is so limited by the others and the harmony of will is so complete that no discord or practical evil could possibly result. But this still leaves both the harmony and the limited independence unexplained.

2. It is objected that the ethical and religious values of the traditional Trinitarian doctrine would be provided for by a divine duality, and that there is no adequate reason for ascribing a distinct personality to the Holy Spirit. To this objection some weight must be allowed. A third person is not necessary to provide either for fellowship within the Godhead or for the divine grace manifest in the incarnation. The common argument for a trinity as over against a duality of divine persons is that the Spirit is necessary as a bond of union between the other two persons. It is the "love" that binds the "lover" and "beloved" together, or it is the uniting bond between subject and object in self-consciousness; and so it is said that "the trinity reduces duality to unity."[43] In this observation, psychologically interpreted, there is some truth. Two persons are bound together by a common object of interest. "The old theologies," says Bishop McConnell, "saw that Father and Son could not vitally be united if each were just the object of the loving gaze of the other. So they made the forthgoing

[43] Trinitas dualitatem ad unitatem reducit.

of the Spirit a mighty enterprise in which each was alike implicated. The fellowship of Father and Son was a fellowship in the Spirit, in the sending forth of the Spirit and in the ongoings of the Spirit."[44] But while this is a suggestive way of putting the matter, and while it is practically important to recognize that "fellowship is an affair of more than two and of at least three," it is still true, as Bishop McConnell admits, that the third factor need not be a person, nor need it be an independent object, it might be a common ideal interest. If the Holy Spirit were a metaphysical bond of union between Father and Son, it would have to be regarded as a profounder type of being which embraced the other two within its own unity; and this would be at complete variance with the traditional conception of the Trinity. There is, as a matter of fact, nothing in either the idea of love or of self-consciousness that warrants the ascription of personality to the Spirit.

3. In view of the difficulties involved in the idea of three Persons in the Godhead it is often said, and with some justification, that the use of the word "person" in this connection is an accident, a *damnosa hereditas* which we owe to Tertullian, and that the word did not originally mean what we understand by it, but, like the Greek *Hypostasis,* denoted a mode of being midway between a person and an attribute. But if we adopt this view, it is evident that we lose the moral and religious values contained in the idea of a divine society. Then, too, we have the disadvantage of operating with terms which have no intelligible

[44] *Living Together*, pp. 29f.

counterpart in reality. We know what substance and quality or person and attribute mean; but a mode of being "intermediate between the substantival existent and the adjectival subsistent" is to us inconceivable.[45] We may affirm its existence, but the affirmation adds nothing to our conception of God except perhaps the thought that there are complexities in the divine nature that transcend our understanding.

4. The doctrine of the Trinity was constructed against the background of Platonic realism and has never shaken itself free from its influence. Indeed, it was the Platonic conception of "essence" that saved the doctrine from tritheism on the one hand and from Monarchianism on the other. If the "one essence" which figures so prominently in the Trinitarian doctrine were conceived in nominalistic fashion as a mere general name applicable alike to Father, Son and Holy Spirit, it is evident that we would have tritheism. There would be no substantial bond of unity. On the other hand, if the common divine essence should be interpreted concretely as equivalent to a unitary personality, it is evident that the three "Persons" would lose their individuality and we would have an essentially monarchian view of the Deity. The only way to escape this or the tritheistic conclusion is to accept the realistic or Platonic conception of the divine essence as a fundamental unitary substance which differentiates itself into three personal modes of being and coexists in and with them. Such a conception by subordinating personal-

[45] Cf. F. R. Tennant, *Philosophical Theology*, II, p. 268.

ity to essence provides for both a substantial unity and a personal triality within the Godhead. But it is just this conception of a common essence to which modern thought objects. There is no semipersonal substance common to a number of persons and representing a more fundamental type of being. All metaphysical reality is concrete or individual, and personality is its ultimate form. There is nothing more basal. Essence is an abstraction from it.

5. The traditional doctrine of the Trinity identified the divine element in Christ with the Logos on the one hand and with the ego of Jesus on the other. The identification is in each case open to serious question from the standpoint of modern thought. We do not, for instance, believe in a distinct Logos as did the Greek philosophers. There is, to be sure, a divine reason, but it belongs to the divine personality and is not thought of as detachable from it nor as a hypostatic distinction within it.[46] The presence of God in Christ does not in our thinking naturally ally itself with the Logos nor with any special mode of being in the Deity. We, rather, think of it as the presence of God himself in his undifferentiated unity. And such would probably have been the view of the early church also, if the Divine in Jesus had not been identified with his ego. This identification established a distinction within the general concept of divinity between the Son and the Father, and hence

[46] "Our modern doctrine of God as self-expressive personality," says Richard M. Vaughan, "is the equivalent of the Trinitarian doctrine of God the Son." See *The Significance of Personality* (p. 147), a book of special interest and value from both the personalistic and religious points of view.

it was natural to identify the Son with the Logos. When this double identification had been made, the logical outcome, as even Biedermann[47] admits, was the ecclesiastical doctrine of the Trinity. To the modern mind, however, it is doubtful whether the God in Christ should be identified with the center of his personality, with his ego. Such a view to-day rather suggests the mythological. Then, too, it is difficult to attach any definite meaning to the idea of an "impersonal manhood" in Christ.[48] We find it simpler and more satisfactory to think of him as "a human personality completely and abidingly interpenetrated by God's indwelling."[49] How this indwelling should be conceived may not be altogether clear, but we naturally think of it after the analogy of the divine indwelling in prophets and saints, an indwelling that manifested itself in a new and vigorous life of the Spirit. What differentiated Jesus from all other men was, as Schleiermacher[50] put it, "the constant strength of his God-consciousness which was *a veritable existence of God* in him."[51]

6. One of the chief reasons for the development of the doctrine of the Trinity was the belief that re-

---

[47] *Christliche Dogmatik*, II, p. 60.

[48] Cf. O. A. Curtis, *The Christian Faith*, p. 235.

[49] J. Vernon Bartlet in *The Lord of Life*, p. 129.

[50] *The Christian Faith*, paragraph 94.

[51] Compare the following statement by Professor Edwin Lewis in his admirable work on *Jesus Christ and the Human Quest:* "Let God be conceived as the Eternal Spirit of Sacrificial Love from which all things proceed, and let Jesus be conceived as One who absolutely manifested that Spirit under the conditions of a human life, and all the practical and religious and philosophical value of the idea and fact of incarnation may be retained without entailing the burden of an outworn and impossible metaphysic" (p. 114).

demption was a mystical-metaphysical process which consisted in the communication of the divine life to men and which could be brought about only by such a substantial union of the human and divine in Christ as was provided for by the Trinitarian theory. But with the Reformation a new conception of redemption was introduced which made it a matter of conscious experience and dependent not upon a metaphysical union of natures in Christ, but upon the perfect revelation of God mediated through him. So long as the perfection of this revelation was guaranteed—and this, it would seem, could be done without invoking the aid of a metaphysical Trinity—nothing more was needed to give faith the assurance it craved.

## Contemporary Trinitarianism

Considerations such as the foregoing have led the church to be less insistent than it once was on the orthodox form of the Trinitarian creed. That this creed enshrines great values that must be conserved, is quite generally conceded. There is no widespread movement to reject it. Nor is there any strong conviction that the traditional formulation of it is so seriously defective that it ought to be superseded by a modern restatement. The feeling rather is that the doctrine in its older form is of permanent value, but that it in some respects transcends both the limits of reason and the demands of faith, and that it does not, consequently, have the finality once attributed to it. So far as its underlying motives are concerned we affirm them as confidently as ever. We hold that God is immanent in the world and that he was in some real sense incarnate in Christ. We hold that he is Redeemer as well as Creator, that he is personally present in human hearts as the sanctifying Spirit, and that in his essential nature he is sacrificial love. But that in order to make these affirmations we must also affirm three distinct centers of self-consciousness and self-decision in the Godhead, is by no means clear. God as bare unity, it is true, makes little appeal to us. As modern men we probably would prefer an organic or social tritheism to a rigid unitarianism. For we are more concerned about religious value than about theoretical simplicity or formal consistency. Yet we should prefer both, and we are not convinced that the traditional Trinitarian theory has pointed out the only way in which the highest values in the Christian idea of God can be conserved.

The profoundest movement in modern religious thought has been that away from Platonism and toward personalism. It is this fact more than any other that has given rise to the current dissatisfaction with the clear-cut Trinitarianism of the past. If God in the totality of his being is a unitary personality, it is at least confusing to continue to speak of three "Persons" in the Godhead. The personality *of* God would seem to exclude the older idea of personality *in* God. Hence there is a tendency to fall back upon the psychological as opposed to the social interpretation of the Trinity, and to combine it either with a form of Sabellianism or an agnostic attitude toward the problem. At the same time there is a deep-seated desire not to surrender the religious values of the orthodox theory. The result is that three different ways have arisen, by which the effort is made to retain the essential truth of the older Trinitarianism without committing oneself to its sharply defined personal distinctions within the Deity.

The first consists in saying that the Trinity is a *symbol* of the richness of the idea of God. What God is in the inner structure of his being we do not know. The classical expositions of the Trinity such as that of Thomas Aquinas went too far. They knew too much. They told us that there are in God "one essence, two processions, three Persons, four relations, five notions, and the circumincession which the Greeks call perichoresis"—all of which was logically deduced from the Trinitarian idea. But however logical the deduction may have been, we have an instinctive feeling and firm persuasion that it is altogether too Gnostic. We can have no such insight into the inner being of God as it assumes. When it comes to this dark realm, the best we can do is to use symbolic terms, and it is in this sense that the doctrine of the Trinity is to be understood. We do not know what hypostatic distinctions there are, if any, in the Divine Being, nor what their relations to each other are, but we are confident that we come nearest the truth when we think of God as Father, Son, and Holy Spirit. These are symbolic terms that express the inexhaustible richness of the divine nature; and it is chiefly because of this fact that the church has clung so tenaciously to them and to the Trinitarian doctrine in which they have been embodied.

A second method of combining the religious content of the older Trinitarianism with modern personalism is to revert to ancient Sabellianism—which W. G. T. Shedd has characterized as "the most subtle and also the most elevated of all the forms of spurious trinitarianism"[52]—and to modify it in such a way as to bring it into harmony with the theory of an immanent Trinity. The objection to original Sabellianism was not that it taught a Trinity of manifestation, but that it failed to bring this Trinity into direct relation to the essential nature of Deity. According to Sabellius, the three manifestations—Father, Son and Spirit—were temporary and successive, and hence did not reveal what God really and eternally is. His so-called self-revelations were not actual revelations, and they could not be such unless there were permanent elements in the divine nature corresponding to them. The Trinity of manifestation would not be true to its name if there were no Trinity of essence. The two belong together. We learn the Trinity of essence from the Trinity of manifestation, and the Trinity of manifestation derives its religious significance from the Trinity of essence. This synthesis of modalism with the doctrine of an immanent Trinity or modified Sabellianism, as it may be called, has considerable vogue at present. It affirms that God in his essential nature is all that is indicated by the terms "Father," "Son," and "Spirit," without attempting to define more precisely the character of the distinctions in his being so named and their relation to each other. We call them "persons," as Augustine says,

[52] *History of Christian Doctrine*, I, p. 252.

in order to avoid the necessity of silence rather than because of any definite idea conveyed by the term. Strictly speaking they are not persons, and yet we may say with Dorner that "though they are not of themselves and singly personal, they have a share in the One Divine Personality, in their own manner."[53] An excellent statement of this position in its more positive form is given by H. C. Sheldon in his *System of Christian Doctrine.* "Corresponding," he says, "to the threefold manifestation of Father, Son and Spirit, there subsist in the Godhead, in a certain logical order, eternal and necessary distinctions which enter into the divine consciousness and determine the perfection of the divine life."[54]

The third way of confessing the Trinitarian faith without committing oneself to the traditional "distinction of persons" is to assert the Christlikeness of God. This method of expression has several advantages. For one thing, it fixes attention on what is basal in the Trinitarian doctrine. What led to the development of this doctrine was, as Bishop McConnell says, "not merely the pressure to make a place for Christ in the Divine Life, in the sense of granting him divine honors, but, rather, to carry the Christ-spirit into the Divine, or, rather, to reveal the Divine as throughout Christlike."[55] In other words, what the Trinitarian theologians were fundamentally concerned about was a new ethical conception of God. They affirmed the deity of Christ in order to make cer-

[53] *System of Christian Doctrine,* I, p. 448.
[54] Page 227.
[55] *The Christlike God,* p. 70.

tain the Christlikeness of God. If this conception of God is granted, we have the heart of the Trinitarian doctrine and for practical purposes need nothing more.

Again, the ascription of Christlikeness to God has the advantage of associating our knowledge of the divine character with the *historical* revelation of it in Christ. If we lay the primary stress upon the eternal personal distinctions within the Godhead and upon a pretemporal act of self-abnegation on the part of the second Person of the Trinity, we obscure to some extent the revelational significance of the life and death of Christ. It was the impression made by the personality of the man Jesus that led to the expansion and reconstruction of the idea of God. It was because his life and death and resurrection were Godlike that men came to believe in the Christlikeness of God, and it was because they believed in the Christlikeness of God that they came to believe in his eternal and self-denying love. It was not belief in the self-humiliation of the pre-existent Son that led the disciples to see a divine element in the death of Christ, but the reverse. They saw God mirrored in the Christ spirit and hence attributed to him an act of self-abnegation. Christ was for them the "express image" of the eternal. In this conception we have the basis of all that is distinctive in the teaching of the New Testament and of the church concerning the divine grace.

A further advantage in affirming the Christlikeness of God is the fact that it directs particular attention to his unity. If God is Christlike, he is one both metaphysically and ethically, especially ethically. He is not a "holy obstacle" to redemption in one aspect of his being and an "eager mediator" of it in another. His entire being is holy will, and to speak of him as Christlike is equivalent to saying that he is in his essential nature love. His love is both self-love, a love of goodness, and communicative love. In both respects he was incarnate in Christ, and hence we have a Godlike Christ and a Christlike God.

In such a God there may perhaps be three eternal and necessary distinctions, between whom there is an interchange of affection and who thus enrich his inner life. But that this triune nature is essential to the absoluteness of his love and of his ethical character, is not certain. Without it there would be in him an eternal self-love, a love of goodness, and there might also be an eternal communicative love, ceaselessly but freely creating personal beings. In the latter case he would eternally have objects of his affection even though he did not find them in himself, and thus an eternal and absolute life of communicative love would be possible to him. But however that may be, the Trinitarian doctrine does unquestionably dramatize the divine love in a way that appeals to the imagination and that makes it an effective symbol of the divine grace. This practical value it will always have, and weighty considerations in the way of a theoretical justification of it will always be available. But whatever value, practical or theoretical, it may have, it should not be forgotten that as an expression of the divine love it does not stand in its own right, but is dependent on faith in the Christlikeness of God.

# INDEX